The Devil Wagon in God's Country

The Automobile and Social Change in Rural America, 1893-1929

The Devil Wagon in God's Country

The Automobile and Social Change in Rural America, 1893 — 1929

MICHAEL L. BERGER

ARCHON BOOKS
Hamden, Connecticut
1979

Library of Congress Cataloging in Publication Data

Berger, Michael.
The devil wagon in God's country.

Bibliography: p. 247
Includes index.
1. Automobiles — Social aspects — United States — History. 2. United States — Rural conditions. I. Title.
HE5623.B45 301.24'3 79-17185
ISBN 0-208-01704-6

First published in 1979 as an Archon Book,
an imprint of The Shoe String Press, Inc.
Hamden, Connecticut 06514

Printed in the United States of America

for *Aunt Hannah*

Contents

Preface

"There can be little doubt," observed historian Clyde B. Davis in 1950, "that the automobile and its concomitant, the hard-surfaced road, brought about the most drastic change in our manner of life in the last half century." In the thirty years since these words were written, few have thought to question this or similar conclusions. If anything, our understanding of how the automobile affects our environment, our lifestyle, and even our long-term prospects for survival, has deepened. The motor car seems to be under attack from all sides. Buyers criticize the rising cost of new cars, consumer advocates demand safer automobiles and less environmental pollution, industrial reformers desire to end the monopoly of the "big four" producers by splitting them up, and conservationists suggest that a replacement for the internal combustion engine needs to be found. Most of this criticism is based on post-World War II developments, such as a record output of cars, a sharp increase in population, the creation of an interstate highway system, and, most recently, a shortage of fossil fuels.

As a result, despite extensive investigations of the automobile's impact on contemporary life and of the development of the automotive industry and the men responsible for it, comparatively little scholarly attention was given until the 1970s to the *historical* interaction between society and the motor car. The most significant work before 1970 was John B. Rae's *The American Automobile: A Brief History* (1965), which, despite its pioneering nature, was by definition a survey treatment of a tremendously complex topic.

Furthermore, since recent problems with the motor car appear most severe in metropolitan areas, research has centered on the automobile's impact on city and surburban life. This focus may be unfortunate, for our megalopolises were made possible largely by the motor car's transformation of what had been rural America. In 1928, rural sociologist Newell L. Sims wrote that "the automobile, needless to say, has been the greatest revolutionizing force yet experienced by rural society." Yet not until 1972 was a scholarly study of the effects of the motor car on rural America published, Reynold M. Wik's *Henry Ford and Grass-roots America.* Even here, the emphasis was more on Ford and the influence of his social, economic, and political ideas on grass-roots Americans than on an examination of how the motor car modified rural social institutions, activities, and services.

This study attempts to complement the work of Rae, Wik, and James J. Flink (*America Adopts the Automobile, 1895-1910* [1970] and *The Car Culture* [1975]) by exploring relationships between the automobile and social change in rural America during the years 1893-1929. It relates, analyzes, and synthesizes contemporary observations of the motor car's impact on the family, the community, leisure activities, the church, the schools, health care, and the environment. These observations have been gleaned primarily from autobiographies and reminiscences, biographies, contemporary rural sociological studies, government legislation and reports, popular and trade periodicals, and works of fiction. Since the automobile was viewed generally as a technological breakthrough and its sociological effects were almost immediately recognized, such references contain significantly more primary source material than one might normally expect.

Although my words form the narrative framework for this study, I have quoted liberally from the writings of farmers, residents of villages and small towns, and contemporary observers of rural social change. As a result, this book should provide more of the flavor of early motoring and the personal reactions of typical rural Americans than such a study normally would.

This volume grows out of work first undertaken while I was a graduate student at Columbia University. Although that was longer ago than I care to admit, I am still grateful to Professors Harvey A. Levenstein and Richard F. W. Whittemore for their advice and assistance at that time. More recently, Joseph F. X. McCarthy of Fordham University read and commented on a preliminary draft of this work. I want to thank him for his help and interest over the course of five years.

In preparing this manuscript for publication, when so much depended on others, I had the pleasure of working with Mary Jane Kraft who, besides doing a fine job of typing the final draft, supplied many worthwhile recommendations on style. My editor, Jim Thorpe, initially provided several useful suggestions about the structure of the study and then offered encouragement and patience during an extensive period of revision. As always, I am grateful to my wife Linda for understanding the pressures and demands experienced by an author. Finally, I would like to express my appreciation to John D. Underwood of St. Mary's College of Maryland, who first offered me the opportunity to know the satisfaction of twentieth-century rural American life.

I The Coming of the Automobile

Primarily because of their initial high cost and the poor condition of rural roads, most of the early automobiles were owned by urban dwellers. Those few vehicles which ventured beyond the city limits were generally intent on following a rigid route to their owners' country homes. As a result, for roughly ten years after its inception, the motor car remained relatively unknown in rural America. There was more than humor in the following exchange, popular in the late nineties, between Tommy and Mr. Figgy:

> Tommy: "Say Paw?"
> Mr. Figgy: "Well?"
> "What is the Horseless Age?"
> "Eight. No horse ever gets past seven."[1]

In 1903, when Dr. H. Nelson Jackson and his mechanic, Sewell K. Crocker, successfully undertook the first cross-country automobile trip in their "Winton Motor Carriage," they found that their machine was still very much of a curiosity.

> A toot from the bulb horn on the outskirts of each isolated Rocky Mountain town ended every game of roulette and Twenty-one as the inhabitants — sheepherders, traders, cowboys and starving Indians — crowded into the street to see the "devil-wagon." The novelty of the *Vermont* [Dr. Jackson's motor car] indeed proved as vexing as the hazards of the road. It was bad enough to have to avoid a ravine, but detours caused by human frailty were even more distressing. Already on one occasion a red-headed woman on a white horse had sent Jackson and Crocker fifty-four miles out of their way, as it turned out, in order to pass her house so that her family could see an automobile. Some of the natives of the hinterland had never heard of a car. They thought the Winton was a small railroad engine that had somehow strayed off the track and was following the horsepaths.[2]

While it cannot be said that the rural roads appreciably improved between 1893 and 1903, the daring of the city drivers did. With their improved vehicles, they ventured out into the country, trusting to skill and luck that they could negotiate the quagmires that the "hayseeds" termed "roads." For these early Sunday drivers, the automobile had little utilitarian function. Back in the city, horse and buggy ably transported both people and merchandise. Alternately, the new electric streetcar lines, the "trolleys," offered easy, effortless conveyance. Thus, the automobile could little improve intraurban movement, but it could make accessible for the first time vast rural territory for the pursuit of pleasure. As such, the needs and desires of the urban tourist were destined to come into conflict with the basically traditional way of life of farmers and small-town residents.

Among the worst problems that was to arise, and the one least amenable to reasonable dialogue among the protagonists, was the dislike of the horse for the automobile. Various explanations were offered for this. Some thought it was the appearance or the shape of the vehicle that frightened the animals. Thus, Uriah Smith of Battle Creek, Michigan, offered the unique solution of mounting on the outer dashboard of his motor car the head and shoulders of a horse.[3] Others blamed the antagonism on the sound and smell of the vehicle, particularly when it came close to the horse.

Whatever the reasons, L. E. French spoke for most early motorists when he offered these observations on his 1904 automobile tour of New Hampshire's White Mountain region:

> Let me say right here that automobiles seem to exert a wonderfully rejuvenating influence upon White Mountain horses. Even the most ancient animals apparently go into a trance in which they have the most violent visions of their younger days. The occupants of the vehicles, who in most cases have been worrying for hours over the prospect of meeting an automobile, naturally catch the general excitement, and panic reigns.[4]

In response to this general situation, there grew up an elaborate procedure, compounded of law and experience, to be followed whenever horse and automobile met. Hiram P. Maxim, one of the early pioneers of the automotive industry, describes below the maneuvers he undertook during 1907 and 1908 when his experimental tricycle encountered a horse:

> I slowed away down, creeping along cautiously, prepared to dismount and make a dash for the horse's head the moment he indicated a tendency to turn sharp around, which was usually what did the damage.... When we had approached each other as closely as I considered safe, I pulled over on the grass at the roadside and stopped. This would have to be done anyway, since no horse would consent to pass close to the machine....
>
> Lobdell [his assistant] and I observed our regular procedure, walking slowly up to the horse and speaking to him as we approached. This almost always calmed the animal; the sound of a man's voice exerted a powerful influence. We managed to get hold of his bridle ..., one of us on each side, and we then led him slowly past the tricycle.[5]

Not all contemporary observers were sure that the horse innately feared the automobile. After all, it had learned to live with the railroad and, more recently, the bicyclist. In 1900, Henry Ford, whose cars were destined to dominate the market completely during the 1920s, was asked whether he ever frightened horses and answered that it "depends on the horse. A low-bred, ignorant horse, yes; a high-born fellow, no."[6] Without arguing the lineage of the average farm horse at this time, it seems safe to conclude that enough horses were upset to hinder urban-rural relations and to keep the level of antiautomobile sentiment high in the country until after World War I.

In all fairness, it should be pointed out that some felt that the responsibility for accidents had to be shared by the horse driver. Dr. Frank Billings, in a letter to the *American Horse Breeder*, claimed: "Autos are in no sense so annoying nor are they really so dangerous as the great army of fools who think they can drive and merely hold reins, never hear a team behind them and seldom care or turn out to let you pass by. The roads are full of such idiots, male and female, and, for my part, I had rather they would be packed with flying autos than with the brainless and hoggish idiots who drive the majority of horses one meets on the road."[7]

If a carefully driven motor vehicle was cause for alarm, one in reckless hands could lead to panic, especially if traveling at an excessive speed. Speed was not necessarily something that rural Americans disliked. The trotter "Dan Patch" had become somewhat of a legend to these people, and it was common to see a magazine etching of him hung on a farmhouse wall. But it was one thing to race around isolated tracks, and quite another to engage in such pursuits on the public roads.

On the other hand, in an age before the advent of the automobile speedway, it is not surprising that the motorist should look to the relatively isolated country roads as ideal places to see what the vehicle could "do" when "opened up."

As a result, rural localities set to work to limit the velocity of this new type of conveyance. Frederick Lewis Allen recalled that "speed limits set by farmer-minded local officials were sometimes low indeed: my personal memory tells me — unbelievably but I think reliably — that in tranquil Holderness, New

Hampshire, the original legal limit was six miles an hour."[8] Another authority claims that such speeds were instituted in a spirit of "fairness," in the belief that the speed of the automobile should not exceed that of the horse. He also notes that ten miles an hour was viewed by many early drivers as a pretty good speed when attained on a typical turn-of-the-century country road.[9] By 1920, despite the increased horsepower then available, the typical restriction had risen to only twenty to twenty-five miles per hour in the open country. However, it should be kept in mind that the condition of most roads was still poor, and the automobile technology of the period still limited (especially that of tires and brakes); this led to the conclusion that motor cars were unsafe when driven at speeds in excess of forty miles an hour.[10] Thus, such limits were equal to approximately 60 percent of the speed that automobiles of the day could safely attain, a mathematical relationship which has continued down to the present.

Certainly, speed restrictions were not imposed solely for the safety of the motorist and his passengers. Rural dwellers were just as concerned with what the automobile and its driver might do to them and their property. Despite the precautions discussed above, reports of frightened and runaway horses were common, and some such incidents ended in tragedy. In 1901, Mrs. John L. Guyre was driving her buggy through Midland Park, New Jersey. Her horse became frightened by an approaching automobile driven by Dr. William L. Vroom; she was thrown from her vehicle and later died from injuries sustained in the accident. A suit was brought by her family for damages before the Bergen County Court in Hackensack, New Jersey. The charge of State Supreme Court Justice Jonathan Dixon to the jury is instructive in that it shows the early confusion as to how great a menace the automobile actually was:

> The question is whether the machine driving along the country roads without a horse in front and discharging steam behind is so likely to frighten a horse on the highway and thus endanger the road as to constitute the machine a nuisance.... It does not follow it is a nuisance because it occasionally or exceptionally frightens

> horses.... In order to make it a nuisance its common effect must be to substantially interfere with the people who drive horses along the highway. . . . If this method of locomotion is a common nuisance, and was the approximate cause of death, then the defendant is responsible.[11]

That the public had not yet made up *its* mind is indicated by the fact that after twenty-three ballots, this particular case resulted in a hung jury, even though its members agreed that the automobile was not a nuisance.[12]

Nonetheless, as Charles M. Harger noted in a 1907 magazine article, such incidents involving runaways and speeders, besides leading to low speed limits, "created a prejudice that the local machine-owners must face for months to come.... A sort of local ostracism grows up against the motor-car owners."[13] Furthermore, the fear of meeting a fate similar to that of Mrs. Guyre led many farm women to avoid personal travel as much as possible, thus compounding their already intense feelings of isolation. (The problem of the isolated farm woman is treated in some detail in chapter 2.)

Certainly rural motorists must have cringed at some of the references to automobiles and farmers in contemporary advertisements. An ad for Murine, "a tonic for the 'auto eye,'" contained the unflattering couplet: "As they dash down the pike, without quaver or hitch / the farmers in front of them take to the ditch."[14] If this was what the motorist boasted of, rural America wanted no part of it.

Harger maintained that rural motorphobia was largely the fault of city tourists.[15] While this was certainly true when most car owners lived in urban America, the motor vehicle was as prone to be dangerous in the hands of rural dwellers as in the hands of their city cousins. Thus, in his novel *Plowing on Sunday*, Sterling North, recreating life on a southern Wisconsin farm of 1913, described the attitudes of both two new rural vehicle owners and a menaced female spectator:

> Peter Brailsford and Dutchy Bloom were coming down the road a

> mile a minute on their motorcycles, and just before they reached the spot where she was standing Dutchy stood up on the seat, let go on the handlebars, and started yelling like a wild Indian. Why he might have killed her! He might have run right over her!
>
> "You better watch out, young man," she shouted after him, shaking her parasol. "You can't go up the narrow road to heaven on a motorcycle. You're just tearing down the wide, primrose path to hell."
>
> The motorcycles were making so much noise that Dutchy did not catch the full import of her remarks, but he turned, nevertheless, and thumbed his nose in answer.[16]

Because of its total divergence from the appearance of the horse buggy and its generally higher speed potential than contemporary automobiles, the motorcycle probably evoked greater fear than the standard four-wheel machine.

THREAT TO ANIMAL LIFE

If the threat to one's person conjured up nightmarish visions, the danger to domestic animal life was just as real, and, judging from reports of the day, more justified:

> Every variety of farm animal could be — and usually was — met in the course of a few miles' run. Horses, mules, cows and pigs displayed an unexpected order of intelligence by getting off the road at the approach of a car. The minds of sheep occupied a niche peculiar to the species. They were wont to be so preoccupied with their ovine thoughts that it was often necessary to nudge them gently with a front wheel to distract them from their stupid reflections.
>
> Chickens! They were the bane of the motorist's life. The approach to a flock of them busily scratching in the dust — always smack in the middle of the road — required thought and finesse, for no power of extra-sensory perception could foretell just what they would do or how they would do it. One could be sure of only one thing — they wouldn't stand still. They were tempermental and

> impetuous. They indulged in impromptu and spontaneous divertisements. They ran in circles, they zig-zagged, they flew for short distances. They did whirling dervish dances and they bounced straight up in the air as if propelled by a land mine — but they never really got out of the way....
>
> The problem was purely one of dodging and outdistancing them, prayerful that not more than two or three would be killed in the process. If such fatalities happened in sight of the farmer's house, it was the unwritten law that the bodies should be carried back and the best possible settlement made. And you couldn't take a freshly killed, unmutilated carcass home for a fricassee even after you had paid for it. No siree, the farmer sentimentally insisted that its last resting place had to be on the old home place — and I'm pretty sure I know where, too; in the pot on the stove.[17]

During the 1920s both the United States Entomological Laboratory and the Illinois Natural History Survey attempted to ascertain the exact animal mortality toll. It must be assumed that by this date farmers had taken certain precautions to keep domestic animals off the highway,[18] and thus the totals are probably lower than they would be for the period 1893-1923. In addition, animals such as pigs and chickens were often removed almost immediately from the road and used for food. Most of these animals would not have been counted by the roving surveyors of these two organizations.

Both investigations covered similar farming territory, and both agreed that most animals were killed on well-surfaced, reasonably straight roads, where drivers could reach higher speeds.[19] (This situation may help to explain early rural opposition to federal and state aid for road improvements.) In a 1924 trip over 632 miles of Iowa roads, 225 dead animals were found, representing 29 species. The investigator concluded that motor vehicles demand "recognition as one of the important checks upon the natural increase of many forms of life."[20] Five years later, a similar expedition of 1400 miles discovered only 234 dead animals, seemingly an improvement of over 50 percent in safety. These figures are somewhat deceptive, however, as approximately 86 percent of the animals found dead in both cases were undomesticated ones.[21] Thus, while farmers were able to keep their domesticated flocks off the road, wild animals were apparently also learning to avoid or dodge the devil wagon.

In fact, an article appearing in 1900 maintained that "animals that had become accustomed to the fleeting, flitting bicycle had already been prepared for the horseless carriage, and it is a backwards beast indeed that is now frightened by a passing automobile."[22] However, the range of the bicycle was quite limited in comparison with that of the automobile, and thus there would be large numbers of uneducated "beasts." Furthermore, dodging a bicycle and avoiding an automobile seem to require somewhat different techniques. The automobile has never really become "fleeting" or "flitting." Finally, there was much in the sound and something in the smell of the motor car which could scare an animal, whereas these aspects were not as prominent in the bicycle.

Not all domestic animals who died in their encounters with the automobile were as innocent as the chickens, pigs, dogs, and cats reported by these 1920s surveys. Harold B. Chase records the following incident in his autobiography, showing, perhaps, that it was not always human beings who misunderstood the motor car:

> A front tire of the Ford had a puncture close to the farm of a breeder of show sheep. I had just finished putting in a spare tube and was starting the wearisome job of inflating it when I noticed a splendid specimen of fine-wool Delaine ram, for which the breeder was famous, walking slowly toward me. Having spent almost every summer in the country, I recognized at once the unmistakable signs of hostility a ram displays just before going into action....
>
> I had no idea of beating a hasty retreat to the safety of the car's seat, so I continued pumping, watching the ram out of the corner of one eye. He stopped about six feet away, surveyed the situation imperiously, lowered his head again, got a firm grip on the road with his hooves and launched his heavy body through the air like a bat out of hell....

When I saw him hurtling through space in my direction, I stepped aside and he hit the partially inflated tire head-on. The shock knocked the Ford off the jack and bounced the ram back on his haunches. A look which combined amazement and increased animosity showed in his eyes and he wasted no time in sighting for a second assault. His hurry made his aim even poorer and his head struck the front axle with terrific force. He dropped limply and lay still. Thinking he was merely stunned, I waited to see what he would do next.

There wasn't any "next." He had broken his neck.... Leaving everything just as it was — the visible evidence was overwhelmingly in my favor and I didn't want to disturb a single minutia of it — I walked the short distance to the breeder's house and reported to him what had happened. He and I had always been on friendly terms, and, after surveying the scene, not a sign of unpleasantness raised its ugly head.[23]

Nonetheless, in the majority of cases, it was indeed the motorist who was at fault. In fact, a 1904 legislative review revealed that the automobilist was in most states "liable for any accident occurring when passing another vehicle or domestic animal. This clause, which has been named the 'pig and chicken' clause by the Automobilists of America, has given rise to much controversy."[24] A great deal of this controversy concerned exactly how much the dead animal was worth. Stephen Longstreet, at the age of twelve, undertook a cross-country motor trip with his grandfather. Although the date was 1919, the events portrayed are representative of conditions that had existed since the turn of the century:

Suddenly there was a blur of color in front of us, then a scattering of gay feathers, a loud lamenting crow of despair, and Gramp pulled up as a large shattered rooster staggered into a mad little dance, fell over on to his back, his tattered feathers at half mast....

A large red-nosed man with a shotgun appeared from behind some apple trees and nodded politely to Gramp. He was chewing tobacco slowly.

"Passin' through?" he asked casually.

"Yes," said Gramp. "This hen just committed suicide."

"Nothin' to live for," said the fat man. "Ain't a hen, it's a rooster. In the prime of life it was too."

"We all have to go. . . ."

"What do you think that critter is worth?"

"No idea," said Gramp, lowering his victim and taking out his cigar case and offering one to the fat man.

"Aigs from his harem, why I got people standin' in line to buy. . . ."

"Wouldn't take a hundred dollars for that rooster."

Gramp said sternly, "Wouldn't give you a hundred. Wouldn't give you ten dollars. Give you five. In gold."

The fat man looked at his smoldering cigar and said, "Pretty good ropes you smoke, Cunn'el. Five it is and two more cigars — *damn* good cheroots. Pardon me, Madame." . . .

The man with the shotgun said, "I'll give him a nice burial, Cunn'el. Only fittin', he was a real Don Jewonnee, rather futt than eat. Pardon me, Madame."

Gramp picked up the victim and shook his head. "I'll just take *my* bird along with me. He broke his neck banging into the front end of the car. A good clean way to go. No suffering."

The fat man unloaded his shotgun and pushed his two extra cigars into the barrels. "It's your rooster, Cunn'el. Nice to have met up with you."[25]

PROBLEMS OF TRESPASS

The tourist, however, was not always just passing through. He was frequently looking for a pleasant spot to stop and picnic, and when he did so the question of private versus public property inevitably arose. Actually, this situation was not a new one. Rural dwellers living close to large population areas had experienced a similar problem in the 1890s with the bicycle. City folk, limited only by roads and their own energy, had swarmed into the country and picnicked where they wanted on what they wanted — frequently including the farmer's animals, vegetables, and fruit.[26] With the coming of the automobile, the radius of these depredations increased.

Even when tourists requested permission to use property belonging to privately owned farms, there were still problems to be resolved. Because rural and urban areas had long been isolated from each other, a "culture gap" had developed. In particular, customs necessitated by the lack of mechanization in rural life had been forgotten by the second- or third-generation city dweller. Farmers' wives frequently found themselves doing battle with well-meaning city tourists who were nonetheless destroying valuable resources:

> Now the way to our well lies down a hot path through the garden. In weather like this I make sudden sullies, not more than three a day if I can help it. The bucket operates laboriously with a windlass. We can't let the visiting gods manage it themselves because in the first place our well, like any other worth having, is our refrigerator. The rope on the southeast corner carries a pail containing any meat or fish we have on hand. The rope on the northeast supports the cream. It requires a certain amount of skill to steer a bucket without putting our precious water supply out of commission altogether. In the second place, these travelers never know how to treat a well. I have seen them take a sip out of a glass and throw the rest down the well. They will wash their hands in the bucket if you don't stop them. . . .[27]

THE RURAL REACTION

The reaction of the rural population to these problems was predictable. In not so subtle ways they made it perfectly clear to the motorist that he was not welcome. At the same time, laws were proposed that aimed at rendering the motor car at least ineffective, if it could not be totally banned. Such proposals stood a good chance of becoming law. State legislatures characteristically were dominated by rural representatives, because of archaic methods of districting that were not overturned until the Supreme Court's "one-man, one-vote" decision of 1962 in *Baker v. Carr.* Furthermore, the country dwellers for whom these representatives spoke had proportionally fewer automobiles than their urban or suburban counterparts, and thus an antiautomobile stance was politically advantageous.

On the local level, even more opposition could be expected, and the results were more radical. In the late 1890s, the town of Mitchell, South Dakota, aware that two residents of Pierre had constructed a motor vehicle, passed an ordinance forbidding its use on Mitchell's streets.[28] As late as 1905, certain counties in West Virginia still had similar laws on the books.[29] According to one authority, police sometimes were empowered to shoot at a car's tires and to erect barriers made of ropes or chains across a road.[30]

When the automobile *was* allowed to use the public highways unmolested, American ingenuity guaranteed that others would have fair warning of its approach. One law required the motorist to ignite a Roman candle upon sighting a horse-drawn vehicle.[31] In Vermont, each automobile had to be preceded, at a distance of one-eighth of a mile, by a person of mature age carrying a red flag.[32] Not all regulations pertained to the open road. The Iowa Legislature passed a motor law that included the following section: "The traveling motorist is ordered to telephone ahead to the next town of his coming, so that owners of nervous horses may be warned in advance."[33] In Belleville, Illinois, auto enthusiasts were required by ordinance to carry a bell and ring it fifteen feet before reaching each street intersection.[34]

Such laws, however, became rarer and rarer as the first decade of the twentieth century came to a close. They were replaced by a new breed of legislation, exemplified by this portion of the Connecticut state highway law that was in effect in 1908:

> Upon approaching any person walking in the traveled portion of any public highway, or a horse or any other draft animal being led, ridden, or driven therein . . . , the person operating a motor vehicle shall have the same under control and shall reduce speed. If such horse . . . shall appear to be frightened, or if the person in charge thereof shall signal so to do, the person operating such motor vehicle shall bring the same . . . immediately to a stop and, if traveling in an opposite direction, shall remain stationary so long

> as may be reasonable to allow such horse or animal to pass, or, if traveling in the same direction, shall use reasonable caution in thereafter passing such horse or other animal.[35]

But, as Richard H. Lee, president of the National Motorist's Association, observed in 1924: "The automobile ... came too fast for its critics. The laws could not be made to apply with sufficient sureness and swiftness to stop the rascals from scaring the horses. So we arrived at the period where people took the law in their own hands...."[36] Tacks and glass were strewn over country roads by rural residents that wanted to rid themselves of the danger of motor vehicles. Rope, and sometimes barbed wire, was run from tree to tree across a road to impede traffic. (The latter action was found to be most expedient at twilight.) Stories even circulated of farmers placing rakes and saws in the roadway, with their teeth positioned in such a way as to wreak havoc with the automobile tires of the day.[37]

Unfortunately, rural anger at the devil wagon sometimes became directed at the occupants of the machine. A 1905 issue of the *Gloversville* (N.Y.) *Daily Leader* reported an incident where a farmer attempted to horsewhip a passing motorist for no apparent cause.[38] *Horseless Age* described *another* auto shooting case the same year from South Carolina, in which a farmer attempted to prevent a Pope-Hartford from overtaking his horse and buggy by shooting his pistol over the heads of the car's occupants.[39]

While such activities obviously were malicious, they did not have the force of law behind them. More serious from the motorist's point of view was the early development of the "speed trap." Until state laws were passed to curb (but not eliminate) them, they were the bane of the motorist's existence.

Devious methods were designed to trap the unwary. Particularly lucrative and significant targets were the participants in the Glidden Tours, held annually between 1905 and 1913. Named after Charles J. Glidden, who had donated the awards, the tours were supposedly long-distance reliability runs. The winner was the vehicle that needed the fewest repairs along the way, not necessarily the first to complete the trip. The purpose of the tours was to show that automobiles had become so reliable that they could be driven over all types of roads with great dependability. Unfortunately, the tours often became races as well and as such were fair game for the local police. By making the trip as difficult as possible, local officials may have hoped to discourage the participants from entering the next tour and thus retard the general acceptance of the automobile. During the 1905 run, *Horseless Age* reported:

> In passing through Leicester, Mass., on their way to the mountains several of the tourists exceeded the speed limit over a measured course at the foot of a hill, down which it was found desirable to travel at considerable speed in order to attain sufficient momentum to climb the next hill easily. Constables evidently had anticipated this and so laid in wait and caught the number of eight, for whose arrest they swore out warrants....
>
> Following payment of the fines the tourists left ... in a close procession with their machines draped with crepe ... A pace of 15 miles an hour was maintained to the Leicester town line, where the band was set down, and the parade went through town at about 2 miles an hour. One stop was made in front of the Leicester Inn and another in front of the home of Policeman Quinn, who served the warrants, and appeared against the tourists.[40]

Such traps were not established solely for the Gliddenites, though people who could afford to engage in such antics were frequently viewed as millionaires by local residents.[41] The average motorist began to be affected by traps set up at such strategic points as just south of Albany, New York, on the Post Road. Public antagonism began to build, and the automobile associations started to pressure localities to abolish them.[42]

Eventually, such agitation led to the inclusion in state highway laws of provisions that either forbade municipalities to regulate speed, such as in New Jersey,[43] or heavily circumscribed their power to do so, as in New York, where every

> city or village shall ... have placed conspicuously on each main public highway where the city or village line crosses the same and on every main highway where the rate of speed changes, signs of sufficient size to be easily readable by a person using the highway, bearing the words "Slow down to --- miles" (the rate being inserted) and also an arrow pointing in the direction where the speed is to be reduced or changed, and also on further condition that such ordinance, rule or regulation shall fix the penalties for violation thereof similar to and no greater than those fixed by such local authorities for violations of speed limitation by any other vehicles than motor vehicles....[44]

THE TRANSITIONAL YEARS

Even a negative practice such as establishing speed traps provides evidence of the coming acceptance of the automobile by rural America. All this attention crowned the motor car with an aura of permanence. Farmers and small-town residents were learning that there was money to be had from the devil wagon. Yet the money collected through speed traps, highway toll gates,[45] and expensive auto ferries[46] — all of which caused ill-will and augured declining profits in the future — was a pittance compared to what could be grossed if the tourist business was actively courted. This realization was slow in coming. In the meantime, the rural population engaged in legalized highway robbery. The price of overnight accommodations was doubled, and sometimes tripled, for automobilists seeking lodging. Rural "mechanics" charged motorists prices they would never have dreamed of for the repair of buggy or farm equipment. Farmers demanded what the traffic would bear, and it was plenty, for renting a team to pull out a car mired in mud.[47]

Although probably exceptional, C. H. Claudy's account of two tourists who ran out of gas in the countryside in 1911 does show both the lingering disrespect for the motorist and the dawning realization that he could be a gold mine on wheels:

> Here is a short tale of a confiding person who, fuelless, bought

> stove gasolene at a farmhouse. The farmhouse was twelve miles from the nearest town. The hour was five in the evening and a storm coming. The farmer at first refused to sell. Doubtless he had visions of towing us into town. But his brother or hired man or son — the relationship is not clear to us, save that it was of the devil, — whispered unto him, and the gasolene was obtained. It was also paid for. And we started thankfully enough. We stopped, too, in a few rods. And start and stop, start and stop, start and stop, was our method of procedure for fifteen minutes. Then we gave up, sent for the farmer, were towed back to his house, bought a dinner, paid lodging for blanket and floor accommodations, paid for a tow to Bridgeport the next day, and left of our good money no less than fourteen dollars with our host.
>
> Proof? We'd have hung him if we had it. But of moral certainty that he watered the gasolene before he sold it, not one of five of us, all old to the game, doubts.[48]

To the farmer and residents of small towns in the country such actions were always justified by the belief that because big-city interests had cheated them out of a large portion of their hard-earned profits, they were entitled to get even in a small way. Unfortunately, the distinction between who should and who should not be taken advantage of quickly became blurred. The connotations of evil and wealth had been so well riveted to the automobile owner that it soon mattered little where he dwelled. Thus, Bellamy Partridge recalled: "At Brad Cowan's harness shop a carriage robe [used to protect clothing during rides over unimproved roads] cost a dollar and a half. Anybody could buy one for that price. But if you went there and asked for an automobile robe, it would cost you three dollars — for the identical robe."[49]

Partridge claimed that such actions were exceptional and attributed them to the fact that some townspeople were economically dependent on horse-related businesses and thus feared that as motor power replaced horse power on the farm they stood to lose financially. Partridge himself "never saw any personal hostility to the motorist ... and, in the main, the motorist received more kindness from the rural populations than was usually his due".[50] Nonetheless, it is difficult to believe that the evidence of animosity presented in this chapter was solely economically motivated, though some of it obviously was. On the other hand, many acts of farmers and small-town businessmen who still believed in helping their neighbor have doubtless gone unrecorded. As a contemporary automobile historian has noted, neither the farmer's *national* periodicals nor his Grange ever went on record as opposed to the automobile per se. Thus the reactionary opposition we have cited was of a local variety.[51] Since there is a tendency in history to dwell on points of conflict rather than harmony, the following account by Louise Closser Hale of her encounter with Farmer Campbell should be considered more than an exceptional case:

> He saw me from a distance swinging my motor hat and goggles at him for there was a surrey in front of the house and I feared he might go off in it before my arrival. He did go off upon discovering my advent, disappearing behind the house to return before I had explained my mission to his wife. He was dragging several feet of chain. "Which one?" was all he asked as we climbed into the surrey. It developed that it was the second one. The cars generally stick in the first mud hole which we had manipulated without any great effort....
>
> Mr. Campbell furnished the chains and Mr. Mann's big car [a fellow traveler] pulled us out backward, pulled us away from Mount Vernon and its quagmires for the unregenerate....
>
> The situation was Virginian to the end. Mr. Campbell refused any gift beyond the gift of thanks.[52]

For the better part of two decades, rural America had passively observed the growth of the automotive industry. While country people had frequently reacted violently to the results of automobile production, they had not sought to become actively involved in controlling its future. Basically, there were four reasons for this behavior. First, most farmers continued to believe that the automobile was a plaything of the rich and that motoring was a sport. They could see little utilitarian value for the automobile in their own lives. Second, those cars that had penetrated rural America had often experienced engine or transmission difficulties. Too many motor vehicles had to be towed back to town by the farmer's team to inspire much confidence in the car's mechanical dependability. Third, machines that ran well on the surfaced roads of urban areas frequently encountered insurmountable difficulties trying to navigate what country folk termed "roads." Because the latter were unlikely to be substantially improved in the near future, the function of even a mechanically perfect vehicle in a farming area was open to serious question. Finally, before the assembly line and mass production were introduced to automobile manufacturing, the price of motorized transport was just too much for most rural dwellers. The cost of a new car ranged from $1,000 to $5,000 at a time when a good horse could be bought for one-tenth that price.[53]

These four obstacles — utility, reliability, roads, and cost — guaranteed, according to one automotive historian, that until 1912, "except in a few great wheat-growing states the motorcar made no inroads on the farm, and comparatively little outside the cities."[54]

SIGNS OF ACCEPTANCE

Even while the automobile was being damned by many rural Americans, there were other, more hopeful indicators that the motor car would eventually be accepted, albeit slowly. In the following selection from a 1904 issue of *Horseless Age*, what begins as a typical description of a runaway team turns into a revelation of the determination of one farmer, who was by no means uncommon, to "break" his horse to the automobile:

> The first word I recognized from the farmer as the outfit came rushing toward us was "Whopee, I've got him. I've got him. Old Bill and I can hold him. I never had that cuss just where I wanted him

> before. Say, I'm glad I met you; that's worth a dollar. That cuss ran away with me when he saw one o' them mobiles three days ago and busted my buggy all to pieces. I've got him this time; me and old Bill." While this was going on, the off horse, at his master's command, had stopped and braced himself to stay, while the near horse was on his hind feet, pawing the air and making lunges for every cent he was worth. Seeing the off horse settle down with such intelligence, I fully realized why the farmer was so sure that he and "old Bill had 'im."[55]

Before the automobile could hope to dominate rural transportation, most contemporary observers believed it would need to do more than merely establish its right to the road; the motor car would need to show its superiority to the horse. As it turned out, there was to be room for both, each with its own clearly circumscribed sphere of activity. But at the end of the first decade of the twentieth century, many people felt it was an "either-or" proposition. The dissimilarities of the two types of conveyance were emphasized, rather than their complementary traits. Witness the observations of William Allen White in 1912 on the advantages of his horse, "Old Tom":

> He makes no claim to speed, but his carburetor always works, and while he has but two cylinders he brings his guests back in one piece and leaves them at home rather than downtown at the undertaker's to be assembled by total strangers into their aliquot parts.
>
> What if he isn't speedy? ... Old Tom may not have a windshield or speedometer. But what would he do with them? He is fully equipped with a few kind words and a whalebone whip.... Princes and potentates, fair women and brave men have lolled luxuriously among the $4 springs of the surrey behind Old Tom and have seen Emporia and Lyon County whizz by them at four miles an hour without fear or anxiety. They knew they were safe. He will go longer... on a forty-cent bale of hay than these new-fangled vessels of wrath fitted into destruction with a bucket of gasolene and a cord of rubber.
>
> Then ... there is this important thing to say of Old Tom; while, of course, it is difficult to get new parts when he breaks, yet after all

he is paid for, and there's no ninety-day note turning up every season to make the years a melancholy procession on the other side of the street from the bank....[56]

On the other hand were comments from rural automobile owners, such as the following statement of a gentleman who could see only good in his recent $1,500 investment:

It has answered every purpose to which I formerly put my horse. It has infinitely increased my sphere of activity and my pleasure. I can make a seventy-mile run now where I used to be sorry to go fifteen, and the astonishing part of it all is that it costs me less to maintain than my horse — in fact, not more than half as much. It may be that I am lucky, but I can't see why, with care, anyone could not duplicate my experience. I don't go after records, or eat up the roads; I don't make "joy rides" after a wine dinner, and I don't forget to oil things when they need it, nor to tighten a nut when it works loose; but neither did I forget to feed my horse or grease the carriage.... When I kept horses, and the hired man left, my household was thrown into a panic. Many a time I have lost hours from business to feed or water the brute. In the winter, when I close up my country place for six months, I have been forced to find the horse a boarding-place, since he wouldn't obligingly hibernate. He had to eat and be cared for, and a nearby stock farm boarded him for $12 a month.

The automobile costs me nothing to board when not in use, and I have actually been able to run it some months for as little as the $12 my horse cost without any use.[57]

The debate over the economics of keeping a horse vis-à-vis a car was to be a long and eventually indecisive one. A pre-1910 advertisement for the "McIntyre," an automobile produced by the W. H. McIntyre Company of Auburn, Indiana, stated that "it cost no more than a good horse and buggy — cost far less to keep — do more work in less time than three horses."[58] An early *Scientific American* writer reported that "from the statements of hundreds of users, it is found that the average cost of upkeep is not more than two-thirds that of keeping a horse."[59] Thus, in both initial outlay and maintenance, the automobile was superior — or was it?

An article appearing in *Country Life in America* noted that "a good car costs five times as much as a good horse and carriage," but suggested that it be regarded as an investment since "the life of an automobile is practically indefinite, with care."[60] However, it would have been difficult to convince many in 1909 that an automobile would outlast a good horse and carriage. The average life of a motor vehicle at that time was just five years.[61] As late as 1920, the *Farm Journal* was saying that "it is *probable* that the cost of maintenance of horses and equipment and the depreciation due to road work, makes transportation more expensive by horses than by the use of automobiles."[62] (Italics mine.) In the end, it was decided that certain functions were best and most cheaply performed when accomplished by a horse, and others by motor power. As a result, the horse generally was relegated to the field, only to be replaced eventually by the self-propelled tractor.

Some of the early hostility to the replacement of the horse by a machine must be attributed to plain sentimentality. After all, the economic argument in favor of the animal had little validity when one considered the time saved, the increase in potential haulage per vehicle, and the reserve power always available with the automobile. This emotional attachment can clearly be seen in the following poem:

The Horse he is a kind beast
And uses every care.
But the Motor is a blind beast,
And doesn't see you're there.

The Horse he is a mute beast,
And hardly says a neigh.
But the Motor is a brute beast,
And roars around all day.

The Horse he is a mild beast,
And lets you pat his head,
But the Motor is a wild beast,
And butts you til you're dead.[63]

As one student of American country life has observed: "The automobile made over our lives; but the auto never gave us the warmth of the living animal — a friend, or sometimes an enemy, but never impersonal."[64]

Even those who accepted the automobile frequently endowed it with animate characteristics. Thus, Louise Closser Hale, in her 1916 tour of Virginia, commented that she was "rather proud that we held to the road so well and hesitated only momentarily in the deep holes. It makes me feel sorry for an engine straining to do its level best, and I am impatient when they are shut up in a garage after a hard day's run without any appreciative oil or grease or kerosene in the cylinders. One might as well let a horse go supperless to bed."[65] It may well be that the citizen of "Plainville, U.S.A.," circa 1920, who felt that "the trouble with cars for a farmer is they don't have colts and they don't make manure," had more than economic matters on his mind.[66]

GENTLE PRODS FROM THE MANUFACTURER

Although the rural dweller had not always been aware of the advantages of the automobile, those who sold the latter had long recognized the potential profits to be derived from the former. Not until 1920 did the federal census show more people living in populations of over 2,500 than in smaller groups. By 1930, a full 40 per cent of the population still lived in such sparsely populated areas. Automotive manufacturers consequently devoted considerable effort toward wooing this market. As early as 1900, the Keystone Motor Company of Philadelphia advertised that their "Autocycle" was "BUILT FOR COUNTRY ROADS."[67] An ad for the pioneering curved-dash Oldsmobile was headed "The Passing of the Horse" and noted: "The silent horse power of this runabout is measurable, dependable and spontaneous — the horse-power generated by supplies of hay and oats is variable, uncertain, and irresponsive."[68] The effectiveness of these ads is shown by the fact that the Olds was the first automobile to sell on anything approaching a mass scale. In 1909, the Maxwell became the first car to be advertised in farm papers and country weeklies, its builders spending $2,500 in a two-month experiment. Results were so good that the company continued this policy and soon was joined by other manufacturers.[69] The appeal to the farmer gradually became more direct, using the rural idiom at times, as in this wording for the 1911 Brush Runabout: "You can use the Brush in numberless ways — going to town, 'getting 'round' the farm, taking produce to market and bringing back the supplies. The women folks can use the car for visiting or shopping, or the children for going to school."[70]

One year later, Hupmobile placed an advertisement in the May 4 issue of the *Rural New Yorker*. A portion of the text is interesting in its emphasis on the reliability of the automobile and the use of what would be termed today "the soft sell" testimonial:

> "I was pulling through the mud along by a farmer's house. Just in front of the house was some water, and I thought I would have some fun; so I let my motor die slowly and stopped for a chat. I asked him if he would get his team and pull me out. He answered: 'There are not two teams in the country that could do that.'
>
> "Then I told him that I would have to pull myself, and he said: 'I guess you can stay with me until the mud dries up a little.'
>
> "When I was ready to go on, I started up as if nothing had happened.
>
> "*He said he was going to have a car of that kind.*"[71]

Not all the dealers had to start from scratch, relying on advertising, both printed and word-of-mouth, to popularize their particular vehicles. Farm implement dealers, with reputations already established, began to manufacture automobiles or to serve as sales representatives for others.[72] Both J. I. Case Threshing Machine and International Harvester produced early motor cars. The latter's 1907 "International Auto Buggy" had a removable rear seat, making possible its conversion into a light delivery truck.[73] Such convertibility was an early strong selling point. Many wagon manufacturers, believing the farmer to be their best customer, also began a transition to the manufacture of motor vehicles. The most successful of these was Studebaker.[74]

Mail-order houses, whose dependence on the isolated rural resident was well known, also sought entry into an obviously expanding market. In 1898, Montgomery Ward had had two electric vehicles made for them as advertising gimmicks, although their catalogue explained, "We are sending them to the small towns of the Union so that those who might otherwise never see a horseless carriage will have the opportunity. . . ."[75] In 1909, Sears, Roebuck and Company began an ill-fated attempt to manufacture and sell their own complete vehicle through their catalogue. Although such assembled automobiles proved financially unprofitable and were dropped from the Sears catalogue, both Sears and Montgomery Ward continued to sell automotive supplies through the mails.[76]

Although manufacturers realized the potential of the rural market, it was often difficult to secure a sales representative in the desired area. The business was too risky to be counted on for one's total income, and it therefore became a side enterprise for many that were otherwise employed. Retired farmers, when they could be enlisted, often turned out to be ingenious salesmen, knowing the "farm mentality" as they did. Floyd Clymer recalls an incident in Berthoud, Colorado, which exemplifies this:

> There was a fast-talking old farmer in the area who had taken to the "gas buggy" and was dealing out Fords for Henry. One of his neighboring farmers was looking for just the right automobile, and the old codger proceeded to give his friend and prospective buyer a demonstration. The buyer had heard down at the barbershop that several drivers, gripping their wheels for dear life, had tried to crawl up a steep quarter mile of hill from the road to his house. He promised to buy a Ford if he could be shown that it would climb the hill. "Be glad to," said the farmer-salesman, and he started up the hill. . . . The jalopy did fine until about halfway up the hill, when it began to buck and cough. The quick-witted salesman cramped the wheels over and swung into a side lane. He pushed the reverse pedal and backed into the hill road again, remarking with great

> pride, "You see, this hill is really nothing. I can even back up it." At the top of the hill, the buyer, in great wonderment, signed the order.[77]

(He learned later, no doubt, that the rear-wheel-drive Model T had better traction when in reverse than in any of its forward gears.)

Probably as many "demonstrations" were offered to rural dwellers by contemporary owners as by dealers. The car was such a novelty that a ride in one without incident was frequently enough to sell the vehicle. As a 1911 issue of *Motor Age* editorialized: "Those farmers who already own cars are big advertisements in the selling of other machines. Society works along the same lines in the country as in the city, and where one farmer has a car, there is immediately bred in his fellow farmers a desire to own a better one. The very fact of farmers without cars seeing others pass and repass their homes in cars stirs up and creates the spirit to buy."[78]

Manufacturers also realized the importance of participation in social activities of a rural character. Thus, in 1912 *Horseless Age* was hailing what it called an "elaborate display of automobiles" at the Indianapolis State Fair.[79] On a more local level, car owners in Walworth County, Wisconsin (population 3,250), organized their own auto show in 1914. Local agents representing fifty different makers purchased exhibition space.[80]

These advertisements, demonstrations, and exhibitions had their desired effect, as the trade publication *Automotive Industries* noted. Not only had total sales in towns smaller than 10,000 inhabitants surpassed those in larger centers, but the future seemed to depend on sales to the farmer and small-town resident.

> Out in those areas referred to as "the sticks" by most of the sophisticated urbanites who make up the bulk of factory personnel; ... out there where salesmen are still drummers in rural sections, the little villages and towns of less than 10,000 population, the

basis of American automobile growth is being made more solid every year.

Here are a few of the reasons why these towns . . . are of such vast importance to the manufacturers of motor vehicles in America today:

About 55 percent of all the motor vehicles in use are in towns of less than 10,000 population.

About 58 per cent of the entire population of the United States is located in these small towns.

About 57 per cent of all the service stations are in these towns.

Every conspicuously successful manufacturer of low priced cars has more than 70 per cent of all his dealers in these areas.

The four leading producers of high priced cars have a greater percentage of their retail outlets in towns of less than 10,000 population than have any of their less successful competitors.

One further fact of major significance remains to be added to the list. $3,980,000,000 worth of automotive products of all kinds were sold last year in towns of less than 10,000 population. This huge sum comprised 57.4 per cent of total retail automotive sales throughout the country.[81]

ECONOMIC ADVANTAGES TO RURAL RESIDENTS

Obviously such success was not due exclusively to salesmanship. Rural residents were attracted initially because the automobile seemed to offer economic advantages. (The social effects of the automobile were given little consideration until after it had been accepted as an economic necessity in rural life.)

Cars with removable bodies had been introduced by 1907. In 1910, the Schacht Manufacturing Company of Cincinnati was offering such a vehicle at the low price of $875.[82] As a 1911 article in *Country Life in America* noted:

Such a car carries the family to church, country fairs, and to lectures, theatres and stores in nearby towns; it carries the children to school, while on the farm it takes the owner about his daily circuit in less than half the usual time, carrying along with him, tools,

> lunches, and a laborer or two, if desirable . . . For quick runs to town to carry milk, butter and eggs, an occasional hog, calf or live chickens it is handy; and when some farm machine breaks it saves much delay because of the short time in which a new part may be secured from the nearest supply store.[83]

Within a year, Ernest L. Ferguson was announcing the demise of this combination car in *Scientific American*, claiming that the faults of its "construction so militated against its continuance as a matter of manufacturing that there came from it no large results."[84] Although farmers experimented during this period with carrying light loads directly in the tonneaus of touring cars and with hitching a regular produce wagon to the rear axle,[85] the dissatisfaction with "combination cars" lay almost completely with the manufacturer. By the mid-teens, trucks were available of such quality and in such quantity to enable the manufacturers to abandon the combination option. This, however, is not to say that rural residents discontinued the practice of removing and replacing the rear seat of their touring cars on their own initiative. Despite their early demise, such combination vehicles must be given considerable credit for initially attracting the farmer to the motor car.

Attempts were also made to adapt the passenger car for use in the field as a self-propelled plow or tractor. The Geneva (Ohio) Tractor Company sold an "Adapto-Tractor" for use with Ford cars.[86] In design, it seems to have been similar to the converters at the 1917 Los Angeles tractor show, described by Edward C. Crossman:

> The simplest modification was merely taking off the rear wheels and substituting therefor wide-tread steel tractor wheels with the familiar "Grousers." Steel-tired wheels were substituted for the front wheels. To get the requisite gear reduction for the power and low rate of speed of this tractor, the low speed gear of the car was used. The scheme is not the best possible one, because of the comparative inefficiency of the low speed of any planetary transmission [the type of drive employed in Ford's Model T] and the tendency to heat the motor. . . .

> Possibly more efficient was the scheme, used by various makers of tractor attachments, of bolting on a heavy supplementary axle to the chassis at the rear.... This heavy axle carried the tractor wheels, with tread up to 14 inches in width, while the rear axle of the car was used merely as a jackshaft to drive the wheels.[87]

In regard to the last point, Charles E. Sorensen has observed: "The horse and the plow had been separate, and so, in the reasoning of the day, the tractor that supplanted the horse should be hitched to the plow."[88] However, by 1916 Ford was producing the single-unit Fordson tractor (tractor and plow together), and this was to prove the more successful design.

The use of the automobile on the road and in the field involved simply applying motor power to what formerly had been accomplished by the horse. Far more ingenious were the adaptations developed to lighten the work involved in the various odd jobs around the farm. Cars were used to saw wood, pump water, generate electricity, run small grain mills, and unload hay.[89] In 1909 C. O. Morris described the mechanics of one such operation:

> A Philadelphia friend of mine once showed me how he utilized his touring-car on his farm. We had about an hour's ride in the car to reach his place. The automobile was then jacked up, a belt attached to one of the rear wheels, and in less than five minutes after the car was on the road it was doing duty as a piece of farm machinery.
>
> The belt was attached to a fodder cutter, and the efforts of two of the farm hands were required to keep the machine fed with material while the big touring-car did its work.... To anyone who has seen this sort of work done by hand it was a revelation of the possibilities of applying ready-made power to the machinery of a farm.[90]

Not all automotively inspired innovations were successful. Ellis P. Butler's attempt to create a power washing machine using the same belt mechanism described above led to some major complications.

> Mary [a servant] put the soap in the washing-machine, and the hot water, and the clothes, and I started the engine. It was all that I hoped. Never, never indeed, had I seen clothes washed so rapidly. Luckily, I had thought to nail the legs of the washing-machine to the floor of the back porch. This steadied the washing-machine and kept it from jumping very much. Of course some vibration was conveyed along the belt from the automobile, and Mary had to hasten to and fro, bringing more hot water to refill the washing-machine. It was like a storm at sea, or a geyser, or a large fountain. When at good speed the water hardly entered the washing-machine before it dashed madly out again, and Isobel [his wife] had to help out by putting in more clothes continuously. It used up clothes as rapidly as Rolf's friend's fodder-cutter used up fodder, but I think it cut the clothes into smaller pieces. We discovered this when we hunted up the clothes afterward. We did not know it at the time. All was excitement at the time.[91]

Most important of all, from the rural point of view, were the economies believed possible in the marketing of farm products by automobile. To a certain extent, this belief may have been irrational. As the rural sociologist John M. Gillette has noted, "transportation ordinarily forms a very small part of the marketing costs."[92] Nevertheless, the quantity of writing on the subject clearly indicates that rural residents, particularly farmers, treated transportation economies as a decisive factor when deciding to buy.

A 1920 survey conducted by the National Automobile Chamber of Commerce showed the average farmer driving his car 4,600 miles a year, with business purposes accounting for 78 percent of the distance. It was also found that only 10 percent of the automobiles were used for pleasure driving exclusively.[93] As J. C. Long remarked in *Outlook,* "It is doubtful if the farmer would have adopted the automobile so universally had it served merely to take him more readily to hear Will Carleton at the Lyceum Course."[94]

The automobile, and later the truck, widened the range of the market with which the farmer dealt. With the horse, he had been limited to ten to twenty miles. If the market or transfer point were farther away, the farmer's highway transportation costs wiped out any profits he might receive from the transaction. Therefore, he was really limited to subsistence farming.[95]

By 1928, however, analysts such as Harvey W. Peck were examining the farm depression of the twenties and concluding that

> unlike the manufacturer, the farmer, contrary to what is popularly supposed, is probably not more prosperous because of the automobile. He may have benefited by it in non-economic ways; but something evidently is not increasing the farmer's wealth or his real prosperity.... Used as farm machinery the motor truck and the passenger car economize time, and make possible more work on the farm and an increased out-put of farm products. Since the farmers were already producing all that could be sold at an advantage, this increased out-put may be one of the causes of a declining relative price for agricultural commodities....
>
> The automobile, which is now a necessity, since the hard-surfaced roads make transportation by horses and wagon expensive and dangerous, has tended to increase the over-head cost of agricultural production [as well]. Hence, the automobile causes an increase in revenue and an increase in expense. This probably means a decrease in the net income of the average farmer.[96]

If we accept Gillette's earlier statement about transportation costs, it is possible that in chasing after the false lure of transportation economies, the farmer actually worsened his economic position by purchasing an automobile.

Although the economic motivation may have been paramount in the farmer's mind, at least one Studebaker agent felt that there was a social explanation for the appeal of the motor car: "No farmer ever bought one purely from a standpoint of saving time and money. It's the fun of the thing that appeals to him. I usually cinch a sale after my man has driven the car slowly for a quarter of a mile or so. He is tickled to death with the sport."[97] Nevertheless, overwhelming evidence indicates that the initial impetus for the purchase of an automobile in rural America was the real or imagined economic advantage ownership brought.

WHAT WAS BOUGHT AND HOW

Through World War I, the steadily increasing prosperity of the American farmer helps to explain the fairly rapid diffusion of the motor car in rural areas. After the war, however, farm prices began to fall and continued to do so throughout the 1920s. Still, the *Literary Digest* noted early in that decade that "the farmer with an apparent income below the income-tax minimum is yet a perfectly legitimate prospect for a low-priced car."[98] How can one explain this apparent contradiction?

First, it is important to realize that in the early twenties over one-half of all automobiles were owned by families with cash incomes below $2,000.[99] Second, the widespread acceptance of the installment plan made possible purchases formerly thought to be impossible. Third, buying a car was largely a question of priorities, and many rural dwellers felt that for economic and social reasons the automobile ought to rank high. Fourth, the automobile became less expensive at the very time that rural America had less money to spend. Thus, in 1926, Ford was selling its runabout for $260 and the Model T touring car for $290. In comparison, the latter had sold for $950 in 1909, and as late as 1916, the runabout had sold for as much as $390.

Not only had the market price dropped, but so had the real price. In 1925, according to United States Department of Agriculture figures, the farmer was paying about one-third what he had paid in 1913 for an automobile in terms of wheat, corn, cotton, and wool.[100] These figures increased to the farmer's disadvantage by 1929, but it still took only 59.5 percent of the wheat, 44.7 percent of the corn, 50.2 percent of the cotton, and 38.4 percent of the wool that it had in 1913 to purchase a car in 1929.[101] Prices of two other automotive necessities, tires and gasoline, showed the same trend.[102] (Apropos these figures, it should be noted that at least one automobile distributor was willing to take produce in exchange for used cars in 1920.)[103]

These price advantages created a favorable attitude among farmers toward the automobile business, and this attitude was a significant contrast with their traditional view of manufacturing interests. "Farmers have been friendly toward automotive products because they have realized that the manufacturers have passed on to the ultimate consumer the benefits of manufacturing economies and lower material costs," said *Automotive Industries*. "They don't feel that other industries have been as fair in this respect."[104]

James R. Howard, president of the American Farm Bureau Federation in 1922, expressed much the same attitude and added his opinion of the automobile industry:

> It has taken natural resources to improve our standards of living and given profitable employment to an army of laborers. It developed at a most fortunate time for agriculture, for there were unmistakable signs of a stagnation in the agricultural market. I am not sure, but it is entirely possible that the increased demand for agricultural products created by the development of the automotive industry has paid for the farmers' automobiles.[105]

Whether the automobile industry was responsible for what little agricultural prosperity there was is open to question, but the enunciation of this idea by the president of the American Farm Bureau Federation must have had considerable impact on rural America.

THE QUESTION OF MAINTENANCE

It was also somewhat cheaper to maintain a motor vehicle in rural America than elsewhere. (Obviously, initial cost varied little from place to place.) For instance, the ordinary barn or shed could serve as a garage. Furthermore, oil and gas could be bought in large quantities at wholesale. One of Sterling North's characters in *Plowing on Sunday* "filled the gasoline tank of his Ford from the big, red barrel mounted on sawhorses beside the milk house. . . ."[106]

Finally, the average farmer had had experience with power-driven machinery, especially the stationary gasoline engine, and thus was capable of making some repairs himself.[107] By 1912, a writer for *Scientific American* was claiming that "there has been brought about without definite effort, in fact, automatically in the best use of the term, a service upkeep condition based on knowledge that equals in its experience much of that possessed by the men who are sent out by manufacturers from their service departments."[108] One must take care, however, not to overrate the farmer's mechanical skill, as distinct from his aptitude. *Motor Age* cautioned in its lead editorial for March 18, 1915, that the farmer "has repaired machinery but most of this work has not been of the delicate nature that characterizes motor car tinkering; such repairs being mostly of a makeshift order."[109]

Nonetheless, historian Allan Nevins was probably correct when he concluded that "farmers, as dealers agreed, studied cars more sagaciously before purchase than any other group. . . . Many owned small gasoline engines and knew a good motor when they saw it. They seldom paid more than $1000 for a car; they almost never bought one at second hand; and they cared more for durability than style. Understanding machinery, knowing how to fight out their own battles, and seldom worrying about a little grease and dirt on their clothes, they were ready to service their own automobiles."[110]

Obviously, a cash outlay was still necessary to operate and repair the vehicle. Contemporary accounts indicate wide variation in such expenditures, dependent to some extent on the owner's income. In the late twenties, Carle C. Zimmerman and John D. Black did a study in Minnesota of the "average distribution of net spendable income" among five factors, one of which was the automobile. They found that the average upkeep cost on a farm car was $208, which exhausted 12 percent of the average net spendable income.[111] Interestingly, these figures are significantly higher than similar ones secured earlier in the decade, where it was found that "only" 7.2 per cent of a *gross* cash income of $2,500 was spent on the automobile.[112] (This should be compared with the 14-15 percent found by Zimmerman and Black for a similar income range.)[113] Insofar as these figures can be compared, it would appear that while the relative cost of tires and gasoline were going down during this period, the percentage of farm income being spent on them was going up. It may therefore be concluded that the automobile was an item of increasing priority in the lives of Minnesota farmers at this time.[114]

It should be emphasized that these figures do not represent the total cost of owning an automobile, but only operation and maintenance expenses. In the early thirties, J. F. Steiner of the President's Research Committee on Social Trends estimated the average annual cost of operation, including depreciation, interest on investment, and general upkeep, as being $350.[115] Unfortunately, this amount is an average for both rural and urban America and may also have been affected by the onset of the depression. Still, it is indicative of the added expenses of installment payments and depreciation which were frequently forgotten by the owner in estimating the yearly cost of his automobile.

THE CAR THAT DID IT ALL

In Rodgers and Hammerstein's musical *Oklahoma!*, Curly tries to impress "his gal" by describing the vehicle they will use on their date — "the surrey with the fringe on top." Driven by a team of snow-white horses, it featured yellow wheels, brown upholstery, a genuine leather dashboard, and isinglass curtains. "Ain't no finer rig," he rightly concludes, for turn-of-the-century rural America.[16]

Twenty years later, another vehicle had caught Oklahoma's fancy. "Its function and design were in spirit a utilitarian creation of rural America," Professor George Mowry observed. "It was black, sober-looking, innocent of sophistication or adornment, and without much provision for the comfort of its passengers."[117] Yet there was little question in rural America that the car's practicality more than offset its dull appearance. Stephen Longstreet was not unique in his remembrance of the Model T Ford:

> It was a much better car in many ways than those we had a few years later. It was simpler; it had no battery, no complicated wiring system, no automatic window-lifters or seat-movers to get out of order. We sat over the gas tank and measured it from time to time with a wooden ruler to see if we needed gas. It was not streamlined to uncomfortable sitting space, and it was high enough to keep its crankcase from being broken by ruts, ditches, or low road crossings. It needed no brake fluids, special gasolines, greases, or doctored motor oils. A healthy man could lift it up by a corner for repairs. The fenders needed no expensive repairing, the body no specialist's body work. A jack could still fit under the car, and no chrome wheel shields, fancy locks, or a collection of many unneeded dashboard dials existed. In clumsy hands, with non-mechanical minds, it ran well. Its illnesses were few, and the average citizen could attend to them with dime-store parts. If the radiator leaked, one dropped in a raw egg; the hot water soon sealed all leaks with hardboiled egg.[118]

The popular Model T soon became affectionately known as the "flivver." This synonym, which appeared sometime between 1909 and 1914, is of uncertain derivation. Although the word may be a combination of several contemporary slang terms, Rudolph E. Anderson offers an interesting explanation: "The shaking of the Ford gave a certain amount of exercise to the liver as does riding a horse. A dealer or owner, perhaps in self-defense, explained that the shaking Ford was 'good for the liver.' In typical fashion this was shortened to 'f'th liver,' then further abbreviated to 'fliver,' and lastly 'flivver.' "[119] Historian Frank Donovan has called this reasoning far-fetched,[120] but James J. Bradley, head of the Automotive History Collection of the Detroit Public Library, calls it "one of the best explanations of the derivation of the word 'flivver' I have seen."[121]

Whatever the etymology of its name, the flivver was truly a marvel of mechanical ingenuity; if Longstreet's raw egg did not work, others suggested using a handful of oatmeal or cornmeal to plug the leak.[122] According to a eulogy in *The New Yorker* in 1936, "one reason the Ford anatomy was never reduced to an exact science was that having 'fixed' it, the owner couldn't honestly claim that the treatment had brought about the cure. There were too many authenticated cases of Fords fixing themselves — restored naturally to health after a short rest. Farmers soon discovered this, and it fitted nicely with their draft-horse philosophy: 'Let 'er cool off and she'll snap into it again.' "[123]

Beside the low price, Ford's mass production guaranteed standardized parts, and these were available in even the smallest town. Allan Nevins notes that in 1912 there was a Ford dealer in practically every town of 2,000 or more.[124] As late as 1930, 38 percent of the Ford dealers were still in towns with populations under 1,000; this was true for only 27 percent of the non-Ford dealers. An additional 27 percent of the Ford dealerships were in towns of 1,000 to 2,500. Thus, 65 percent of the Ford dealers in 1930 were located in rural areas (as defined by the federal census). Since non-Ford dealers had 46 per cent of their offices in rural America, Ford's investment in rural areas was almost twenty percent greater than that of all the other makers combined.[125]

A third factor influencing rural sales was the availability of parts. Not all dealers carried accessories or serviced vehicles. In 1929, 92 percent of the Ford outlets handled accessories, while only 70 percent of the non-Ford dealers did so.[126] Complementing this was the fact that Ford was one of the few manufacturers to offer a *reliable* service warranty.[127]

Parts made specifically for the Model T were also available through the mail-order companies.[128] However, because of the time that would have been involved in sending for and receiving the item(s), such business was probably carried out more in fringe accessories than in repair parts. Beginning in 1919, a more likely source of Ford parts was the nearest garage. After January 1 of that year, replacement items were available to any garage at the regular dealer's discount.[129]

To understand what a boon the existence of nearby dealers and parts could be, one has only to read Harold B. Chase's experience of "repair service" in rural Ohio prior to 1912:

> There wasn't a vestige of a garage, repair shop or service station within ten miles of our home and even at that distance, a repair shop was nothing more nor less than a blacksmith shop. The owner was likely to be a brawny, but enterprising individual who was more adept at hammering out on an anvil a farm axle from a bar of cherry-red iron than at making an adjustment on even one of the less complicated parts of the mechanism of an automobile. I drove my limping Ford into one once which displayed a new sign gallantly displaying the words, AUTOS FIXED.
>
> Only two of the four cylinders were functioning. It happened that I was on my way to a place where I preferred to arrive with at least a semblance of clean hands and I hopefully thought this would be a good place to have the spark plugs cleaned, which was a necessary operation about every hour while driving. I left the engine running and took off the hood (it didn't raise), explaining to the "mechanic" my suspicions about the plugs. Whether or not this was his first repair job after audaciously hanging up the sign, I'll never know, but I do know that, instead of testing the plugs with a wooden-handled screwdriver or wrench — a procedure dictated by ordinary caution — he stuck his hairy grimy hand in and grabbed hold of a plug. With a yelp, he almost disappeared in the smoke that hung under the low ceiling of the shop! When he was back down on the ground and sufficiently collected to utter an intelligible sentence, he yelled at me above the clatter of the engine, "Shut that goddam thing off."[130]

Finally, studies conducted in the mid-twenties revealed what rural dwellers had long suspected: the Model T was better built, and it lasted longer. A 1926 investigation at the University of Michigan by Professor Clare E. Griffin made just this point and added that: "The low cost of repairs, the relative simplicity of the mechanism, the fact that many a farmer's boy can do the repair work himself, the large number and wide distribution of the service stations, all would tend to that conclusion."[131]

Homer Croy's physical description in *R.F.D. No. 3* of a well-used Model T, though fictional, provides a fine concluding picture for this section:

> Among the automobiles which had come to town this morning was one belonging to the Decker family, living six miles west of Junction City. It was a Ford, one that had been banged about a great deal and which was used for both pleasure and profit. It never made a trip to Junction City without bringing something in addition to passengers — chickens, plows, machinery parts, milk cans, vegetables; on returning it carried out to the farm nail-kegs, gasoline, wire-stretchers, harness, shorts, bran, stock feed. There was no carpet on the floor; one of the fenders was held in place by a rusted wire, and a crack in the windshield had a piece of yellow paper pasted over it.[132]

This was a far cry from Curly's "surrey with the fringe on top," yet Ford was destined to sell over 15,000,000 Model T's. Although its popularity waned in the late twenties, the flivver, more than any other car, personified the acceptance of the automobile by rural America.

CONCLUSION

The eagerness with which rural Americans acquired motor cars, especially after World War I, is dramatically revealed by the statistics available. In 1911, it was estimated that 85,000 automobiles were used on farms in the United States.[133] By 1920, this number had risen to 2,146,512, according to the United States Department of Agriculture.[134] Finally, figures released by the National Automobile Chamber of Commerce in 1930 showed 9,724,950 passenger cars on farms and in towns of under 1,000 residents. This represented 42 percent of the *total* passenger automobile registration for that year. If one adds the cars in towns of 1,000 to 2,500, the totals become 10,994,325 and 47.6

percent, respectively.[135] (It should be noted that, of these, 4,910,300 vehicles were on farms.)[136]

The authoritative *Rural New Yorker* was claiming in 1924 that "the tendency now is for a country family to own two cars — a light one for quick work and a heavier one for family use."[137] Astounding as this may sound, it seems to be supported by the Department of Commerce's 1920 Agricultural Census. This showed that of the total 6,448,343 farms in America, 1,979,564 or 30.7 percent reported having automobiles. However, the number of cars was 2,146,362.[138] Hence, 166,798 farms, or 8 percent of those reporting automobiles, may have had more than one.[139] By 1930, 58 percent of the American farms had at least one motor car, according to the federal census, an increase of almost 28 percent in ten years.[140]

The advent of some nine million vehicles in twenty years was bound to have wide-ranging repercussions. In 1922, a study of a Traer, Iowa, implement dealer revealed "the first buggy sale in two or three years and in several years records do not show of over four. Not so many years ago dealers with a stock of less than seventy buggies were considered small and daily sales of three were not unusual."[141]

The report cited above is a fine example of the significant changes in rural economic life brought about by the automobile. Nonetheless, the *social* implications inherent in such observations would ultimately affect life on the farm and in the small town even more profoundly. For in changing the transportation habits of rural America, the motor car transformed the very institutions that defined life outside urban areas. The extended farm family, the crossroads rural community, the Protestant church, the little red schoolhouse, the country doctor — these were some of the traditional foundations of rural American life that were destined to be altered radically by the twentieth-century transportation and communications revolution, in which the motor car was to play such an important role.

We turn now to an investigation of how this automotive "invasion" of nine million cars affected the social aspects of life in rural America, beginning with the institution of the family.

The farmer and the motorized city slicker were often not the best of friends. This cartoon is from the 1906 book *Auto Fun*. (*T. Y. Crowell*)

This South Carolina farm in 1927 shows an evolutionary stage between the carriage barn and the two car garage. (*National Archives*)

II. The Farm Family

"No burden," concluded Edward R. Eastman in 1927, "has ever set quite as heavily on farming and upon the farm family as has the curse of isolation and loneliness."[1] The *Yearbook of Agriculture* for 1928 reported that while eight million of the farm population lived within five miles of towns of 2,500 or more, twenty million were even more isolated.[2] A government circular entitled *The Farm Woman's Problems* revealed that members of the average farm family had to travel approximately three miles to reach the local church, five miles to market, six miles to high school and the family doctor, and fourteen miles to a hospital.[3]

Before the automobile, isolated and lonely farmers were always on the lookout for new avenues of social contact. Although most farm families made periodic trips into town or to relatives, Theodore M. R. von Kéler, writing for *Collier's*, noted in 1915 that such journeys were often "an experience to be classed with the hardest work."[4] Similarly, Eastman recalled: "One of the big events of my boyhood was that of going once a year with Mother to 'grandpa's house.' We started with the old farm 'plug' [a worn-out horse] before daylight and we traveled all day long before we came to the end of the journey. All of us, including the horse, whose gait had become slower and slower, were tired out. Today [1927] the same distance can be made with a car in less than an hour."[5]

The farmer was isolated largely because of the nature of his occupation. The old necessity for cooperative economic enterprise had been mitigated greatly by the widespread introduction of farm machinery.[6] Ironically, increased mechanization often led to increased output, rather than more leisure time to visit the neighbors.

Furthermore, as Warren H. Wilson observed, the farm needed constant attention: "The claims of domesticated animals upon the farmer are such as to chain his foot to the homestead. He can go from home only so far as will permit him to get back in time to spray his orchard trees or to cultivate his corn. The only type of farming that permits the farmer a long range is the one-crop farming which may, if he keeps no horse or cow or fowls, give him liberty for certain months of the year. Such farmers are often too poor to travel."[7] Thus, until the introduction of the motor car, the American farmer found the "team-haul" to be equivalent to the radius of the rural community. Known to all within its boundaries, he was a stranger beyond.

Limited as it was to the idiosyncrasies of one community, the farm family had the unenviable choice of adapting to the existing social structure or facing social ostracism.[8] Even acceptance in the local town-dominated community meant only infrequent group gatherings. Rural sociologist Charles J. Galpin noted that, as a result, "such neighbors as farmers have are also exclusively farmers.... The full force of this fact can come home to us only when we establish the minute modifications of ideas in any individual child, attained through the face-to-face contact, conflict, sympathy with children reared in families where the fundamental occupational concepts are different. The city child is under the stimulating influence of a score or more of varied occupational technics. What is true of the child in this respect is true still more perhaps of the adult."[9]

Of all the members of the farm family, the farm wife felt the isolation most acutely. Her trips beyond the farm were infrequent and her tasks at home constantly repetitious. In many respects, this situation was aggravated by technological developments at the turn of the century. Modern conveniences such as the telephone, the automobile, indoor plumbing, and the wonders electricity could bring — all of which were beyond her grasp in the foreseeable future — created a new sense of dissatisfaction. A writer in 1912 noted that "these farm women find themselves in a new civilization, but not of it.... In many cases, from a financial standpoint, they can as well afford the luxuries of modern life as the majority of those who possess them. But, as the wives of farmers, they must give themselves to the land. Their houses go neglected that they may help with work in the fields. Their hands are coarse and rough from assisting their husbands with pressing work on the land."[10]

Sometimes the monotony of her existence was relieved by the appearance of an unannounced salesman. Unfortunately, a short stay by him, which would have proven psychologically beneficial, was not possible. Before country roads were improved to accommodate the automobile, transportation conditions often required that the agent stay the night, or longer. A South Dakota woman wrote the Department of Agriculture on this subject in 1915: "Many a farmer's wife is forced to be a country hotel keeper without pay, and if on rare occasions a man with conscience does pay, it is no compensation, even at regular hotel rates, for the extra washing, cleaning, and cooking thrust upon an already tired woman.... This condition causes girls to desert the farm. It steals their leisure time for which they had planned reading, music, driving, or visiting. They wonder why there is no privacy in the farm home when in the city, town, or village the home is sacred to its owners and their friends."[11]

When the farm woman did leave the farm, it always meant falling behind in her household chores. The ride itself could be difficult, and the town even boring, as noted by a Michigan woman: "I am haunted now by the faces of the women I find myself looking for on the street corners, knowing they have to endure the tiresome driving in uncomfortable wagons over heavy roads behind slow and unattractive horses. I see the long list of purchases to be made in town, then the waiting for all the party to get together, the late arrival home, tired, cold, and hungry, and the extra work to do after dark on account of the half day off."[12]

Because of the isolation of the farm family, parents remained the dominant force in the character development of youth. The possible competition or reinforcement of values by the church and school was not as great as is usually assumed.[13] As Ernest R. Groves wrote in *The Rural Mind and Social Welfare*, country youth could be expected to emerge quite different from their urban counterparts:

> The working conditions of farm life tend to bring into association the several members of a family; for indeed, much of farming in America still remains in some degree a family industry. The son works with his father in the fields; the daughter helps the mother with the housework. Even the recreation of the children is apt to be more under the eye of the parents than is ever possible in the urban environment.
>
> It follows that the rural family performs a larger function along educational lines than would be feasible under different industrial and social conditions. The companionship between parents and children makes it easy for the parents to impress their standards of life strongly on their children. Their influence meets less competition than does that of city parents.[14]

The problem of rural migration into towns and cities, discussed in the following chapter, was largely a youth movement. The isolation and loneliness of the typical farm household simply were not conducive to the social activities and desires of the maturing teenager.

INTRODUCTION OF THE AUTOMOBILE

Although isolation was generally seen as a social evil, it did make the farm home the focus of leisure activities. By contributing to the end of such provincialism, the motor car seriously threatened the unity of the family, though this problem was not seen clearly at the time. "The possession of an automobile means greater frequency of visits and thereby the keeping together of family ties, not a growing apart in ever widening stretches," observed Ernest L. Ferguson in 1912.[15]

Yet the time involved in traveling by horse and buggy had led to prolonged albeit infrequent visits. With the automobile, there may have been less sociability. As rural sociologist James M. Williams observed, "Instead of coming to stay the afternoon, the farmer's family is out for a long ride to some adjacent city and drives into a friend's yard for a few minutes; then away they go."[16] Thus, although the nuclear family may have increased its number and range of acquaintanceships, these probably were not as strong as those that preceded the automobile.

Furthermore, the introduction of the motor car may have decreased interest in the farmstead itself. It was, after all, necessary to go away from the home to enjoy the automobile. The Lynds found that in "Middletown" the motor car was "making noticeable inroads upon the traditional prestige of the family's meal-times at certain points; it has done much to render obsolete the leisurely Sunday noon dinner of a generation ago . . . , and during half the year when 'getting out in the car' is pleasant, it often curtails the evening meal to an informal 'bite' ".[17]

These trips, which were seen as so damaging to family life, apparently developed at a more rapid rate than those longer journeys which were to accelerate the urbanization of rural America. In a volume prepared for the President's Committee on Social Trends, Malcolm M. Willey and Stuart A. Rice concluded that

> longer journeys by more people are now made with relatively greater frequency than ever before. But *an even greater intensification of mobility takes place within circumscribed local areas.* While the average user of the automobile travels on occasion to distant points (with resulting new experiences and contacts) his travel within the narrower limits of the local area increases even more. *Contacts within the community are multiplied out of proportion to contacts at a distance.*... The problem of appraisal is how to balance the effects of these opposing tendencies: on the one hand are more frequent contacts which may be destructive of provincialism; on the other are still more intensified local contacts which may serve to foster it.[18]

Similarly opposing tendencies characterize the automobile's effect on what Sorokin, Zimmerman, and Galpin term "the familistic basis on which rural society was organized in the past. . . ."[19] According to those authors, the family "has lost ground rapidly as nonfamilistic elements similar to those in the city, elements based on contact with persons and institutions outside the family, increase in importance."[20] Thus, it would appear that farm families paid for the loss of their isolation with a decrease in the unity of the nuclear family. By increasing leisure, the automobile had made the farm home more enjoyable and more worthwhile,[21] but it had also provided individual members of the family with the means to pursue separate activities.[22]

When the family did travel together, they were subjected (willingly, no doubt) to the powerful forces of urbanization, which would eventually overwhelm the traditional form of rural life. G. Walter Fiske, writing on the development of rural leadership in 1917, was hopeful that the spread of city customs and ideals would have a positive effect:

> To the extent that these customs and ideals are constructive and adaptable to a wholesome country life, to that extent this urbanization makes for socialization and should be welcomed. Unquestionably, this process, hastened by increasing intercommunication, is rapidly making country life and city life more alike, and is extending the limits of suburban life. It is to be hoped that

> this urbanizing will not destroy the unique social consciousness of rural civilization and make it simply imitative of the city. On the other hand, it is hoped that the city may more effectively teach the country the secrets of socialization, so that the social efficiency of urban life may be reproduced in the country.[23]

Others hoped that, as a result, "the city man, instead of assuming a superior and unsympathetic attitude toward those who have not had the advantages of which he boasts, will come to respect and love the guardian of those natural products and resources from which the imperious city draws its power."[24]

Urbanization, though, is an inanimate force, compounded of many elements. Although the automobile drew the rural dweller and his urban counterpart closer together geographically, it does not necessarily follow that they became friendlier. David L. Cohn is typical of twentieth-century historians and rural sociologists in observing that this was far from true in the case of farmers and small-town residents, even though they continuously came into contact with each other.[25]

While the automobile may have had the potential to alter rural institutional life and mores radically, this was not the prime concern of the average farm family. Their isolation had led them to think in individualistic terms, and their primary concern was enhancing *their* existence, rather than developing the community. The automobile offered a means to this end by providing rapid, direct transportation at minimal cost. One computation placed the immediate cash cost of a country trip for a family of five at eighteen cents a mile by railroad, as compared with only a penny a mile in a Model T Ford.[26] Furthermore, the car delivered you to the door and was faster than a horse-and-buggy, thus allowing longer trips in shorter time.

Farmers traditionally had felt guilty about taking trips, even when the time was available. Their frugal outlook probably balked at the time involved in "gettin' there" as compared to the amount allowed for the actual leisure activity. "One of the values of the automobile is that by its use many a farmer has been given a new realization of the value of recreation," wrote Dwight

Sanderson in 1922.[27] Horace B. Hawthorn found that in Monona County, Iowa, "Farmers took from six to twelve longer trips each year, which carried them beyond the confines of their community into other counties. Ten to fifteen percent of the people took annual vacation tours in their cars, lasting from a few days to several months. A month's trip to the mountains would be beyond the means of the farm family if railroad fares and hotel bills had to be paid for the four or five members; but with a car and camping outfit, the expense is greatly reduced."[28] A Department of the Interior study of motor vehicles entering Yellowstone National Park in 1926 revealed that those engaged in "agricultural pursuits" were most numerous, more than double those of any other profession.[29]

Undoubtedly, such long-distance touring by both rural and urban people had an homogenizing effect on the total population. Walter Burr observed this in Kansas in the 1920s:

> One who has visited frequently during the past few years in farm homes and conversed with members of the farm family has become accustomed to hear them discuss their experiences in Chicago, New York, San Francisco, Miami, Detroit — at the Grand Canyon, in Yellowstone Park, in the Yosemite Valley, in the Canadian Northwest — and wherever else there are highways which can be traveled by automobiles. They put up at the same hotels or camp at the same tourist parks used by the city people. Since the city type has dominated in the past, and has been looked up to by country people as being more highly cultured, the tendency is for country people, as they come in contact with them, to become urbanized.[30]

Much more common than such long trips were the short afternoon or Sunday jaunts that the automobile popularized. According to the Lynds, these trips made "leisure-time enjoyment a regularly expected part of every day and week rather than an occasional event."[31] The advantages of such trips were realized by at least one country writer as early as 1912:

> The pleasure and contentment of the family which the automobile makes possible because of the evening automobile ride

> for diversion or the exchange of social courtesies and the attendance upon meetings of various kinds is not to be overlooked. The great distance that may be covered, at the same time the fact that the evening pleasure with the automobile does not lessen the efficiency of the farm motive power on the following day, as is the case when the farm team must be hitched onto the pleasure vehicle, is a factor which the student of farm conditions should not overlook.[32]

This new mobility effectively doubled the farm family's range of social activities, from six or seven miles with horse and buggy to nine to twelve miles with the motor car.

Such travel supplied information previously unknown to the farmer. Professor Harvey Peck maintained that "the average farmer has long been on a lower economic level than the average urban dweller. Yet this fact, since it was unknown to most farmers, was not a cause of discontent. The farmer was in the same economic condition as most of the people he met. But the newer mobility, and the resulting increase of social contacts, have enlarged the scope of his social comparison. The result is the acceptance or recognition of the higher average standard of living."[33] (The automobile as a factor affecting the standard of living will be discussed in more detail later in this chapter.)

It is also possible, although difficult to prove, that this increased contact brought on by the motor car lowered the rural birth rate. As Sorokin, Zimmerman, and Galpin have observed, the high birth rate resulted in part from the mores of rural family and religious life. "Multiply and replenish the earth" was a Biblical injunction under which farmers stood to benefit both socially and economically. As a result, population control and extramarital sex were condemned as irreligious and divisive of the family unit. The authors go on to conclude that "the family institution, as a union of parents and children and of husbands and wives, has been much more important economically, socially, morally, and biologically in the peasant class than to any other class of society. In the city the individual and his interests are considered first; in the country the interests of individual members should be and still are sacrificed to the family and its interests."[34] Thus, to the degree that increased mobility brought the values of urban America to the countryside, one would expect a change in rural mores and a lowering of the birth rate.

Smaller rural families may have been made more acceptable by the increasing mechanization of farming and the consequent need for less manpower. Furthermore, where electrification and indoor plumbing were adopted, the female's chores in the farm household became fewer and less burdensome. Combined with the shortage of good farm land, these trends constituted substantial motivation to keep one's family small. Rural sociologist Dwight Sanderson noted the reduced size of families in a 1922 study and postulated that the rural family would be "less self-sufficient socially than formerly" and would become fragmented by the formation of community-wide groups based on age or sex rather than proximity.[35]

Not only did the automobile affect the activities of the unified family, it also wrought changes among different family members. Although women often expressed interest in driving their own cars and thus being able to leave the farm when they wished, they often were stymied by the necessity of hand-cranking the motor to engage it. With the introduction of the electric starter in 1912, women drivers became much more common. Unfortunately, as late as 1924, self-starters were still not standard equipment on the Model T Ford, the car owned by much of the rural population.[36] Thus, most farm women during this period either mastered the crank or depended on males for travel. C. H. Claudy offered women some advice on this problem in 1913:

> Get your instructor to show you the gentle art of cranking a machine without effort. Without much effort, that is; some is necessary. But there is a vast difference between the main strength exhibition of the man who turns the engine over because his muscles are stronger than the engine's compression and the knowledge of the little lady who uses her head rather than her strength to accomplish the same task. If the handle be properly engaged and the engine "rocked" to and fro, the heavy fly-wheel will gain enough momentum to help even a weak woman to "throw

it over" with little added strength — and there is a great satisfaction in being thus independent of the services of some masculine biceps.[37]

Despite this problem and the chance of mechanical or tire trouble, the motor car provided rural women with their first opportunity for independent mobility, and there was every indication that they intended to use it. A good example of this philosophy is the following description of a day in the life of an Ohio farm woman which appeared in the pages of the *Rural New Yorker* in 1913:

> One morning she hurried through the morning's work, had the car brought to the house before the men went to work, and after the partly cooked dinner was stowed away in a box of hay in the celler to finish cooking itself she got into the car at a little before 10 and drove 41 miles to her daughter's home; getting there just as the family were sitting down to lunch. The route led through Cleveland, and in mid-afternoon she took her daughter and child and they did some shopping at a great department store, where she could buy much better and cheaper than at home. The daughter went home on a suburban car [an interurban trolley or tram], and the mother reached home in time to put a late supper on the table.[38]

In addition, farm women's clubs were given an impetus by the automobile. It was possible to attend in the afternoon and still be home in time to prepare supper, something which would have been impossible using a horse and buggy.[39]

The motor car became so popular with farm women that it was often preferred and purchased before household appliances. Asked by an investigator from the United States Department of Agriculture why her family purchased an automobile before a bathtub, a farm woman replied, "Why, you can't go to town in a bathtub."[40]

Similarly, Mrs. John Dickinson Sherman, president of the General Federation of Women's Clubs, in reporting on a survey of 296,551 homes, stated that the automobile took precedence over home improvements "*because the housewife for generations has sought escape from the monotony, rather than the drudgery of her lot*. She can and does endure toil, actual physical labor, patiently and cheerfully; but she breaks physically and nervously under monotony. The automobile, the telephone, and talking machine or radio offer the modern homemaker the escape from this monotony which drove many of her predecessors insane."[41]

Not everyone viewed the new mobility of rural women as an improvement. *Motor Age* reported in 1916 on the problems sometimes involved:

> Women of the central Illinois farms emphatically denounce the libel that the egg industry has gone to pot because they are spending most of their time scudding across the country in motor cars and neglecting the poultry yards which have been the foundation of egg production from time immemorial. They assert that the charge that the farmer's wife; her son's wife; and her grandson's wife, instead of looking after the chickens, coaxing them to lay, and generally supervising the industry, are hunting bargains in town, driving across the country in their cars, and drinking in the scenery on tours, is a base falsehood. They propose to fight to the limit, the threatened legislation forcing the farmers' women folk to forego their limousines and cuddel the chicken biddies for the delectation of the public that insists upon omelets.
>
> The women of the rural district declare that they have a right to spin away on a fair day in their cars and become acquainted with their neighbors, and no one can force them to stay at home, ruminating in a poultry yard to keep the chickens ambitious. . . .[42]

What the critics seemed to ignore was that the automobile lessened the chores of the farm woman, and this lighter work load allowed her more leisure time. For example, she no longer had to grow or make all foodstuffs that the family would consume during the year, especially during winter. The farmer's wife now could drive to town or a nearby city to purchase produce shipped in from the south, thereby avoiding malnutrition.[43]

The introduction of the motor car also widened the range of

possible contact for rural youth. A New York State commission reported that: "Rural children are allowed junior licenses for restricted use, but they have gone beyond the limits of the privilege.... A good many of the boys as young as 16 either have automobiles of their own or are allowed the privilege of taking out their parents' car whenever they wish and take girls regularly to country dances."[44] Rural sociologist Newell L. Sims noted, "The complaint is wide-spread that the younger farmers and country youth are seriously neglecting business on this account."[45] Teenagers were able to visit movie theatres and other places of amusement in towns, and as a result all youth moved towards a more standard national set of manners, styles, and diction.[46] Not all rural adults saw such influences as beneficial; particularly troubled were the mothers of these youngsters. "The farm woman knows well enough that many of these influences are not what she wishes for her children, and yet, as an individual, she is powerless to change them," concluded one woman writer in 1924.[47] The social forces set in motion by the motor car could not be controlled by the dictates of a single family or community.

To many, the automobile seemed to threaten the very unity of the family. No longer need its members depend on each other for most of their social satisfaction. Not surprisingly, a study of girls in Pender County, North Carolina, found that in almost one-third of the rural homes there were fights over the use of the car.[48] The Lynds found that boys and girls went riding without their parents approximately forty percent of the time.[49]

Nonetheless, motoring was not the only leisure activity that separated parents and children. A greater percentage of youngsters, for instance, went to movies, listened to radio, and sang or played a musical instrument without the presence of their parents than went automobile riding without them.[50]

A seemingly positive effect was that the enlarged radius of travel led to increased intermarriage between boys and girls living in different geographic areas.[51] These new family links tended to harmonize the interests of town and country. They also represented an improvement from the standpoint of eugenics.

THE NEW MOTORIZED LIFESTYLE

In 1906, Woodrow Wilson, then president of Princeton University, announced that "nothing has spread socialistic feeling in this country more than the automobile. To the countryman they are a picture of the arrogance of wealth, with all its independence and carelessness."[52] He seemed to be expanding on the vision of Robert Bruce, who wrote in 1900:

> Exactly what position it [the automobile] will ultimately occupy it is only now possible to speculate on. Possibly it may in the end be the distinguishing mark of social grade and affluence, much as the private equipages and cavalcades of the early centuries were the outward and visible signs of rank and wealth of their respective owners. . . .
>
> Much will depend upon the condition in which the main high roads of the country are kept. If these are brought, over wide areas, into a condition which will enable them to be traversed in safety, then we may witness a return to them of undreamed of magnificence, and our people of wealth and leisure may move from county seat to county seat and tour from city to city, or from one social resort to another in all the pomp and circumstance that lavish expenditure can buy and emulation spur them on to.
>
> This seems to me to be by no means a far-fetched imagination because it should be noted that the old-time aristocracy did not adopt the railroad because they liked it, but because the road inns on the old coach roads died out when the railroad took over routes. The automobile will circumvent this, because by its increased capacity to cover distance it will enable travelers by it to reach towns further apart and provided with hotels capable of appropriately entertaining such guests.[53]

The automobile was eventually purchased by a much broader social spectrum than these writers imagined, but possession of a motor car nevertheless had considerable impact on the social ranking of a resident of rural America. Traditionally the farmer who owned a special rig for trips into town on Saturday or to church on Sunday was acknowledged to be "well fixed," as opposed to one who used his work wagon for all occasions.[54]

For the most part, the expensive horse and buggy was replaced by the automobile, though there was a status order beginning with the Model T Ford and going up. As one contemporary writer put it, "A better passenger car now assumes the status of a social necessity. The new car ... is justified by its improvement of the immaterial conditions of the farmer and his family."[55] Another pointed out, "The motor car has stolen into the vantage-point formerly occupied by the home; it has become the most widely accepted symbol of a man's ability to purchase luxuries.... A home is more visible; but it does not accompany its owner from point to point, and its cost can only be roughly approximated by a layman."[56]

On the other hand, *the* car of this period for rural America was undoubtedly Ford's Model T. Its vast numbers and low price gave a democratic quality to automobile ownership. An article appearing in *Collier's* maintained: "In the country ownership of a car does not create a new line of social distinction. The country car is a good deal of a neighborhood jitney; one youngster with the privilege of the family car is likely to bring two or three loads of passengers to the dance on Saturday evening."[57] It appears, then, that the attitude of the rural dweller toward the automobile depended on his income, with the richer more likely to view the motor car as a status symbol. In fact, two modern students of the automobile refute Woodrow Wilson by arguing that "by creating a desire for individual ownership, the car did much to keep the United States away from socialism."[58]

Nonetheless, ownership of an automobile did make it possible to choose one's friends more selectively. It therefore did much to decrease sociability among neighboring families. "Before the days of the automobile mere propinquity made neighbors more or less intimate," wrote James M. Williams in 1926. "Today the automobile enables farmers to pick their associates much as do people in cities. The intimate friends may be miles away."[59] This process may have been accelerated by the fact that the passenger car and truck allowed families to move away from the poor land

In Hayes, South Dakota, the Model T had by 1925 become as important for efficient farm management as the barn, the tractor and the out buildings. (*National Archives*)

The old and the new means of rural locomotion pose with their owners in 1928 on a South Carolina farm. (*National Archives*)

near the railroad to the more fertile areas farther inland.[60] Such movement would tend to break up old friendships based solely on neighborliness and make new ones harder to come by, because of the relative increase in the distance between farms.

In consequence, as one study of a rural New England community revealed, the traditional criteria for assigning social status (family background, personal qualities, possessions, etc.) could not be applied with certainty. While these measures were still valid, distance and mobility created a social situation in which people came to be judged by superficial appearances, and even the measures of social status became confused.[61]

It was also noted that automobile drivers did not stop to offer rides to pedestrians as often as did drivers of horse-drawn vehicles. Most motor owners claimed that this was *not* because they felt it to be below their station, but their explanations seem rather lame on examination. One writer for the *Rural New Yorker* in 1917 tried to answer the question of "Why the Car Driver 'Moves On'":

> When the man changes to the auto he does not undergo a change of heart, but he finds he has changed his steed. The horse-driven vehicle is light, moves slowly and is easily stopped and started, but the car is heavy, stops and starts slowly and must be driven at from 12 to 20 miles per hour for efficient running, so stopping and starting mean great strain and wear on brakes, tires, gears and the whole car.... If people understood the matter from the auto driver's side they would not expect to be stopped for, nor resent it when passed by.[62]

If mechanical reasons were not sufficient justification, the rural motorist suddenly became concerned with the morals of the hitch-hiker. This was still a topic of discussion in 1923:

> It may seem a churlish thing to refuse a ride to some man or boy who turns to look meaningly at your empty seat, or, directly to signal you to stop. Unless under exceptional circumstances such rides should not be given, for they can only encourage irresponsible

> men and boys to wander about the country at the expense of passing motorists, and if, by such refusals, you chance to discourage some college student who is "hiking" from coast to coast on a vacation trip, instead of going to work, you will have done one of your fellows a real service.[63]

Not only did the car itself sometimes serve as a criterion for social standing, it may also have made those inside it more conscious of their personal appearance. Traditionally, farm families had been made conspicuous in towns or cities by their distinctive clothing. In fact, one writer for *Country Life in America* in 1911 thought this a positive virtue: "Maybe some of you will think I am dropping to a lower level when I number as a ... great joy the farmer has the Joy of Old Clothes. Perhaps that doesn't fully express my meaning. I want to class under this head the comfort which comes through a sense of personal freedom from all merely artificial conventions, whether those of dress or of other things."[64]

Nonetheless, such attire had often been an object of ridicule by the urban observer, lending credence to such terms as "hayseed" and "hick." As Edward R. Eastman observed, the real reason why the farmer had no new clothes was that he had no place to wear them. "He had little money for good clothes and with the exception of church, few places to go where 'store clothes' were needed. Not until recently have farm people been doing much traveling. When they did go, it usually was with a horse and caring for a horse is not particularly conducive to the wearing of good clothes. But the automobile has changed all that. The farmer has become a cosmopolitan. He takes long trips with his whole family as often as anybody else."[65] As if to counter the *Country Life* writer cited above, Charles M. Harger maintained that such changes in apparel signaled a new "self-respect" on the part of the farmer, brought about under the aegis of the motor car.[66] The automobile also seems to have been directly responsible for certain changes in women's fashions.[67] For example, long skirts had to be shortened so that women could easily manipulate the floor pedals of a motor car.[68]

While automobile travel seemed to demand different clothing, it also provided a means for securing that clothing. A study of 1,328 midwestern farm families at the time found that they traveled an average of nineteen and a half miles to buy clothes.[69] As a result, "country stores were no longer scenes of long Saturday purchasing expeditions when fathers and mothers picked out clothes for their children and made them like it," notes Thomas D. Clark. The piece-goods trade was on the wane; ready-made clothes were bought because they were up-to-date, even if they were of inferior quality.[70] It therefore became increasingly difficult to distinguish farm families from their town and city counterparts by what they wore.

CONCLUSION

First, it should be emphasized that the motor car is an inanimate machine. As such, the automobile neither caused nor was to blame for any changes that took place in rural America between 1893 and 1929. Rural families used the automobile to fulfill what they felt to be their needs and best interests. Furthermore, the motor car was one of many technological innovations that affected country life during this period. The appearance of rural free delivery, the telephone, motion pictures, radio, improved roads, and rural electrification coincided with the introduction of the automobile. It is all but impossible to identify any one of these factors as the major instrument of change.

With this in mind, one can still ascertain trends that were accelerated by the rural family's adoption of the motor car. For one, the isolation and loneliness described at the beginning of this chapter all but disappeared. The farmstead was accordingly transformed into a more enjoyable and worthwhile place to live. Leisure-time pursuits, the church, and education all became more accessible to the rural family.

However, most of these new contacts were impersonal in nature and involved urban people and institutions. As this interaction became more intense, it threatened the unity of the rural family. The inputs into their lives increasingly came from sources over which rural residents had little control and from people with different views of the meaning of life. In addition, since the motor car enabled individual family members to split off from the whole, the type and degree of these contacts differed from person to person.

To understand why rural life changed as quickly as it did, it is important to remember how the automobile was adopted. The motor car was not introduced by government fiat, nor were funds voted for its acquisition by the village council. Purchase was an individual act. Whatever transpired was the result of the sum total of millions of individual social actions. In fact, it is possible to conclude that the changes came so suddenly (well within one generation), and the individual family had so little control over them, that it became impossible to stop the collective revolution that individual families were putting into motion. If one family owned a car but did not believe in Sunday driving, there was no way to prevent one's neighbor who did. The very breakdown of isolation effected by the automobile made it increasingly difficult to control actions by bringing familial and/or community pressure to bear. The wider became the effective unit of living, the easier it became to adopt the anonymity of the large town or city.

Finally, family life simply became more complex. No longer did one choose friends, recreation, and religion on the basis of proximity. The new associations included people from geographically separate units, with differing social, political, and economic viewpoints. Time had ceased to be the barrier it once was. Certain traditions no longer seemed to operate. The rural family was forced to accommodate itself to a new world of flux.

Prosperity in 1929 rural Virginia: a stately home, a functional automobile and a barefoot boy. (*National Archives*)

A muster of motor cars at the annual farm picnic. (*National Archives*)

III. The Rural Community

Harlan P. Douglass, in his classic study of the rural small town, described a typical day in the life of the townspeople. It is an interesting contrast to the lot of the farm family pictured in the previous chapter.

> The little townsman has already greeted his fellow this morning as he splits the kindling or feeds his chickens in the back yard. His wife has called a "good morning" to her neighbor during domestic processes, or compared notes on infant diseases over the fence.... All day the incidental contacts of life continue, varied and shifting. There is leisure for humour, for human intercourse for its own sake. . . . There is pause in the day's work; noon, with the school children trooping home; the return of the business man to dinner; the comings and goings of women to market or club; the daily exodus of half of the inhabitants when the train comes in; the equal interest in the baseball club; the concourse of the whole town at fight or fire. This is social richness and complexity as compared with farm environment....[1]

Still, as Douglass also observed, the distance that one could negotiate on foot defined the town neighborhood.[2] Thus, although town dwellers routinely interacted with a greater number of people than did those living on farms, this interaction was limited to a small, circumscribed area. In this respect, residents of rural towns also suffered from isolation — different in kind, perhaps, from that of the farm family, but not necessarily in degree. One writer on the question went so far as to say that "before the automobile was available at a moderate price, the people in the smaller towns were the most isolated of any of our people. The people in the larger cities had the use of the trolley cars, and the people on the farms had horses and buggies, but very few people in the small cities and villages had any means of transportation regularly at hand."[3]

Townspeople had always taken a selfish view of their role in rural America, and this had frequently strained town-country relations. Professor Charles J. Galpin summarized their divisive attitudes in *The Social Anatomy of a Rural Community*: "The banker, store keeper and blacksmith knows [the farmer] ... as the goose that lays the golden egg. The problem is one of pleasing [him] ... and getting his trade without building him and his mind, capacities, and wishes, into the community fabric."[4]

A study done for the Institute of Religious and Social Research in the mid-1920s found that, far from eliminating this friction, the automobile sometimes exacerbated it:

> In two communities a storm in a teapot arose because of the assumption on the part of the village that all farmers drove automobiles. In one case some hitching posts were removed and in another the village government connived at the removal of a low watering trough which had stood for years at the intersection of two main streets and which had become an obstacle to automobiles driven rapidly through the center of the village. Even though a majority of the farmers did operate cars these acts were interpreted by all as unfriendly to the rural interests.[5]

Lewis Atherton may have been correct in observing that, during the first third of the twentieth century, rural villages and towns suffered by aspiring to become great urban centers. Rather than trying to establish cultural, social, and economic ties with the farming element, they rejected the cultural similarities and common heritage that tied them together and sought to establish a new identity.[6] This desire of small-town America was abetted to a degree by the introduction of the automobile. Communities came to be thought of in terms of time more than geographical space.[7] What was true for the farm family also held for the townsmen: "Spatial distance under modern conditions bears little relation to social distance. Physically adjacent population groups may be interrelated in an economic or symbiotic manner and yet live in vastly different social worlds."[8] A new, complex social and economic organization was developing all through the rural community. Professor Roderick D. McKenzie of the University of Michigan observed this result:

> By reducing the scale of local distance, the motor vehicle extended the horizon of the community and introduced a territorial division of labor among local institutions and neighboring centers which is unique in the history of settlement. The large center has been able to extend the radius of its influence; its population and many of its institutions, freed from the dominance of rail transportation, have become widely dispersed throughout surrounding territory. Moreover, formerly independent towns and villages and also rural territory have become part of this enlarged city complex.[9]

The significance of the wider rural community was not lost on government officials in Washington. In 1915 the rural free delivery (RFD) of mail and parcel post was changed to take advantage of the new conditions. Unfortunately, the Post Office Department's reach toward efficiency exceeded its grasp of the social attitudes regarding mail delivery in rural America. The automobile was employed as an aid in reorganizing many routes and as an excuse for eliminating others. (In the latter case, the postal authorities believed that the farmer now had greater access to the town post office and that the savings to the postal system were worth the small inconvenience such trips would cause.) One consequence of this reorganization was that many farm families found themselves on different routes, sometimes with new addresses. This change often meant that they were receiving their mail from towns with which they had no real social or economic ties, and that their identification with a certain community, sometimes built up over generations, was seriously weakened. As Wayne E. Fuller has noted in his study of RFD, more than just sentimental attachment may have been at stake in these mail route changes: "The farmers wanted to be identified with their community, the place where they traded and went to church and sent their children to school. When they needed medicine, they wanted to telephone their doctor in the village and have him send it out with the rural mailman. When the mailman started from a different town than that in which their doctor lived, this kind of service was impossible."[10]

Nonetheless, it was argued that all progress carries with it some *temporary* disruption. To counter criticism of the changes, postal officials could emphasize that many rural communities were receiving their mail one or even two days earlier because of motorization, and in some places the number of deliveries per day had increased.[11] Whether the social benefits of improved postal service (such as the prompt delivery of a daily newspaper from a distant city) offset the loss of identity through a particular post office is left unanswered by the literature.

DEMOGRAPHIC CHANGES

It was not only the small-town resident who yearned to be part of the big city. The desire for urbanization was shared by the farming class as well, evidenced by both the large number of children who left the farm for the urban metropolis and the determination with which retired farmers decided to spend their last days in town rather than on the farmstead. Both of these developments took their toll on the integrity and vitality of the farm household.[12]

Obviously, much of this migration was prompted by the social isolation and economic conditions on farms. What particularly bothered sociologists of the period was that a large proportion of these migrants were the potential leaders of rural America. They tended to be young, progressive in thought, and more dynamic than the individuals who were left behind.[13] Professor E. A. Ross feared that a visible moral decline in the community would result.

> The roads are neglected, which means less social intercourse and a smaller turnout to school and church and public events. School buildings and grounds deteriorate, and the false idea takes root that it pays to hire the cheaper teacher. The church gets into a rut, fails to start up the social and recreative activities which bind the young people to it, and presently ceases to be a force. Frivolity engrosses the young because no one organizes singing schools, literary societies, or debating clubs. Presently a generation has grown up that has missed the uplifting and refining influence of these communal institutions.[14]

At the time, such developments were seen as catastrophic for the country as a whole. Many leaders, including Theodore Roosevelt,[15] felt that the vitality of the nation depended on constant transfusions of new blood from rural areas.

As long as the urban milieu presented social and economic advantages over that of the country, the migration of rural dwellers to the towns and cities would continue unabated. What was needed was a means of introducing the conveniences of modern, urban life into the rural environment without upsetting moral and physical benefits that were believed to characterize country living. The automobile was one of several means of doing this. Henry Ford claimed that "a very decided drift away from the farms was checked by three elements — the cheap automobile, the good roads over which the farmer might travel to market, the moving picture theater in the community where the farmer and his family might enjoy an evening's entertainment."[16] One should add the introduction of radio and the advent of indoor plumbing and rural electrification in the 1930s as other contributing factors.

By 1916, one observer of rural Montgomery County, Maryland, postulated that, as a result of the automobile, "the young people no longer yearn to get away, simply because they have discovered that they can go when they like, and their easy touch with the outside has rubbed off the glamour."[17] Another spokesman stated that the automobile "has saved the farm," but "not in the way you might think. It didn't keep the boy and girl on the farm, but it provided the farmer with means for getting people from the town to take their places."[18] The last viewpoint seems to be supported by more contemporary evidence than those of Ford and the Maryland resident.

Thus, while the automobile did not mark a return to the status quo of the nineteenth century, it seems to have provided an aid to the continued viability of country life. A good example of this development was the new attitude of the farm laborer. John North Willys, the automobile manufacturer, gave his impressions on this subject in a 1919 interview with *Country Gentleman* magazine:

> Some years ago workmen in the big towns used to go to the shops and factories on roller skates. The farm laborer can't do that. But he can own his own machine. And many of them do.
>
> The little car is getting to be quite as much a part of the farm laborer's equipment as the bag of tools is the carpenter's. It makes him independent. If he can pull up and get out any time he likes, he doesn't want to. He's contented. That's the moral value of it.[19]

The automobile also allowed the farm owner to pick up his hired help in town after breakfast, return them there for lunch, and drop them off at night in time for supper. This would have been particularly appealing to farm women, who had traditionally complained about having to feed and house "strange men" and their bad influence on the family household. It also was a way of adjusting to the large-scale emigration of female labor from the farms into town and city offices and factories. Formerly this group had attended to the domestic needs of the male help that lived on the farm.[20]

A careful study of the actual population shifts in rural America between 1900 and 1930 reveals several important facts. First, the depletion of the rural population was relative, not absolute. In 1920 there were 1,599,871 more people in rural areas than in 1910 and 5,791,875 more than in 1900.[21] In 1930, there were over two million more rural dwellers than in 1920.[22] However, while population in rural villages and towns rose 3.6 million in the 1920s, the farm population dropped by 1.2 million. It appears that while large numbers of farmers were indeed migrating, they were going only so far as the country villages and towns, which were becoming a proportionately larger segment of the total rural population.[23]

This movement *within rural areas* should not obscure the fact that the greatest absolute population growth was taking place in cities and towns of over 2,500 people. Between 1920 and 1930, these larger communities increased by 14.6 million, as compared with 2.4 million for the rural areas.[24] As a result, the rural population dropped from 48.6 percent of the total population to 43.8 percent, even though there was an absolute increase of almost two and a half million people in rural areas.[25] Many were simply moving completely out of rural areas into the expanding urban centers.

It therefore appears that the automobile did *not* "save the farm," which lost ground against competing population centers. This suggests that physical isolation may not have been the only objectionable element in farm living. One writer surmised as early as 1912, "The real 'isolation' ... is social.... If physical isolation were the cause of the discontent, modern improvements in methods of communication would do much to bring contentment. It is noticeable, however, that in those communities best provided with modern conveniences the drift cityward is most rapid. The more closely men are drawn together, the more surely does the old order pass."[26]

Furthermore, the passing of the old order, made possible by farm mechanization, meant that fewer people were needed. It can therefore be argued that townward migration would have

The Rosemonts, Californians of the early 1920s, in a classic American family picture. (*Rosemont family archives*)

A Farm Bureau agent pauses near evidence of horse traffic to chat with a resident of Malta, Montana in 1919. (*National Archives*)

On a summer morning in 1930, a rural resident of York County, Maine enjoys the ritual of receiving the mail. (*National Archives*)

In 1914, this home demonstration agent drives to a meeting through the Montana snow. (*National Archives*)

happened even without the automobile, via the railroad, for instance. (Note that we are discussing permanent migration, not commutation.) However, the automobile may have encouraged many farm families to move to relatively small towns, from which they traveled to more industrialized districts for the workday or to farming areas to visit relatives. In this respect, the automobile created an agreeable social compromise in the face of economic necessity.

Finally, the automobile, as a modern method of transportation, helped to eliminate duplicate economic and social services which had existed principally because of poor methods of communication. Certain villages were eclipsed by their "twin" neighbors. This was especially true in those regions which "were thickly settled long before the coming of the railroad and the automobile. In a region where the ordinary methods of transportation were the ox cart and the horse and buggy," argued C. Luther Fry, "it is but natural that villages should have sprung up close together, since farmers could not easily travel long distances to trade. With improved means of transportation, particularly with the coming of the motor car, rural people suddenly were enabled to travel far greater distances than formerly."[27] In writing about this phenomenon, Professor John H. Kolb concluded:

> It has been clear that not every town and country community can expect to have its own social institutions if attention is to be given to efficient service at economical costs. In these days of easy communication and transportation, no one community lives to itself.... This inevitably means specialization, a sharpening of the function of this community as compared to that. By all means farmers and their families need their own neighborhood life and organization, but it has been evident from ... studies that they can hardly hope to maintain such social institutions as the high school, library, or hospital without taking into account the neighboring town or village.[28]

SUBURBANITES

Before the introduction of the motor car, people who lived

beyond the city limits in "country homes" had been forced to live near the railroad right-of-way. The automobile enabled them to settle on land that lay elsewhere. In many cases, farm land was converted into country estates for the rich and small bungalows for the urban working class.

The concern of this study is not with the majority of suburbanites, whose primary focus remained the urban metropolis. These people, as one writer phrased it, practiced "the art of living in the country without being part of it."[29] Rather, our focus is on what rural sociologist Harlan P. Douglass termed the "rural suburb." Its population did not commute to work in an urban area. Rather, rural suburbanites lived, worked, and played in what had originally been a farming environment. They depended very little on the nearby city.[30] This did not mean, however, that such suburbs were dominated by the rural way of life. On the contrary, the "new" urban ideas and values tended to overwhelm those that had previously existed in that area of the country. In the words of Douglass:

> These Goths and Vandals from the city are Americans just as the natives are, but they have different standards of living, of dress, of household appointments, of expenditure. Their manners are more formal. In social life, in recreation, in religion they are not like the original people of the town. They have different cultural interests. More of them are college-bred with "highbrow" notions. As citizens they have novel ideas. They demand more public improvements, more expenditures through taxation. They bring in churches of new denominations, organize new clubs, and separate themselves from the older population in many ways. The older leaders are ignored, outdistanced, ultimately they are defeated politically.[31]

Since World War II, the culmination of these developements has become visible. According to the 1970 census, more people live in suburbia than in either rural or urban America. However, in the 1920s such communities remained the exception rather than the rule. Approximately 40 percent of the population remained on farms or in rural villages and towns. Their lives continued to be influenced primarily by rural interests and attitudes, though these were coming under increasing attack as motorization brought with it urbanization.

ROAD IMPROVEMENT

Obviously, most of the changes in the rural community cited so far were dependent upon the full acceptance of the automobile, which in turn often led to the systematic development of country roads. "One of the first coincidents with the introduction of the free-moving carriage," the *Independent* editorialized in 1903, "must be a great impulse given to improvement of roads."[32] That magazine would have had little trouble in enlisting the support of an observer of the unlucky contestants in the 1907 Glidden Tour:

> A heavy rain had fallen over night . . . and the soft, pasty mud which that powdered dust made, was a study in physics and chemistry. It was slippery, slimy, treacherously dangerous ooze, the like of which, the contestants had never seen before. The roadbed itself, was hard, and this covering of slime from a foot to two feet deep, made just the correct combination for fancy skidding. The cars floundered around in it like so many mired pigs. . . . The State road was full of great holes, the depth of which could not be ascertained until the car plunged right into them. Frequently they were deep enough to force the driver to back out and try to sail around them. Between the towns of Java, Swanton, Delta and Bryan [Ohio], the car the writer rode in, continually skidded around at right angles to the road and into ditches, although the most expert driver was at the wheel. This alone accounted for the car not upsetting, when a turtling seemed unavoidable in several instances, and all passengers were ready to jump.[33]

Although the need for good roads was obvious to many, the movement made little progress until the 1920s. In his 1919 novel *Free Air,* Sinclair Lewis used literary license to portray conditions on Minnesota country roads similar to those described above:

"The road ahead was a wet black smear, criss-crossed with ruts. The car shot into a morass of prairie gumbo — which is mud mixed with tar, fly-paper, fish glue, and well-chewed, chocolate-covered caramels."[34]

The explanation for this continuing problem is somewhat complex. Two points mentioned in chapter 1 are relevant here. First, poor roads were financially lucrative for some farmers, who earned extra money by pulling stuck vehicles out of the mud. Second, the depredations of the rural landscape and wild life caused first by the bicyclist and later by the early motorist were large deterrents to road improvements.

In this regard, the importance of the urban bicycle craze of the 1890s should not be underestimated. The antagonism it engendered in rural America was to give those who opposed good roads in the twentieth century a heritage upon which to draw. Lloyd R. Morris describes the fate of highway improvement proposals in the nineties:

> An incipient "good-road movement" ... aroused their [farmer] opposition, the more savagely, perhaps, because it was sponsored by prosperous city folk whom the farmers regarded as their oppressors....
>
> It was, if anything, intensified by the antics of city-slicker cyclists. These were of two breeds: the "scorchers" who, imitating celebrated professional racers, were maniacs for speed, and the members of the Century Road Club, who wore badges laddered with gold bars, each of which certified to the pedaling of one hundred miles in eighteen hours. Both the "scorchers" and the "centuries" streamed out through the countryside, crouching over their handlebars, scaring nervous farm animals and spattering villages with mud in their demoniac pursuit of "records." This, surely, was bad enough; but there was worse to come. For presently the stern public morality of American farmers received a shattering jolt. Incredibly, there flashed by a "tandem" bicycle — and for it, one half the motive power was being furnished by a woman; probably young, necessarily short-skirted, and therefore obviously abandoned.[35]

Thirdly, since most early automobile owners were wealthy, if not urban, the average rural resident resented being taxed for what appeared to be someone else's pleasure. Condemnation grew more heated when much of the new state and federal aid went for long-distance tourists roads and interurban links.[36] As one Arizona woman put it: "The first great need of this community is good roads. Not automobile roads. The State and county have seen that nearly all the money spent for roads in this great fruit country has gone for automobile roads, and we poor farmers' wives must travel over the roughest of roads in poor vehicles."[37]

Finally, *Scientific American* voiced the opinion of many when it observed: "It costs little more to keep a horse when he is driven over roads inches deep in mud than when he is used on a city street — or, for that matter, than when he is hibernating in the barn."[38] While this was technically true, studies in the mid-twenties were to show that horses could haul several times as much on a macadam road as on a unimproved one.[39]

Although several organizations, such as the 1910 Farmers Union convention,[40] went on record as supporting good roads between farms and markets, the factors cited above kept improved highways to a minimum before 1920. In fact, many cars continued to be run on "tall" wheels so that they could safely negotiate the high centered country roads [41].

Nonetheless, several elements at work from 1916-1919 were to bring about a significant change in rural attitudes towards roads. First, the federal government held to its policy of denying rural free mail delivery to communities where roads were impassable. Even the 1915 plea of Mary Doane Shelby failed to move the government from its stance:

> Don't you think, Mr. Secretary [Secretary of Agriculture David F. Houston], that bad roads are a very good reason for having a free delivery of the mail? Isn't it better for one responsible man to go over the road than that ninety families should have to send for their mail or go without? . . . In these stretches of country where money is not plentiful, and where the farmers and their wives are dependent

> upon their own physical exertions for everything necessary for living, Government and newspaper urging doesn't take us very far on our way toward good roads. When we shall have automobile roads we shall not need rural delivery. In the meantime we are paying our taxes and are really a part of the United States of America, although we should hardly realize it save for sentimental attachments.[42]

Second, schools in some areas presented a somewhat similar situation. Consolidated schools, which generally had better equipment and teachers and which separated students by grade, were made possible and accessible through the provision of good roads. Where roads were impassable, communities refused to provide public transportation of pupils to the schools.[43]

Third, agitation for the building of transcontinental motor roads, and the actual beginning of one (the so-called Lincoln Highway), did much to awaken rural America to the advantages of good roads. Drawing on the bitter experience of the nineteenth-century railroad boom, when towns had rapidly decayed when the railroad passed them by, rural leaders took measures to guarantee that any interstate route would run through their particular trade center.[44] Typical of the concern shown was the reaction of Homer Croy's fictional "Junction City" to a proposed interstate highway:

> It would be a splendid asset to the town; it would put Junction City on a direct line of communication; bringing thousands of tourists and automobile parties each year. And then there was the matter of the mail-order catalogue. More and more, farmers were buying from mail-order catalogues. The small towns in the county were slowly decaying; the stores were being boarded up — the more enterprising farmers were buying them for granaries. Villages were dying out, the towns were getting the trade, and now the larger towns must contest among themselves. With an automobile highway open during winter and during the heavy rains of spring which turned wagon roads into mires, the farmers would come to Junction City to do their "trading" instead of going to rival towns and sending their money away to Chicago [mail-order houses].[45]

Fourth, it was a mark of distinction to live on a paved street,[46] and there was also good reason to believe that farm land near improved roads increased in value.[47] Property values were to increase even more with the suburban land boom of the 1920s.[48]

A fifth reason for rural residents to support good roads was the dawning realization of the social benefits they afforded. Traditionally, "at the very season when farm work is light and social intercourse feasible, at that season the highways have been impassable," notes a 1905 road expert.[49] Furthermore, agricultural labor was more likely to seek employment on farms that had easy access to social and recreational facilities.[50]

Finally, as one writer observed as early as 1915, the adoption of "the automobile and motor truck ... made the conditions of the roads of the country of direct interest to all."[51] As a result, beginning around 1912, state and federal governments made substantial funds available for constructing these new roads.[52] In 1919, Oregon introduced a new tax on gasoline to help pay for highways. By 1929, all states were collecting revenue by this method. This helped to temper the argument of large property owners, farmers in particular, that they were shouldering a disproportionate amount of the tax burden for roads.[53] Still, such benefits were mainly for *state* highways. Two-thirds of the highway revenues raised by towns and cities continued to come from road taxes and local budget appropriations.[54]

Increased state and federal involvement was more evident in the changing methods of constructing and maintaining rural roads. Formerly this had been a purely local concern. As John M. Gillette observed, "Each district is apt to be regarded as a law unto itself and its roads built without reference to those beyond its borders."[55] In fact, most of the road work had been done by farmers, who preferred to "work off" their taxes rather than pay them in cash. "No taxpayer would pay a dollar, when he could come and make mud pies on the road all day and visit and gossip with the neighbors and save his dollar too," said humorist Bill Nye, only half in jest.[56] As a result, an 1899 writer for *Forum* magazine felt that "our average country highways are little better to-day than they were at the close of the Civil War."[57]

Martin Dodge, director of the newly established Federal Office of Public Road Inquiries, summed up the situation from the technical angle in 1905:

> After the rights of way have been cleared of their obstructions and the earth roads graded into the form of turnpikes, it becomes necessary to harden their surfaces with material which often must be brought from distant places. In order to accomplish this, expert skill is required in the selection of materials, money instead of labor is required to pay for the cost of transportation, and machinery must be substituted for the hand processes and primitive methods heretofore employed in order to crush the rock and distribute it in the most economical manner on the roadbed....
>
> The local road officer now not only finds himself deficient in skill and the proper kind of resources, but he discovers in many cases that the number of persons subject to his call for the road work was greatly diminished. [58]

Often when local money or labor was not sufficient, "Good Road Days" were proclaimed for a given area. These usually involved the entire rural community, not just the farmers, by declaring a business "holiday" for the time necessary to make the repairs. All materials and work were donated. Such an event took place in Summerfield, Kansas (near the Nebraska border), around 1920, as described by a resident of that town:

> When the time came, the entire community turned out in force — men with horses and road tools of every description, men with axes, spades and shovels — and also a dynamite squad for blasting out trees and stones and stumps.... A large tent was erected centrally located to the work for the purpose of serving meals for the men. The ladies of the community were out in force to serve the meals. Each evening the tent was provided with seats and a stage and entertainment furnished for the large crowds in attendance. Amusements consisted of music and a variety of entertainment; also some very prominent speakers from each state to preach the gospel of good roads.[59]

As the states, and to a lesser extent the federal government, took over the function of highway building and upkeep, road work as a social activity disappeared from the rural scene.

It is interesting to note that one modern student of the automobile, employing mathematical correlations, has apparently shown that, up until 1914, "there is no tangible evidence that the automobile first diffused more rapidly in those areas [states] in the United States with the best roads or that the automobile led in the short run to better roads in those areas where it was most widely adopted at first."[60] If this is also true of the following decade, and applicable to rural America *in particular,* then the "good roads" debate was largely irrelevant to the spread of the motor car.

LEGAL ASPECTS

Bruce Smith observed one result of this new rural highway network: "Extensive areas, without becoming cities in themselves, have acquired many of the characteristics of urban development. This process originated in improved transportation, the decline of agriculture, the rise of new industries in small towns and hamlets, and the influx of an heterogeneous population which has been drawn from the cities to the land, and to its mills, its forests, and its mines. The commission of certain types of criminal acts appears to have been stimulated by such unsettling changes."[61]

This is not to say, however, that before automobiles and good roads, crime was unknown in rural America. In the late nineteenth century, a *New York Evening Post* article stated, "Rural life is montonous and hard, with nothing in it to stimulate the imagination and refine the taste. The closest observers will soonest admit that by consequence the grosser forms of vice and crime in rural communities abound more than in great cities with all the slums counted in."[62] In the country, wrote Dr. Earnest A. Hooton, "one must rape, murder, or behave."[63]

Yet, with the introduction of the automobile, dwellers seemed more likely to resort to deviant behavior. The personalized character of town and country life, which had been an effective deterrent when the community was small and interaction common, was disintegrating. Gossip and social ostracism were no longer sufficient weapons to be used against people whose social lives violated traditional community standards. The tightly knit neighborhood was being replaced by looser, impersonal arrangements.[64]

This breakdown of community cohesiveness made local crime less risky. *Motor Age* reported accounts of thieves using automobiles, who had been "wreaking havoc" in the rural areas surrounding Sandusky, Ohio in 1908. Typical was the loss experienced by farmer August Fischer, who had twenty-four bushels of potatoes stolen by two men in a motor car.[65]

Such incidents, however, were considered petty in comparison with the activities of roving *urban* criminals. *Country Gentleman* magazine was concerned with the "Return of the Bad Men":

> At periods when the roads are in the best condition for fast motor-car driving, raids upon smalltown banks in the upper Mississippi Valley are of almost daily occurrence....
>
> The favored form of attack in recent years is the day-light hold-up, usually a swift affair of the duration of not more than three or four minutes. The bandits drive quietly down the main street to the bank door. While one man smashes the local telephone switchboard so that help cannot be summoned, others dash into the bank and hold up the cashier....
>
> Away they speed then, striving to throw off the pursuit by zigzagging and fast driving. Often they cause their own undoing by this speed recklessness, so it is important to keep upon their trail as long as possible.[66]

A play entitled "Good Roads," published in 1929, expressed the opinion that rural people were no longer safe in their own homes. According to one character, the new state road was responsible for "bringing the riff-raff of the city out here where folks is used to living decent and righteous."[67]

To make matters worse, law enforcement officials in the country were unprepared to deal with such "professionals." "Even if he can spare time from collecting the fees which fall to him as spoils of his office," observed C.R. Henderson, "he has no natural or acquired qualifications as a detective; he is both awkward and ignorant. Local agents of peace and justice have only a local knowledge of persons bent on crime, usually those who are most harmless, stupid inebriates, naughty boys whose mothers have neglected to spank them."[68]

It was not enough to equip a sheriff with a motor car so that he could speed quickly to the scene of the crime. "Law violators may rush into the country, commit a crime and then escape to a large city before the sheriff can arrest them," Charles R. Hoffer observed. In response to this problem, Americans began to press for "state police systems which have been established in several states, [and] have proven to be an effective addition to the existing law-enforcing agencies in rural territory. When equipped with motorcycles, these officers can go from one county to another very quickly, and if their headquarters are located at strategical points, police protection is available in practically every county."[69] As early as 1914, a system similar to what Hoffer proposed had worked successfully to apprehend an accused murderer near Harvard, Nebraska:

> The motor car as an aid in the pursuit of criminals was given a most severe test in this county last week, when 1,000 machines, transporting 2,500 armed men, were used in pursuit of the murderer. . . .
>
> They came from every direction and from every town and hamlet and farm in the county. In the meantime the police kept track of the fugitive by the aid of telephones. In this manner the murderer was tracked to a hayfield, which was entirely surrounded by motor cars, loaded with men and guns. The posse fired a number of shots at random into the hay, but were unable to dislodge the murderer, who was known to be armed with an automatic pistol. Finally the dry hay was set fire and a line of motor cars followed in the track of the flames through the field, [thus dislodging the man]. . . .

> The successful pursuit of the murderer showed the value of the motor car when used intelligently, in a matter of this kind.[70]

Yet at least one expert on rural crime felt that there was still room for the horse in crime work:

> The eastern states here under review are covered by a network of excellent highways which admittedly require motor patrol. Yet there is not one of these but has certain large sections which are as eddies in the current of motor traffic that flows not far from their doors.... If these communities are to be served at all, it must be through the medium of an observation patrol which moves slowly from point to point and which does not count as lost the time which may be spent at rural post offices and general stores.
>
> So the state trooper must amble across country, making friends for the force and for law and order as he goes, following the little-frequented lanes and byways, and piecing together scraps of information which may lead to the prosecution of a felon, the commitment of a dangerous lunatic, or the relief of a stricken family. For this work, mounted patrols are clearly preferable to motors. Speed has no relation to it. On the contrary, it is highly desirable that the patrol be carried out without regard to considerations of time. It cannot be done in haste.[71]

The changing conditions brought on by the automobile also affected the courts and the lawyers who practiced in them. The small-town lawyer, for instance, lost social status, primarily because he met new urban competition. He simply could not compete with either the quantity or the quality of services offered by the urban legal profession. Whereas geography and a sense of community had formerly given the small-town lawyer a monopoly on family and business practice, he now found himself losing out to the same forces that were pulling the social and economic activities of farmers and small-town dwellers toward the city. Just as important, his ability to impress the locals with his education and knowledge of the law was seriously lessened when his background and experience were compared to those of urban partnerships and title guarantee companies. The mobility made possible by the motor car dealt a serious blow to the practice and prestige of the small-time lawyer.[72]

The automobile made it possible to include larger population areas in a single judicial district, and the inefficient local courts came in for their share of criticism. Modern rehabilitation programs were impossible on the local level, because there simply were not enough prisoners to justify a comprehensive effort. Nevertheless, each community felt compelled to maintain its own penal institution, which, regardless of size, had to have a full complement of administrators. One possible solution to this problem lay in the consolidation of services. As sociologist Walter Burr observed, "In rural areas there are many cases where from three to eight counties might now be merged into one great legal unit with one set of officers and one set of institutions."[73]

Yet, improvements introduced into this system, such as moving juvenile court to the cities because they were theoretically so easily accessible, met resistance. As Kate H. Claghorn found:

> This law is not in high favor with the town justices of the peace, nor with possible complainants scattered through the rural sections, for the reason that the prosecution of a delinquent child now means that complainant, child witnesses, and constable must all make the journey to the city for the first hearing, and perhaps also for adjourned hearings, and that much loss of time and money will result therefrom. Several cases come to the investigator's notice in which the complainant refused to act when he discovered how great would be his own personal inconvenience.[74]

CONCLUSION

The contributions of the motor car to changes in the structure of the rural community largely mirror those that were examined earlier in relationship to the family. The insularity of town and village life ended forever when swift, relatively inexpensive personal transportation became available. Communities that had been the hubs of large geographic areas found themselves unable to compete with the attractions of more urban localities. The social and economic growth of the small rural town was retarded or, in many cases, reversed.

In a sense, the concept of a rural *community*, as opposed to a cluster of economic units (farms), ceased to exist. It gave way to the metropolitan area and the suburb. Such a transition was bound to disrupt traditional lifestyles and to necessitate significant adjustments within rural families and in the nature of their social and economic interactions. The new mobility meant that geographical factors were no longer the major determinants of where one worked, shopped, or played. The population began to shift toward more urban areas, while the automobile guaranteed that the *individual* was free to live where he or she wanted. Many of the certitudes of American life, especially the stereotypic views of rural and urban living were therefore called into question.

However, none of these changes would have occurred so quickly, or had such an extensive impact, if the advent of the motor car had not been followed by the movement to improve country roads. Although the automobile had more stamina and speed than the horse, these advantages were meaningless whenever the roads turned to mud. It is probably no accident that the great post-World War I boom in automobile ownership coincided with significant advances in both the quality and maintenance of rural roads. While most country residents favored these developments, at least in principle, they probably got more than they bargained for when horse-drawn wagon ruts were transformed into "highways." The elementary fact that good roads run both ways, that the urban dweller might be just as interested in traveling out to the country as the farmer to the city, may have been grasped, but certainly its long-range social ramifications were not. Family life, the structure of the community, education, recreation, religious institutions, and health care were all to be changed significantly.

The double-edged nature of the good roads movement, and of the acceptance of the automobile itself in rural America, can be

Rural road conditions in 1919 near Dumfries, Virginia, on a highway supposedly linking Washington, D.C. and Richmond. (*National Archives*)

Many an early motorist reached his destination only with the help of the farmer's horses. (*National Archives*)

A solitary gasoline pump, a water tank and free air were the essentials of this Ohio service station in 1923. (*National Archives*)

Outside Freehold, New Jersey, a home demonstration agent demonstrates the womanly art of changing a tire in 1919. (*National Archives*)

seen in their effects on legal profession. Law enforcement officials became more effective, but the motor car also made outlaws more efficient. Crime and its punishment were removed somewhat from the local level and were better managed on a regional or even statewide basis. As such, the former roles of many village and small-town policemen and lawyers were either eliminated or altered to become supportive of more centralized authority. The social status and prestige of such people in their communities were diminished accordingly.

The legal profession was not alone in experiencing changes engendered by the automobile age. Before examining the fields of religion, education, and medicine, it is necessary to conclude this examination of the rural community by looking at the automobile's impact on leisure.

IV. Leisure

Historically, rural recreation involved a group of neighbors assembling at a centrally located farm and making some economically productive activity "fun" by virtue of the group effort. Typical of such activities were husking bees and barn raisings. "Our trouble," wrote Warren H. Wilson in 1923, "is that we cannot continue the husking bee. It does not fit our present needs."[1]

Even where work had been separated from leisure, as it sometimes was in the small town, social activity still centered in the home. As late as 1927, one rural sociologist was observing that "for the most part, meetings, entertainments, parties and dances, which constitute the chief stream of social life, are held from house to house."[2] As a result, home standards were often synonymous with community standards.

Yet, these "home" social activities came to seem insufficient as the twentieth century moved into its second decade. Ernest R. Groves summed up the situation just before the automobile had its major impact on social life:

> The people of the country take life too seriously and are too much engrossed with material interests. They do not play enough. Too

> little provision is made for recreation.... Rural people cannot share the advantages of modern life to a reasonable degree unless they can obtain opportunity for a quantity of play experiences. The craving for play has been greatly stimulated by modern conditions, and the leisure resulting from labor-saving machinery has been largely expended in more abundant recreation. Yet the farmer has relatively fallen behind. He has lost many of the enjoyments of his predecessors, notably those that were characteristic of pioneering days. To be sure he has gained others. Especially he has borrowed recreational facilities developed in the cities; but compared with the city dweller he has suffered loss.[3]

Warren H. Wilson concluded as early as 1912 that "if it be allowed that there is a vital connection between work and play, it follows that the situation in which play is concentrated in given communities and work is distributed over other communities, the allurements of the communities in which recreation is provided will prove almost irresistible."[4] For the rural dweller, commercialized amusements had traditionally been synonymous with urban areas. This had been especially true for the farmer, who had never enjoyed taking his leisure in the village because of the underlying economic antagonism between town and country.[5]

This did not mean that recreational activities were unavailable to the rural resident. As Edmund deS. Brunner notes, there quite possibly may have been too many opportunities — but not, unfortunately, of the type that was increasingly sought after 1910. "The organized social life of villagers is characterized by considerable competition for the leisure time of the people; by a marked degree of overlapping of effort; by a lack of any comprehensive plan for caring for all the chief social needs of the community.... It is possible that the overplus of organizations accounted for the relatively small amount of commercialized recreations in villages."[6] When such commercialized amusements were available, as in the western town of "Belleville" (population 2,367), they easily outdrew the traditional means of leisure. The table below, adapted from the YMCA magazine, *Rural Manhood,* emphasizes this point:

TABLE 1

ANNUAL PATRONAGE AT SELECTED SOCIAL ACTIVITIES IN "BELLEVILLE"

Activity	Patronage
Moving pictures	105,000
Church services	93,600
Pool and billiard games	90,000
Agricultural fairs and farmers meetings	12,400
Church socials and picnics	8,696
Lodges	8,692
The Chautauqua	5,600
Baseball	2,870
Public dances	2,300

Calculated from Harlan P. Douglass, *The Little Town: Especially in Its Rural Relationships,* rev. ed. (New York: Macmillan Company, 1927), pp. 24-25.

The majority of rural residents, however, had few opportunities for such activities before the automobile era. The situation described by a West Virginia supervisor of rural schools may have been more typical: "About the only means of social intercourse that many rural communities have may be summarized briefly as follows: an occasional entertainment at the schoolhouse, an occasional party or dance, and the associations of men about the country stores and blacksmith shop. Farm women have, as a rule, less leisure than men, and generally fewer opportunities to enjoy that which they have."[7] In addition, farmers were generally avid readers, particularly of newspapers, periodicals, and government farm publications.[8]

Most historians believe that the youth of rural America were even worse off than their parents in regard to the variety of leisure activities available. "The boys of that time in a country town had to make a good deal of their own fun," as one observer remembered. "We skated on the rivers, creeks, and ponds in the winter time and went swimming in the river in summer."[9] The "we" is important here, for as Carl C. Taylor has pointed out,

"Before the day of the automobile and the consolidated school, it was almost impossbile to find a group of rural boys of approximately the same age who got together often enough to make . . . organized games possible. . . ."[10] With the larger farms created by mechanization, and a lower birth rate, children were even fewer and farther apart by the end of World War I.[11]

Yet at least one farm woman felt that the children's recreational opportunities were enviable:

> All the day long they are as busy as bees, sliding down the hay, playing in the carpenter shop, building a dam across the brook to turn a watermill, climbing trees, hunting the hens' nest, hitching up the calves, playing hide and seek, or earnestly building a fort to stand strong and firm against imaginary Indians.
>
> Though child playmates may be few there are always the pet lambs, the curly-tailed pigs, the colts, the calves, the chickens and ducks and turkeys, the farm dog and the furry kittens, besides all the wild things of the woods and fields and treetops to give them companionship in their play. They are too busy and happy ever to feel lonely even in the long summer days.[12]

Regardless of which of these views is historically correct, the recreational environment created between 1910 and 1920 changed the ways in which both adults and youths used their leisure time. Movies, bowling alleys, and skating rinks appeared even in small towns, and their advent significantly disrupted country life. As early as 1911, one writer answered the question of "Why Young Men Leave the Farms" by bemoaning that the new types of leisure activities "furnish entertainment that produces no leaders, that makes the country boy turn his eyes toward the town for his amusements."[13] These amusements were made more accessible by improved roads and the motor car.

According to Professor Jesse F. Steiner, the automobile also tended to multiply friendships based on age, sex, and similar interests, as opposed to those dependent on family relationships and geography. The latter had been predominant in the horse-

and-buggy era.[14] "This change," noted rural sociologist Charles R. Hoffer, "has increased family responsibility, for somehow the children must be taught to evaluate and interpret the contacts that they have."[15]

This new responsibility was not always willingly undertaken. As one experienced social worker observed, "The average community considers itself apart from its young people, is quite often ashamed of them, does not understand them and lays the blame for young people's restlessness to the jazz band and automobile instead of facing the charge of negligence and lack of sympathetic understanding in its own scheme of living."[16]

CHANGES IN THE TRADITIONAL FORMS OF ENTERTAINMENT

The coming of the automobile had a profound impact on many traditional rural institutions of leisure. Changes in the attendance and content of the state fair were typical:

> By reducing the time-space element it [the motor car] stimulated both an increase in attendance and an increase in exhibits. No longer were state-fair visitors dependent upon the railroad for transportation and upon hotels and private homes in the city for lodging; now they could drive to the fair in their own automobile and camp a few days on the grounds, or more often return home after the evening performance. Formerly it was usually the farmer himself, in need of a new bull, or ram or desirous of investigating a new plow or binder, who, after outlining to his wife and the boys the week's work to be done at home, took the train to the state fair. It was, in numerous respects, an expensive trip, not often to be undertaken except in case of necessity and then commonly by only one member of the family. But the automobile has revolutionized the customs of fair-going. Now the farm family is likely to rise before dawn, do the morning milking and hustle the cows off to pasture, snatch a hurried breakfast, and, locking the house and leaving the collie on guard for the day, set out in their automobile for the fair.[17]

As a result, the very character of this institution changed. No longer was the program confined to animal exhibitions, equipment displays, and after-hours agricultural discussions. The fair adapted itself to the influx of women, children, and the nonfarming rural population. It offered lectures and discussions that were keyed to the interests of these groups. Just as importantly, the entertainment element of the fair was greatly enlarged.[18]

The state fair was one of many factors that tended to urbanize the rural population. In particular, it further developed the taste for commercial amusement as opposed to the traditional variety. Many of the fairs established permanent locations on the outskirts of cities, where they could draw from the urban, as well as rural, population. Amusements were therefore introduced that catered to visitors whose interest were not primarily agricultural. As Wayne C. Neely describes in his classic study of the agricultural fair:

> Hippodrome acts, spectacular fireworks displays, automobile races, airplane demonstrations, even such bizarre attractions as head-on railroad train collisions, came to be customary features of the entertainment program The recreational aspect of the fair is of course as old as the institution itself, but only in the present century has it come to involve lavish expenditures in the manner providing periodic popular spectacles.... In days when the automobile was permitting rural people to go to state fairs in larger and larger numbers, these amusement features benefited fairs by giving this group diversion not only different in amount from what they had known before, but different in kind as well.[19]

Dancing had historically been another popular means of rural entertainment (except in those areas where religious doctrine frowned upon it). "Old-timers tell of riding from forty to fifty miles in a buggy or of walking thirty miles to Sand Creek and back in order to trip the light fantastic," recalled Albert Blumenthal.[20] Dances usually were held in public buildings, under community auspices and control.

In response to the automobile, however, roadside dance establishments were created, where "immoral" dancing and illegal drinking were often possible, far beyond the watchful eyes of inquisitive neighbors and relatives. One crusader against the evils of such places drew upon federal reports to show that

> there were many fly-by-night dancing places in the rural districts. They are generally vicious. It does not take long for the reputation of the latest-established place to spread far and wide, and for patrons to arrive from long distances by means of the automobile. Some of these disreputable resorts are found in decent little communities that hardly realize they are infected until there is a local epidemic of immorality.
>
> The barn dance, which used to be an innocent rural festival, has become largely a commercial and vicious enterprise. A barn is rented by someone for a few dollars. The patronage is not only from the farming community but from the small towns round, and there is absolutely no supervision.[21]

The above should not be thought of as a singular observation by a biased commentator. A field worker for the New York State Crime Commission made similar observations in the mid-1920s. Reporting on activities outside two dance halls in Manz, New York, a hamlet of 200 inhabitants, he noted, "About fifty cars were parked on the road and in the fields surrounding the dance halls. . . . Couples and groups were shouting and laughing, getting in and out of automobiles. Some couples were parked in the darkness, in their cars, and were heard only by the worker during his inspection. Some cars had occupants who apparently had been drinking. The lack of supervision, utter darkness and liquor gave opportunity for misbehavior."[22]

THE COUNTRY STORE

A third institution affected by the motorization of rural America was the general or country store. Besides their economic function, such stores had traditionally served as informal town meeting and rest areas. In 1931 Charles M. Wilson colorfully recalled the day's assemblage:

> Its company encompases the entire scope of rural humanity, young and old, landed and landless, ragged and replete. Old country men who have spent their hearty years testing out the glamorous fecundity of flesh and earth gather to re-live old times. Old wives come for a speculative hour of barter, and look serenely upon the world which they no longer have cause to fear. Countryside sages in faded overalls ponder over lost causes and impossible allegiances. There are sun-browned scholars in the first toils of book learning; yearning maidens grown restlessly romantic; bare-footed urchins bent on devilment; fuzzy-faced farm boys come to observe the ways of commerce and prosperity; little girls with classic names and sun-browned legs come to buy a spool of thread or a nickel's worth of shoe buttons, and in the course of buying listen to the words of great and knowing men.[23]

Even if the country store had not served as a social center, its economic function would have provided both townspeople and farmers with the majority of their social contacts. What Charles R. Hoffer observed for the farmer could apply as easily to the village dweller: "The farmer comes in contact with the merchant more frequently than with any other agency in the community. He visits the store oftener than he does the school. He engages in conversation with the merchant more frequently than he does with the minister. And it not infrequently occurs that the clothier, the grocer, or the hardware dealer knows more about the farmer and understands his mental attitudes better than any other person in the community."[24] (This state of affairs was abetted by the bargaining which usually preceded any purchase in these stores. The advent of mail-order catalogue competition, with its set price, gradually led to the abolition of this practice.)[25]

Unfortunately, town and country merchants were not above using this social relationship for economic advancement. Thus, when many perceived a threat from the urban mail-order houses, their initial response was not to reorganize their stores for greater efficiency and lower prices, but rather to plead for community loyalty. One country newspaper asked on behalf of local merchants: "When your baby died, did the mail-order house send its sympathy? When your crop failed, did it offer to carry you a while? When your daughter was married, did it send a present? Has it helped build the churches, the schoolhouses, or the bridges of the community?"[26] Yet, by 1930, even this appeal would have been on shaky ground. By that time, economic control had passed from purely local interests to the more aloof urban financial wizards who cared little about the social concerns of their customers.[27]

Contemporary reports are full of contradictions as to whether the village and the general store were dead, dying, or enjoying a revival economically.[28] These conflicting reports seem to verify the remarks of a village editor who wrote: "When the automobile brought us into competition with the outside world, the town was dazed. Then stores modernized and prices were reduced. A couple of the inefficient places gave up. There was consolidation. Now we're served by the optimum number of agencies and are holding our own against all comers." (Incidentally, such competition was probably also responsible for the end of much of the remaining financial exploitation of the farmer.)[29]

But the price that many of these places had to pay for economic survival was their decline as social institutions. A merchant in an eastern town of 1,200 was happy to boast that he was attracting "quite some business from city people who have found that our prices are a bit lower, and who would rather drive to a pretty village like this than put up with the congested traffic and bad parking conditions in R——."[30] The arrival of such people probably tended to dissipate the neighborhood feeling that had existed previously in local stores. In conjunction with the introduction of sanitary packaging, it also meant that the pace of merchandising was quickened, and thus the store owners and employees had less leisure time and diminished interest in the local residents who camped in and around the establishment.[31] If one accepts the idea that those who spent considerable time in such stores were frustrated actors, it can only be assumed that they became dismayed by this lack of audience and left, looking for a more receptive public.

The social functions of the country store were also undermined by the introduction of the delivery wagon, and later the motorized delivery truck. As early as 1912, one storekeeper was asking his colleagues, "Do you know that for about what it costs you for one delivery boy and bicycle — two parts of the time — and for the expenses of a horse and wagon and a man to take care of it and run it, you could run a nice automobile delivery cart that would increase your delivery radius at least five miles and save no end of time and be the finest kind of an advertisement for the progressiveness of your store."[32]

When people began to telephone orders in, it became almost unnecessary to set foot in town at all. This development was abetted by the introduction of standard brands and prepackaging, which guaranteed quality sight unseen. Furthermore, in at least one Illinois village of 525, the grocer dispatched trucks directly into the country loaded with merchandise, and these served as traveling markets.[33]

The appearance of the roadside farm market had similar consequences. Because of the high volume of traffic on some roads, farmers could profit from keeping such establishments. Some country and suburban dwellers therefore didn't go to the local village for foodstuffs at all. The canned merchandise could be purchased in the larger trade center, and at neighboring farms fresh vegetables, berries, and fruit could be had at much lower prices than in stores.[34] These produce stands usually were run by farm women and therefore provided another antidote to the isolation and loneliness discussed in chapter 2.

Finally, to a great extent, the old-time general store was a victim of time. Many services and functions were now handled less expensively and more efficiently by others. The same technological advances that had made possible the automobile had also created a revolution in farm machinery. The size and complexity of these implements meant that they were an impractical commodity for the small country store, and, special establishments therefore developed to sell and service them. Similarly, the introduction of refrigerated train cars made it possible to market "fresh" meats and produce year round; this was often done by specialty stores, many of which delivered.[35] More often than not, these new services and functions were performed by businessmen located in urban areas or large rural towns.

Neither the farmer nor the small-town resident looked with favor on these developments. Time and again they showed their willingness to shop at home if the town merchants would adopt modern merchandising techniques, including specialization of functions, which would make their prices competitive with their more urban neighbors.[36] As John H. Kolb and Edmund deS. Brunner have noted, "trading with friends and neighbors of years standing, when on a satisfactory basis, is often more attractive than with outsiders."[37]

Still, there did seem to be a general trend towards shopping in larger areas.[38] However, a University of Nebraska study cautioned its readers *not* to form the opinion that

> the automobile and good roads have been the only factors causing the shift in trading to the larger centers.... Certain stocks have been declining in the small towns for years before the advent of the motor car. The growing tendency in the last few decades for people to go to the larger centers to shop is the result of many factors. The last quarter of a century has witnessed the definite passing of the frontier in agricultural states.... The result is that the rural community has become much less self-sufficing and now people go to the city for many articles once made at home. In the same time the standard of living of people in rural communities has risen. Advertising, both locally and in popular-priced magazines, has been a demand-creating factor. Railroads catered directly to the shopping public by improving the passenger service to the larger centers. Rural mail deliveries and the telephone have brought the farm closer to the city. Full recognition should be given to these forces, but at the same time the fact must be emphasized that the

> motor car has been not only the most important single factor but also an agency facilitating the action of other forces working to this end.[39]

In some respects, as David L. Cohn has noted, the old-fashioned country store was replaced eventually by another form of general store — the gasoline filling station:

> In its versatility it provides the needs of the car by way of oil, gasoline, air, tires, and services; then, without blinking an eye, it serves sandwiches, beer, soft drinks, or complete meals to the car's owner. Frequently is also sells staple groceries, notions, tobacco, and toilet goods, while on Saturday nights it becomes a dance hall whose clients move to the music of a juke box....
>
> In small towns and villages it is the hangout for youngsters that the poolroom once was, and the station attendants and "car-hops" are generally teen-age boys who are friends both of the hangers-on and of the customers. The filling station, moreover, is a place of light and movement in small communities that go to bed soon after dark. There is a state of suppressed excitement about it as cars come out of the unknown and go out again into the unknown. The hangers-on watch the comings and goings, guess what the occupants of the car may be up to, and — who knows? — one may be suddenly snatched up and carried off to a dance at Crystal Lake, thirty miles away.[40]

Thus, the old, leisurely atmosphere of the country store had been lost forever.

NEW FORMS OF AMUSEMENT

Another aspect of the changed recreational habits of rural America was the *constant* availability of commercialized amusements. Events like fairs, church socials, sporting events, bees, etc., took place periodically, whereas the newer entertainments were regularly available. "Amusement is no longer something to be taken in large amounts from whatever source may be available; the general supply is a relatively steady one from which people can make a number of choices," observed Wayne C. Neely,[41] Chief among the new forms of leisure made accessible by the motor car was the motion picture show. Commenting in 1926 on the impact of the movies on the farm community, Samuel R. McKelvie observed, "When good roads began to develop, interchange of ideas became easier. Inventions such as the steam engine, the telephone and telegraph, the automobile, linked the world closer together. Then came moving pictures, not only to speak but actually to show what other men and other women are doing. With the advent of the moving picture, it may be said that the last barriers which separated the man on the isolated farm from his neighbors in the cities were hurdled."[42]

If we accept the assumption that people "live" the movies they watch, it is not difficult to explain the rural popularity of the movies. While there is no *actual* physical activity on the part of the viewer, he or she may become so involved in the action on the screen that there seems to be. This entertainment was not work disguised as leisure, nor was it necessarily socially beneficial. It was the out-and-out escapism that the rural dweller sought after an arduous day in the field or store. Best of all, thanks to the automobile, it was available when, and generally where, one wanted.

Movie theaters also served as community meeting places, where all members of the family could gather and interact with other community residents. Just as importantly, such interaction crossed religious, ethnic, sexual, and educational lines in a way not possible in any other rural institution.[43]

The relaxed informality surrounding the newer amusements appealed particularly to the farming element. The weekly band concert grew in popularity as a result. As Lewis Atherton observed, "Informally dressed adults sitting at ease in cars around the band stand or courthouse square, milling youngsters with candy and popcorn, and a rather sedate program of music lasting something over an hour characterized the band concert. While listeners express approval of popular numbers by sounding their horns, they seem to like most of all the easy informality of the occasion and the excuse which it provides for a pleasant evening drive."[44] Such evenings were often combined with an "open-air" movie projected upon a white building or a large canvas. Merchants made the most of such activities to lure potential customers.[45]

At the same time that the automobile seemed to be dividing the business loyalty of the farmer among several trade centers, his social contacts remained concentrated in one area, according to studies done in the 1920s.[46] "Because the farmer came to town at a time when village society was needing his financial and moral support, farmer leadership became dominant and active in all social and economic affairs," claimed Horace B. Hawthorn. "The automobile also brought the farmer to the city, but not as an active social participant; it secured his trade and banking, but not his personality or leadership."[47] As a result, two members of the President's Research Committee on Social Trends concluded country people had established a fair degree of interdependance with the villagers in social, educational, and religious matters.[48]

Thus there seemed to be a renaissance in communitywide social activities. People began to realize that the automobile could not only take their neighbors to the city to hear "big name" entertainers, but could also be used to bring these entertainers to them. For instance, in Woodbury County, Iowa, several villages imported talent ensembles from Sioux City.[49] Furthermore, as Kolb and Brunner note, "The automobile and good roads make it possible to organize inter-community leagues of many kinds, kitten-ball [softball] for women, men, girls or boys, men's baseball leagues, quoit-pitching tournaments and tug-of-war contests.... Plans may include eliminations until a county play-off is arranged in order to select a team to go to state finals; for example, to the State Fair."[50]

Yet there can be little doubt that many traditional forms of entertainment passed from the scene.

In the presence of the movies, the village debater's words stuck in his throat, and no one cared any longer how the word phthisic was spelled.... The village fiddler faded into the mist and with him the whole tribe of rural musicians who played the organ, thumped the piano, strummed the guitar, or twanged the jew's-harp. The movies, the phonograph, and, later, the radio took their places. Girls no longer learned "accomplishments" with which to amuse boys in their parlours. Now they danced with them twenty miles from home, and might cover the area of a county before the evening had ended. The centripetal influence of isolation upon the farm home was weakened. The family gathered less often around hearth or lamp after the day's work was done. Faery lands forlorn no longer lay over the inaccessible horizon, but were well within reach of Mr. Ford's ubiquitous car, while the passport to them was not the golden fancy, but the price of a few gallons of gasoline.[51]

TOURISM

The automobile also made possible new recreational activities that could be enjoyed without joining specialized groups. Probably the most recognized example of this was the growth of motor tourism following World War I.

Although the motor car was not directly responsible for providing long periods of leisure, it did make it possible to use them more economically when they arrived. It actually may have created the pleasure vacation for the masses. As Elmer Davis claimed in 1932:

> The pioneer conditions that made indolence suspect and leisure unknown discouraged the habit of traveling for pleasure; a man had to do traveling enough when he was going somewhere for a purpose; till good roads were general — and that is a matter of the last dozen years — there was not enough fun in it to make it worth while unless you expected to do something or see somebody at the end of your journey....
>
> Then suddenly, the automobile came within the reach of every one. There were immense distances to be covered and a machine capable of covering them; and in large parts of the country it was necessary to travel immense distances to see anything different from what might be seen at home.[52]

As with so much else connected with the early history of the motor car, the rural environment was at first ill equipped to deal with the automobile vagabond. This was evident to the motorist when he tried to decipher which way to go at the numerous country crossroads. By way of explanation, Bellamy Partridge offers the following observation on road signs in rural America: "The countryfolk, with their intimate familiarity with local landmarks, paid little or no attention to their signboards and probably never missed them if they collapsed and were carried away. The city motorist, however, accustomed to a street sign on every corner, began to feel lost when he had passed beyond the city limits. . . . An attempt was made to develop some cooperation on the part of the localities where signs were most needed; but this resulted only in cynical smiles by town officials and county boards of supervisors who were not at all anxious to encourage the city motorists to make use of their roads."[53]

Incidents involving lost tourists, many of which seem humorous in retrospect, were common. Carl G. Fisher, developer of "Prest-O-Lite," one of the early methods of auto illumination, recalls the problems that could arise less than ten miles from a large city:

> Three of us drove out nine miles from Indianapolis, and being delayed, were overtaken by darkness on the return trip.
>
> To complicate matters, it began to rain pretty hard, and you know automobiles didn't have any tops on them in those days, so we all got pretty wet.
>
> We guessed our way along as well as we could, until we came to a place where the road forked three ways. It was black as the inside of your pocket. We couldn't see any light from the city, and none of us could remember which of the three roads we had followed in driving out; if, indeed, we had come that way at all.
>
> So we stopped and held a consultation. Presently, by the light of our headlamps, reflected up in the rain, one of us thought he saw a sign on a pole. It was too high up to read and we had no means of throwing a light on it, so there was nothing to be done but climb the pole in the wet and darkness and see if we could make out some road direction on the sign.

While the Great War rages in Europe, tourists stop to admire the view from Rabbit Ears Pass Road in Colorado's Routt National Forest. (*National Archives*)

City families at a 1922 country outing along Riverside Drive in Memorial Park, Drayton, North Dakota. (*National Archives*)

> We matched to see who should climb. I lost. I was halfway up the pole when I remembered that my matches were inside my overcoat and I couldn't reach them. So down I had to come, dig out the matches, put them in my hat, and climb up again.
>
> Eventually, by hard climbing, I got up to the sign. I scratched a match and before the wind blew it out I read the sign.
>
> It said: "Chew Battle-Ax Plug" [brand chewing tobacco].

Added to this problem was what Frank Farrington has called "the sore trial of eliciting intelligible information regarding distances and destinations from the honest country person, who himself always knows exactly what he is talking about but lacks the ability to make anybody else understand it."[55] This condition was somewhat alleviated by the publication of automobile "blue books," which gave detailed directions that often contained physical descriptions of landmarks such as trees, rock formations, and fences.

Meanwhile, automobile clubs pressured state legislatures to erect signs, and in desperation sometimes hired private parties to do it for them.[56] Louise Closser Hale ran into a honeymoon couple in Virginia who were engaged in such work: "The two young hearts were spending their honeymoon sign-posting the best way to Hot Springs for the automobile club of a large city. The back of the tonneau was full of neat wooden placards with the names of the towns painted thereon. "Danger" in red, arrows with Hot Springs on them, like the banner of Excelsior, and band boxes for milady's hats. As their honeymoon was just as important as sign-posting a road already very decently marked, we did not deplore his lack of activity in the getting out and nailing up directions."[57]

After many *more* successful efforts, rural America found itself being transformed into a new vacationland. In certain country areas, this new vehicular traffic was reminiscent of that which had existed in prerailroad days. During those times, stage coaches, men on horseback, and families in farm wagons formed a regular procession through the country, stopping at "taverns" at night for food and lodging. With the advent of the railroad, this traffic dried up. The motor car and good roads brought this trade back into rural America. "Tourists Lodged" signs began to appear in front of farmhouses, and forces were set in motion that were to have profound social and economic effects.[58]

Given the early reaction of rural residents to the automobile, it should not be surprising that the new long-distance tourist elicited varying degrees of sympathy from the natives. One writer for *Country Gentleman* thought there were two major schools of thought on the subject:

> The glad-hand theory proceeds from the belief that automobile tourists may have money or at least friends. The segregation theory, on the other hand, is based on the conviction that they have neither, and proceeds accordingly.
>
> The glad-handers provide signs and conveniences galore for the gasoline strangers — banners, green grass, traffic cops and natural gas. And camping assistance clear up to that pinnacle of modern civilization, the bungalow camp....
>
> The segregation towns focus their attention on the dubious quality that the transportation element has injected into the touring public. [Those who figure they can live cheaper on the move than at home]. They provide "public" camp grounds as a sort of restricted district for gasoline campers, where the most noise can be made and the least damage done. The public camp ground and the railroad freight yards are apt to be side by side, so that cinders and empty tomato cans can be conveniently tossed back and forth...
>
> It's hard to say which town has the best of it. If the tramp is what he appears to be, the glad-handers are out of luck. In the morning they might find even the statues missing from the city square. On the other hand, he may be a millionaire. During a period of automobile travel, the two are apt to look almost alike.[59]

In the end, the immense economic potential of tourism seemed to be decisive. Since tourist camps were virtually unknown until after the war, the early tourist trade tended to "resuscitate" the small country hotel temporarily.[60] Some hotel owners claimed that extensive renovations were undertaken to accommodate satisfactorily the increase in female tourists brought on by the motor car.[61] But this revival was short lived; by 1922 there existed 600 motor camps or courts, and in 1925 over 5,300.[62]

It is difficult to measure the *social* impact of this tourist traffic. However, one tourist couple who was traveling near Boonville, New York, in 1930 commented on the fact that their two-dollar room in a farm home "afforded the advantage of giving us an opportunity to talk with the family; an opportunity of value to those traveling and interested in the community through which they pass."[63]

Besides the obvious exchange of ideas, one author claimed that there had been a "complete change in attitude toward the world in general, for instance. The [farm] women who went out to meet their first 'strangers' with their knees shaking under them, have now the calm poise of women of the world. They can size up strangers with an unerring eye, and be perfectly at their ease about it ... in other words their knowledge of human nature is several hundred per cent enlarged."[64]

On the other hand, rivalry among families to secure the tourist trade often strained old friendships, and this became more acute as the commercialized motel took away the bulk of their business. In addition, antagonisms developed between those families who wanted to attract tourists and others who felt that the increased traffic and commercialization would spoil the neighborhood.[65]

Much more objectionable, from the community's point of view, were the large number of tourists who planned to "camp out" and generally did so when and where they pleased. L. F. Kneipp concluded in 1924 that, as a result, "the first tentative provisions for public campgrounds were purely defensive measures. For the growing army of automobilists created new conditions of hazard; hazard to public property through the thousands of campfires kindled daily by men who, however well-intentioned, knew little about the care of fire in the woods; hazard to public health due to contamination of watersheds through the assemblage of thousands of people upon areas where no provision for the maintenance of good sanitary conditions has been made."[66]

However, such establishments, particularly when they charged admission, helped to keep away the less desirable tourists. At first, motor camps were free. The public or private interests that owned them made a profit by selling automotive supplies and food provisions. But, as a 1927 writer for the *Magazine of Business* observed,

> In a free camp many who were not vacation campers set up their abode in increasing numbers. It was easy enough. Just drive an old rattle-trap car inside the gate, put up a tarpaulin for a tent, borrow utensils and food from your generous neighbors — tramping rubberized! These "white gypsies," foraging farmers' crops, stealing like real gypsies, have placed an odium upon many otherwise wholesome camps. The out-of-workers, the gasoline bums, the pay-as-you-go fellows, the hard-luck kids, and a small but troublesome proportion of downright criminals, all but ruined some fine camps.
>
> But the pay camp eliminated most of this riff-raff; besides, when the camp went into the "pay" class it had funds adequate for police protection and for a salaried superintendent with police power to order on their way the undesirable who might be able to pay the fee.[67]

As a result, such supervised camps were encouraged, and probably not solely for economic reasons. It is easy to lose sight of the fact that, with the introduction of the Model T, many of the rural campers were farmers and small-town people from other areas. Persons engaged in agricultural pursuits were twice as numerous in national parks as those associated with any other professional class.[68] There is no reason to believe that the situation was different in the town camps. Farmers in particular probably were quite pleased by the democratic atmosphere of these places. As one contemporary observer stated, "Informality is the password, snobbery is taboo, every man is your 'neighbor,' and all are bound together by an almost unbelievably powerful tie — the dust of the open road."[69] This state of affairs was in sharp contrast to the prevailing town-country and urban-rural attitudes alluded to earlier. Furthermore, as Willey and Rice were later to point out, "the patron feels none of the embarrassment [in the tourist camp] that he thinks might come with entrance into an urban hotel in the clothes of the road."[70]

Thus, for economic and social reasons, rural interests fostered the development of such camps, taking care always to see that the "wrong element" was kept to a minimum. In the end, they may have helped themselves more than they realized. The mushrooming tourist camps provided an impetus for developing country park land further. The latter, in turn, easily could be equipped as a playground.[71] This development not only struck a blow at rural isolation but provided for the further development of local recreational facilities.

CONCLUSION

The first third of the twentieth century witnessed a true revolution in the concept of leisure for rural Americans. What had begun as an occasional, work-related activity, performed in the home or the local business establishment, was transformed into a totally separate aspect of life that was constantly available and frequently engaged in beyond the confines of rural America itself.

While the automobile was not solely responsible for these developments, it was a major contributing factor. RFD, electrification, and eventually the radio helped bring elements of the nonagricultural world into the country, creating yearnings that could not be fulfilled because of geographic separation. It was the motor car that was eventually to break down this barrier.

These developments were to have profound effects on rural social life. The changes, when they came, were not gradual but abrupt. The traditional leisure world of rural America remained largely the same until its "death" in this period. It had always resisted the commercialization and the purely recreational nature of amusements found in urban places; as a result, the modifications that might have created a new type of leisure ethic never developed. Therefore, when the allure of urban recreation was combined with relatively easy and inexpensive access, the transformation that took place was almost total.

At first, these newer types of amusements were available only in the cities and the larger towns. With time, they spread into rural areas, easily overcoming the moribund institutions with which they briefly competed. Traditionalists may have hoped to confine such recreation to urban locales. But in attempting to do so, they were running counter to powerful economic and social forces, including the acceptance of the automobile in rural America, that were homogenizing American civilization and making the uniqueness of country life less attractive.

The transformation of rural leisure broadened the recreational activities available to both farmers and small-town residents. In so doing, it probably helped to overcome some of the social dissatisfaction that existed among these groups in the years 1893-1929. No longer need they enviously read and hear about the exciting new world of the twentieth century, knowing that they could only partake of it by renouncing their rural way of life. Now, thanks to the automobile, the new amusements were easily accessible at night, on the weekends, or during short motor vacations.

At the same time, however, participation in such activities was bound to "contaminate" country life. The negative aspects of commercialized recreation were unavoidable. To the extent that these engendered unlawful acts and immorality, rural residents could not hope to be immune. Contemporary accounts, while bemoaning these developments, seem to show a general willingness to tolerate the unwanted side effects in exchange for greater social satisfaction.

That rural America itself might become a recreational setting was not seen initially by its inhabitants. Their somewhat myopic view concentrated on exploiting urban recreational riches or preventing the commercialization of their own traditional leisure activities. They had difficulty imagining what might bring large numbers of vacationers out into the country. In a sense, they took for granted what thousands of urbanites sought: fresh air, large expanses of greenery, and relatively uninhabited areas. It did not take long for automobile tourism to become a major recreational activity, and when it did, rural America found itself the object of leisure pursuits as well as a partaker in them. With this development, there could be little hope of preserving traditional rural society and the leisure activities that were part of it. The isolation that had made them possible no longer existed. Rural and urban residents would now jointly formulate the recreational habits of America and share the resulting leisure activities together.

V. Religion

Three major problems had traditionally plagued rural religion: "overchurching"; nonresident ministers; and town-village competition. Before discussing each of these weaknesses, it should be emphasized that all of them existed before the motor car was introduced to rural society. Thus, while the automobile may have accelerated certain trends, it can not be said to have caused them.

A typical example of the problem of too many churches was Bellville, Ohio, where, in 1917, there were 5 Protestant churches with a combined seating capacity of 1,675. Yet, the town had a population of only 913, 534 of whom were members of local churches.[1] During the same period, Edward Eastman reported that 14 percent of the rural communities in the United States had no Protestant churches at all.[2] Thus, not only were there too many churches, but they were unevenly distributed.

Either extreme — intense church competition or complete lack of institutional religion — had a disintegrating effect on the community. No one group, argued rural sociologist Paul L. Vogt, had the power to organize the community, because its leadership was not recognized by nonmembers and therefore its influence was limited to a minority of the population.[3]

Many of these churches continued to exist only because they

were receiving "home-missionary" aid from more established and wealthier churches of the same denomination in the cities.[4] Even so, while money might buy buildings and provide for their upkeep, trained men of the cloth were also needed and they were in short supply. It thus became necessary, as Walter Burr remembered, to institute "circuit" or "out-station" plans:

> My father started his ministry in the United Brethren Church in Southern Indiana as a circuit rider. No one point in the area that he covered was more important than another point. He had his pony and saddlebags, and would ride on a two-weeks' tour through the forest, visiting little settlements or neighborhoods in the interest of the church. The places visited were separate and distinct units with no socially organic relationship to each other. This plan ... grew into the peddling of a sermon from place to place by a man who had no community interest in his spiritual customers.... Under this system the church which he served with the greater part of his time and near which he lived was in a town, and he drove his horse and buggy a few miles into the country Sunday to preach a sermon to a group of country folk assembled in a school house or in a country church building. This ... came alarmingly near to being an exploitation of a group of farmers by the town churches in order to obtain money for the support of a city preacher.[5]

Because of this shortage of clergy, religion in the more rural parts of America was frequently limited to a weekly service, with little or no personal visitation or church-sponsored activities in between.[6] Harlan Paul Douglass and Edmund deS. Brunner noted that some circuit ministers served so many churches that they could not reach every one each Sunday. As a result, 13 percent of the village churches and over 60 percent of those in the open country were not used each week.[7]

This difference between town and country churches is important. Throughout the period under discussion, the open-country church suffered more than the town and village ones, though all found themselves declining as the percentage of the population that were church members decreased.[8]

As noted previously there was a general townward trend among the rural population for such services as shopping and leisure. Not surprisingly, this trend was accompanied by a similar movement of religious institutions. John H. Kolb and Edmund deS. Brunner felt:

> It illustrates the desire to enjoy the better-trained ministers and richer programs of village and town churches, to worship in large congregations and thereby benefit from increased social opportunities, and to follow into the church the village people with whom they participate in other activities....
>
> Village churches rarely, if ever, absorb all the constituents of abandoned country congregations, many of whom cease going to church altogether, especially if they do not own automobiles.[9]

One reason for the loss of parishioners was that many former members of rural churches were unwilling or unable to adjust to the centralized nature of the village or town institution.[10] No doubt this was partly because the ministers of most such congregations were more oriented toward the city than the country. Warren H. Wilson claimed that farmers sensed this orientation and therefore did not become involved with the village or town church.[11]

Still, the rapid growth of town churches, coupled with the urban clerical orientation, shows the intensity of the desire to attend less rural churches. In 1920, approximately 23 percent of the people belonging to village churches and 6 percent of the members of town churches lived in the open country, reported Kolb and Brunner. A decade later, this had increased to 40 and 24 percent, respectively.[12]

CONSOLIDATION OF CHURCHES

Consolidation had its major impact during the same period that the automobile made its greatest inroads into rural America. As this statement from a rural California minister shows, the automobile had both positive and negative effects on the country church:

> In 1874 I was sent to a ten appointment charge [serving as minister for ten separate communities] in Minnesota. The rule was that every township must have a Sunday school and a preaching service every two weeks, if possible. Twenty years later I visited that circuit and found that it had been reduced to four appointments, this change being accounted for by better roads and conditions of travel which allowed farmers to attend village churches. Ten years later, after the introduction of the automobile, this same area was reduced to two appointments.
>
> A year ago I visited an old friend who drove me over a part of the old circuit, and as we passed six of the school houses where we used to preach he told me that not a service or even a Sunday school now existed, in spite of the fact that the population had nearly doubled. I said to my friend, "I suppose these people attend the church in town." "No," he said, "not one in ten. They are only tenants and have no automobiles or other means of travel, and as they are only here for a short time and are so poor, they do not attend church because they feel they cannot afford to belong to a church."[13]

Thus, although the quality of "churching" probably increased, certain groups without the new technology found themselves effectively deprived of religion.

However, they need not have been. "I remember well," wrote Warren H. Wilson in 1924, "the first pastor who testified in a meeting of his brethren in Montana to the gospel use of the automobile. He employed it for visiting the remote ranchers 'above the ditch' on the semi-dry lands."[14] In ways like this the motor car could bring religion to those who had previously been inaccessible.

Indeed, sometimes the automobile itself became the church, as described below by historian David L. Cohn:

> The peripatetic preacher flowers lushly among Negroes of the rural South. There an eminent divine may "pastor" churches spread over two or three states, the road to Damascus being cleanly paved

> and traversed by him in a once magnificent Packard limousine now fallen upon evil days. Sometimes such a toiler in the vineyard of the Lord may hold services in as many as three or four churches in a single day. Such is the miracle of the spirit which allows no fatigue and the car which knows no distance. Some Negro sects — such as the Know the Truths or the Never-Die-Sanctified — can afford neither a regular pastor nor even a church building. Services are therefore conducted by a car-riding preacher in a plantation cabin belonging to a member of the sect.[15]

Similarly, *Motor Age* reported in 1916 that a Congregational minister in Centralia, Kansas, "devised a way to give his members who own motor cars the fullest measure of pleasure from them, and at the same time maintain the attendance at Sunday evening service. He preaches on the church porch, where the orchestra and choir also are placed, and he invites the motor car owners to park their cars in the yard and street, and listen."[16]

It soon became clear, however, that it was the church's responsibility to see to it that changes like those cited above were controlled in its best interests. A 1923 writer voiced such a concern in *Christian Century* magazine:

> Good roads increase the ease of communication and make church going more regular. They permit the church to reach out to a wider field and thus increase the area of its influence.... Those who want better churches [must] agitate for better roads as a means of obtaining them....
>
> But now there arises another problem with the coming of quickened transportation and communication. The rural church was centered in a neighborhood of small radius. Like the rural school it must be within easy riding distance for the horse vehicle and the poor dirt road. With the coming of hard surfaced roads and the automobile the old neighborhood grouping expands into a modern country community..... The families that are ambitious enough to covet better education for their children also covet better advantages in church and religious instruction. The town church, with its resident pastor, graded Sunday school and young people's organizations, invites attendance by offering more adequate

> religious training. As a result the more advanced and abler of the farm families are steadily being drawn off from the rural community, and the rural church loses leadership.[17]

One solution to this problem was to consolidate open country churches with those of the same denomination in villages and towns. Not only did this tend to lessen rivalry within sects, but according to Professor Walter Burr, it made the rural church a "going proposition." Economies of scale allowed for a resident preacher, a deaconess, and even other assistants, all of whom performed their functions daily. "Instead of coming from a little family neighborhood to an inefficient old building to listen to a peddled sermon," Burr concluded, "they come now in their automobiles from many miles away to listen to their resident pastor."[18]

In a 1921 article entitled "Motorizing the Rural Church," O. R. Geyer summed up the changes wrought by the automobile:

> The decline of the old-fashioned church first engaged public attention at about the time the automobile was gaining a foothold in the country districts, and from that day to this has continued with ever increasing force. Perhaps the chief reason for this has been the important part played by the automobile in annihilating distances and in bringing about a larger and better community spirit. Where three and four churches were deemed necessary a generation or so ago, because of poor roads and thinly settled districts, one church today is doing the work of its predecessors with much greater success....
>
> Church leaders as a rule are strongly convinced that the change is for the better. They are giving full assistance to the work started through the agency of the motor car and good roads, because they realize the necessity of the new rural church. An illustration of the good that is being accomplished in this change is the fact that church membership is constantly increasing [in absolute terms] as the number of rural churches decline....
>
> This change has brought about an increased social life, and has made possible flourishing community churches serving large populations. Those churches lacking in the elements which make

> for a larger and better social life in the community are doomed to disappear, and there is certain to be no great mourning over their loss.[19]

THE AUTOMOBILE AND THE SABBATH

As one observer remembered it, "Sunday was the Sabbath in the horse-drawn days, with a simple, quiet program. Church in the morning, big Sunday dinner, nap or a jog of six miles to Steward and back in the afternoon, cold supper, church in the evening, a bit of reading and bed."[20] Above all, Sunday was the Lord's day, when one put worldly thoughts and pleasures aside to contemplate religious teachings and the hereafter. Nonetheless, by the turn of the century, transportation developments were beginning to change what was viewed as "proper" Sunday behavior.

Like the automobilists that followed them, bicycle advocates first experienced the condemnation, and then the approval, of Sunday pleasure travel. In 1896, the Presbyterian minister in Monroe, Wisconsin, requested that bicyclists stop organizing group visits to neighboring localities on Sundays. However, another minister was able to justify Sunday bicycling in a broader examination of morality in general. He noted, according to Lewis Atherton, that "there was no more harm in a bicycle 'spin' on Sunday than in a drive with horse and carriage; less, as a matter of fact, if the horse was tired."[21]

Still, the automobile did contribute to a decrease in rural church attendance, if not membership. One writer for *Scribner's Magazine* maintained in 1922 that "in good motoring weather I have attended Sunday-morning services from Waycross, Ga., to Manistee, Mich., and it would be hard to find any pews emptier anywhere."[22] An elderly pillar of the church stated: "I never missed church or Sunday School for thirteen years and I kind of feel as if I'd done my share. The ministers ought not to rail against people's driving on Sunday. They ought just to realize that they won't be there every Sunday during the summer, and make church interesting enough so they'll want to come."[23]

The latter point is important. The automobile made possible visits to urban churches, where the quality of services and sermons was generally higher than in rural America.[24] After such visits, many wanted to go to the best or not go at all. In addition, rural residents increasingly were able to listen to the nation's outstanding preachers on the radio.[25] Thus, whether a particular church would grow often depended on image rather than deeds. For many rural pastors, this was bad news indeed.[26]

Not all churchgoers were equally affected by the automobile. There seems to have been something of a generation split, with the younger people more willing to innovate. Ruth Suckow's 1924 novel *Country People* showed the reactions of three generation of the same rural Iowa family to the motor car:

> It was a wonder to Emma [the mother] to sit on the porch on Sunday afternoons and count how many vehicles went by. But grandpa wouldn't even try to count. "*Ach*, no! no! no!" was all that he would say. This was all so wicked on Sunday!
>
> August [the father] had kept his hands on other things, but he couldn't keep the boys from using the car. When they took their girls, it wasn't an all-day occasion, as when Frank had got grandpa's old buggy to drive Lottie to the fair. They went out on Sunday afternoons when they felt like it. August would go out and find the car gone again. It was no use trying to stop them. Emma thought it was dreadful for the boys to "pleasure-drive on Sunday," against which the Richland Methodist Church was making a last futile stand, as against cards and dancing; but both she and August got used to it. All the young people seemed to do it. But one thing August said: if he ever heard of his boys driving to a Sunday baseball game, they would never have the car again.[27]

The reference to baseball should be emphasized, for it indicates that the automobile was not solely responsible for making the Sabbath more secular. For instance, Lewis Atherton recounts that in Hillsboro, Illinois, the Chautauqua, a church-related institution, agreed in 1915 to allow Sunday boating by its members on the community lake. The directors even discussed the possibility of permitting children to swim on the Sabbath, provided it did not compete with any religious activity.[28]

The automobile seemingly could also be a tool of the Lord for those who refused to attend Sunday services. Bellamy Partridge, in describing the motor troubles of a Mr. Dorlon, suggested that the automobile could reflect one's religious conscience. "His favorite place for breaking down seemed to be in front of the cemetery. Somehow he managed to stall there two or three times every day. . . . Eventually this inability to go past a cemetery began to get under Mr. Dorlon's skin, and he admitted to me privately that he was being given a premonition. . . .

"Mr. Dorlon came around to our office and made his will. He began to go to church assiduously, twice every Sunday, and he never missed the Thursday night prayer meeting."[29]

Similarly, Louise Closser Hale, one of the early women to use the automobile for touring, observed that many of her mishaps occurred on Sundays. "I believe now that motor cars are deeply religious," she concluded. "One may observe in the Monday morning papers the harvest of accidents of the day before. It must be very painful to a highly moral motor car to carry around a lot of joy riders who ought to be in church knowing better. I suppose when the occupants become too joyful for the day, the car bucks and throws them out. 'Steering gear goes wrong,' reads the newspapers — but the other motors know!"[30]

Some ministers, however, reported a 1928 writer for *Christian Century,* were willing to try out the advice of their congregationists who maintained that communion with nature, easily accessible through the use of the motor car, was a religious act of the highest order:

> The peripatetic ecclesiastic had dedicated this vacation Sunday to the Lord of heaven and earth. He would join the caravan of "blue-domers"; he would take his religion out of doors, where God smiled and spoke to burdened business men. In serene solitude he would

> drive his car over smoky and smelly roads, oblivious of all but the deeper invisible realities. To the care-free accompaniment of the motor he would raise hymns of joy to the God of breeze and field. Religion today would be pure awareness and grateful communion. No problems, no duties, no symbols, no institutions, no rationalism, no questioning or doubting. Man should not intrude his disturbing companionship into the calm of spiritual being.
>
> The fragrance had not yet left the dewy grain. Good will and song and prayer expanded my soul. Speeding under such circumstances could not be wrong; it was but the winging of the eager spirit.[31]

Even the conservative Baptist weekly *Watchman-Examiner* was willing to concede that the automobile could perform a religious mission, provided it was properly identified as such.

> An esteemed subscriber to *THE WATCHMAN—EXAMINER* suggests that in the interest of church advertising as well as in the interest of the Lord's Day observance, it might be a good thing for Christian men who use motor cars to reach their church services, to carry some kind of refined but universally used placard or pennant which would signify that the car was being used with a religious end in view. This novel suggestion strikes us forcibly. . . . There ought to be some way in which Christian people using motor cars for laudable purposes might be distinguished from the multitudes who have no regard for God or the Lord's Day.[32]

Despite all the rhetoric, the automobile had undoubtedly made the church more accessible to the rural dweller. As *Motor Age* observed in 1919:

> Many a farm family's supply of steeds is limited and on Sunday in the old days the horses were turned out on Sunday to graze and enjoy a well-earned day of rest. If it was extremely hot or extremely cold, if it was muddy underfoot or snowy underfoot or slushy underfoot, going to church was a laborious task, a task which more than one person found easy to shirk. Walking to church meant half the day gone, a late dinner and half the afternoon as well as all the morning gone.

> With the motor car, however, there is a big change. Even the farmer in the remotest rural district may wait until the last minute, jump into his car and go to church, attend services and be home in less than the time it used to take him to get there alone. His car needs no rest, and the trip consumes so little of his time that it does not seriously cut into the time he himself requires for relaxation at the end of the week. Indeed, the trip to church is a relaxation in itself.[33]

That country men and women took full advantage of this opportunity appears doubtful. The available evidence shows that rural church attendance and membership never rose above 40 percent of the population.[34] These statistics seem to indicate that the church was never the pervasive factor in country life that it is often made out to be. This is not to say that rural America did not possess a strong moral and ethical value system. Rather, it implies that socially acceptable behavior was possible without an institutional superstructure that attracted the majority of the populace.

Because the church was in trouble before the motor car made its major impact, the automobile can at worst share the blame with the weaknesses mentioned earlier in this chapter. As Cohn observes, "The platitude that a man's strength is proved only when he is tempted, may here be applied to the church in the sense that its pull is evidenced only when it competes successfully with the pull of other things — in this case, the car. . . .

"Man's mystical yearnings toward godhead were not killed by the jalopy, and the probabilities are that the car has left both the church and the average minister — more earnest than inspired — just about where it found them."[35]

A survey in the mid-twenties tried to ascertain the direct effect of the automobile on church attendance. Pastors were almost evenly divided on whether the motor car was harmful or beneficial.[36] In the words of a doctoral student writing in 1928, "It would appear that any unit of activity or any mechanical object can be, at some time, emotionalized into a moral issue, at other times, rationalized into a technical expedient."[37]

MORALITY

Above all, the church was concerned about the automobile's seeming contribution to immorality. Rural America had always sharply contrasted itself to the sin and degeneracy of urban areas, and most American people and institutions assumed such a contrast. At the University of Missouri in 1871, the course in moral philosophy and twelve lectures on "Evidences of Christianity" were required of all students *except* those in agriculture. The catalogue opined that such requirements "may not be so necessary for a farmer. He communes with nature so much [that] his moral powers are better developed."[38] Such notions were widespread, and rural youth were therefore allowed to work and play together with little adult supervision. It was believed that their upbringing would guarantee proper conduct.[39]

Wrapped up with this philosophy was the current mode of transportation. As one 1901 magazine writer observed, "the moral influence of the horse is also very noticeable to one who studies human beings. There is something noble about a horse, and his intelligence is so nearly human that he humanises [sic] those who love him."[40]

Beneath this facade, however, country living was not all that good and clean. Unfortunately, the automobile was later held accountable for some vices that had been well established before the advent of the motor car. Edward A. Ross noted in 1917 that "'hanging around the streets' is rife and 'haunting the pool rooms' is growing. Cigarette smoking is general among the boys and meets with little or no parental opposition. Sex consciousness arrives early and, in the absence of competing interests, the effects are alarming.... [This is] precisely what my be expected under the three conditions of lack of wholesome and innocent recreation, absence of religious influences, and want of parental supervision."[41]

Rural immorality had been restricted largely by the tight-knit quality of the community. However, this quality was seriously threatened by the automobile. Frederick Lewis Allen hypothesized that "one of the cornerstones of American morality had been the difficulty of finding a suitable locale for misconduct."[42] This cornerstone was now crumbling.

Two schools of thought have grown up as to whether the automobile itself was responsible for a change in the moral standards of the time. One group, which included people like John Keats, believed that "the total number of wenches tossed on back seats was at first probably no greater than that theretofore tossed in haylofts."[43] Similarly, Albert Blumenthal reported that "when it is suggested that the automobile facilitates sex diversions at the present day,... older residents reply: 'It wasn't very hard to get out of the city limits during the horse-and-buggy days.' "[44] As Edward R. Eastman has noted:

> The "sowing of wild oats" is an ancient custom, in which every generation has had its part, the variations not being in the wildness but only in the methods. With the modern automobile, young folks can go fast and far and they certainly seem to be handy with "petting." But there were a good many old farm horses ruined in other times by long night drives, and there are many critical fathers and mothers of today who have forgotten how convenient the old farm "plug" was for petting parties — only they called it "spooning" in those days instead of "petting," when they were frank enough to refer to it at all.[45]

On the other hand, as Robert and Helen Lynd have correctly observed, "buggy-riding in 1890 allowed only a narrow range of mobility; three to eight were generally accepted hours for riding, and being out after eight-thirty without a chaperon was largely forbidden. In an auto, however, a party may go to a city halfway across the state in the afternoon or evening, unchaperoned automobile parties as late as midnight, while subject to criticism, are not exceptional."[46] Furthermore, "with the aid of an automobile and the device of leaving the dance an hour or so early, a girl can 'pulla wild party' and still return home at a time which does not arouse the suspicion of her parents," observed Blumenthal.[47]

Finally, the motor car was evolving toward something like a living or bedroom on wheels. Completely enclosed cars increased from 10 percent of total production in 1919 to 90 percent by 1929.[48] Beginning in 1920, built-in heaters became available as optional equipment, although devices employing charcoal bricks had been used as early as 1902.[49] Floyd Clymer claimed that open buggies and wagons had accustomed people to braving bad weather while sitting in a vehicle,[50] but his perspective probably differed from that of the rural youngster who declared, "They all say that summer is the time to do your stuff and you've got to have an automobile to get much. Petting is a seasonable pleasure all right. It's too cold around here most of the year to do it and be comfortable."[51]

The automobile also seems to have been directly responsible for certain changes in women's attire, just as the bicycle had been earlier.[52] "Since a position behind the steering wheel was hardly conducive to such 'cumbrous paraphernalia' as bustles, hour-glass corsets, layers of fluffy petticoats and towering coiffures," Wilfred Leland observed, "women quickly decided that the time had at long last come for them to appear in public in some semblance of the shape that their Creator had given them."[53] In addition, long skirts had to be shortened so that women could easily manipulate the car's floor pedals.[54] To those who felt that similar changes necessitated by the bicycle had been demoralizing and degrading, these new innovations must have been just as disconcerting. Furthermore, since bicycle riding had largely been limited to urban people, the alterations brought on by the automobile may have been more abrupt in rural America than elsewhere. Yet this point seems to have been little discussed in the writing of the day, and it seems safe to conclude that it was a moral factor for only a small number of rural residents.

Unfortunately, there are few statistics to document any change in sexual mores brought on by the motor car. The available information often seems contradictory. For example, the Lynds found that "of thirty girls brought before the [Middletown] juvenile court in the twelve months preceding September 1,

1924, charged with 'sex crimes,' for whom the place where the offense occurred was given in the records, nineteen were listed as having committed the offense in an automobile."[55] On the other hand, when an investigator returned for a follow-up study to an Iowa prairie town in 1923 to determine the effect of the radio, phonograph, movie, and automobile, he concluded that there had been little change in the moral standards.[56]

David L. Cohn's remarks below seem to offer the only conclusion warranted by our sketchy data:

> It is a maxim of medicine that "syphilization and civilization" go hand in hand. So do the automobile and contraception. It is the combination of these two that has brought about monumental changes in the sex behavior of the country. The car — unlike the horse and buggy — enables a couple to evade prying eyes and consequent social censure. Knowledge of contraception then permits them to avoid the biological consequences of their physical relations. Thus instincts and desires which might have been repressed at another time through fear of detection and dread of childbirth are given free play, with results so profound and so pervasive as sharply to differentiate Americans of the automobile age from their predecessors of the horse and buggy era.
>
> It is fallacious, of course, to conclude that the car is at fault, since it is obviously an inanimate machine which the owner puts to such uses as he sees fit. It is equally fallacious to conclude that Americans in the past were morally "better" than they are now. . . . One must ask whether their alleged higher standard of "morals" arose out of conviction or out of the fears which invention has reduced to a minimum for their descendants.[57]

Curiously, the same machine that was superficially assumed to lower moral standards was responsible for the demise of an institution often accused of the same crime — the livery stable. Lewis Atherton observed that the latter was frequently viewed as only slightly better than the town saloon. It was seen as a place where men went to dissipate their time by loafing, playing cards, and drinking. In addition, stable owners were condemned for their numerous vices, which included the use of profanity and an apparent avoidance of all religious activity.[58] One investigator even concluded that the livery stable was a common environment for the murderer:

> It was no mere whim of preachers in the 1890s that produced the countless sermons against livery stables and fast rigs. Anyone who makes a study of crimes involving women during this period must be struck by the number of females who never returned from buggy rides. An even greater number of females, so ancient rounders say, returned from buggy rides in a condition which was, as a vivid phrase of the time had it, worse than death. But leaving "sin" as compared to crime out of the matter, it would appear in retrospect that a pretty girl's progress from the livery stable was often direct to the morgue.[59]

Such condemnation obviously made the livery stable a place of acute interest for young country boys, who often found amusement of a quite innocent variety there. In 1927 a writer for the *Saturday Evening Post* nostalgically recalled that a small boy "could get horseshoe nails there, if he failed at the blacksmith shop, to make into a ring that he figured would come in very handy if he should ever get into a fight with the thief who stole his collection of turtle eggs. He hung on the lies of the loafers as they winkingly told of strange far-away places where they had never been. . . . After a rain he found plenty of horse hairs there to try the snake-making experiment in the mud puddles."[60] Such stables, combination rent-a-horse establishments and storage garages, fell on hard times as the automobile took over the transportation functions of the horse in rural America. The motor car must therefore be credited with eliminating what most rural mothers felt was a morally offensive institution.

Another positive effect of the automobile was the growth of the Town and Country Departments of the Young Men's and Women's Christian Associations (YMCA and YWCA). One spokesman for the YMCA claimed that "the introduction of the automobile into our plan of operation has made it possible to reach more than twice as many communities as formerly."[61] By the end of the 1920s, the YMCA had established itself in fourteen hundred rural communities.[62] Its traditional work of organizing rural youth for everything from Bible study to athletic contests to boy-and-girl socials was therefore brought to greater numbers of country dwellers.

In a 1925 article in *Survey* magazine, Joseph K. Hart summarized the interaction of religion, morality, and the automobile:

> The automobile, and its impersonal power, have come to stay. They have a reality that is not possessed by phrases. But the machine and its power does not threaten morality, or education, or even religion. It threatens only those forms of morality, education and religion that depend upon phrases, or hocus-pocus, for their continuance. The automobile and power are real: they are of the universe. The morality, or education, or religion that is also real, that is *of* the universe, will have as much chance as the machine, or power, for continuance. But the automobile does not hesitate to change — in the interests of use, and in the face of new discoveries and inventions. Can morality, or education, or religion dare the same test? Any other sort of morality, or education, or religion will necessarily vanish along with all the other unrealities that the race has set its emotions upon in the various credulous moments of history; or, it will linger for a little longer, in some stagnant by-way, or belated mind, which assumes that by threats, or by prayers, or by legislative enactments, it can turn the course of the stream of time or dam up the flood of the years. . . . [63]

CONCLUSION

The church in rural America had historically been a local institution and frequently a powerful force unifying the community. The vast distances that separated families and neighborhoods made this a logical arrangement. Nonetheless, it helped create such problems as over-churching, nonresident ministers, and religious competition among towns and villages.

The various forces that urbanized the American population

during the first third of the twentieth century — of which the automobile was a particularly significant one — were destined to alter these conditions radically. As mobility increased, it became possible to consolidate the efforts of the individual religious sects and to centralize their activities regionally. As a result, the quality of the ministry improved, and the absolute (but not relative) number of people attending church correspondingly increased.

Nonetheless, changes in the rural religious experience, particularly in the less densely populated areas, came so quickly that they often had a disintegrating effect on the community. Where the church had served as a unifying institution, linking the families of the open country together, the transition to a town-centered church tended to disrupt the integrity of the old neighborhoods. In the face of these changes, many people felt at a loss as to how to order their religious lives.

Consequently, rural religious practices became more ambiguous. A good example of this ambiguity is the attitude of both ministers and lay people toward the sanctity of the Sabbath. In the past, the relative immobility of the rural population had made "going to church" a full day's event. The automobile made it possible to engage in all of the religious activities normally scheduled for Sunday and still have time for recreational pursuits. It therefore became necessary to redefine the nature of proper conduct on the Sabbath.

Just as importantly, the new mobility provided an excuse for many rural Americans to desert their local churches on Sunday. Although attendance at town or city churches was frequently offered as an explanation for this behavior, the motor car was often the *means* by which many people diminished the importance of religion in their lives. (The origins of the desire to do so are more difficult to discern.) Thus, although total church attendance increased during this period, there was a significant downward trend relative to the population as a whole.

In such transitional times, it is not surprising that the more religious sought and found in the automobile a scapegoat for changes in the church of which they did not approve. The motor car's greatest impact on rural society coincided with significant modifications in the nature of the rural church and an apparent lowering of moral standards. While the automobile probably was not totally responsible for these changes, it was apparently an important contributing factor. At the very least, it made more visible activities that the rural community would have traditionally viewed as antisocial. While such conduct no doubt was engaged in previously, the strength of the local neighborhood or community had kept its existence submerged. With the weakening of many local institutions, including the church, it now became possible to display one's lack of religion or "immorality" more openly and with a minimum of censure.

Nonetheless, there is substantial evidence that the motor car strengthened rural religion in many respects: the presence of resident ministers, weekly religious activities, and involvement in the social life of a wider community. The vehicle that ostensibly took people away from the church could also be used to literally bring the church to them, in the form of motorized chapels. Areas formerly without any religious institutions could now be reached with some regularity. The benefits of consolidated churches were no longer the sole province of urban residents; country dwellers could partake of them as well.

In sum, the impact of the automobile on rural religious life was complex. Whether that impact was positive or negative depends largely on one's point of view. While it can be said with certainty that the motor car played an important role in an era of religious change, any qualitative assessment of these changes must be subjective.

VI. Education

If the occupants of the first automobile to penetrate rural America had bothered to stop at the local district school, the famed "little red schoolhouse," they would have found it largely unchanged from pioneer days. In a single room, poorly heated in winter and poorly ventilated in fall and spring, were collected from eight to thirty children, distributed over the full range of eight primary grades. The school was ill equipped by urban standards, and what education took place there generally could be credited to the expertise of the teacher. She, unfortunately, was often poorly trained for her task, and lack of supervision by her distant superiors compounded her problems.

Probably most important of all, these schools were generally dead ends. As a rule, there were no high schools in rural areas. Those that existed were located in towns and cities and maintained by them. As a result, those few country boys and girls who desired to enroll were treated as nonresidents and were charged tuition.

In addition, town and city high schools were in different school districts from the country schoolhouses, and their educational policies were therefore outside the control of farm owners and workers. Consequently, the curriculum rarely focused on agricultural subjects or interests.[2] These conditions did not result from antiintellectual forces but rather from small school districts and local taxation policies that were inadequate to provide decent secondary schools in rural areas.[3]

Historically, the district school had served as the neighborhood social center, and the district boundaries had themselves defined the neighborhood.[4] This school role was undermined to the extent that families sent their offspring to the town institution and established other contacts there.[5] As country residents increased the number and variety of their social contacts in more urban areas, the local district school became an administrative anomaly.[6] As Professor Walter Burr observed in 1921, "With the coming of the automobile, this tendency to recognize the larger area as one community was greatly emphasized. With this condition apparent, the district school begins to fail, because, although its development was a recognition that education is a community function, it does not have a community scope in the new order of things, and therefore does not permit the larger community to function educationally."[7]

An obvious reason for maintaining the district school was the opportunity that it afforded for visits between home and school. One 1912 study of rural schools observed that "there are few homes represented in the school and all are within walking distance, so that a teacher who desires to do so may hope, without too great an expenditure of time and effort, to visit all of her pupils and their parents in their homes. Acquaintance and friendship with the teacher make visiting the school easier for the parents."[8]

In answer to such persuasive arguments, the *Journal of Rural Education* carried an article entitled "Do We Want the County as the School District?" Its author, Professor C. W. Stone, argued that, thanks to the automobile, larger schools were possible while maintaining parental involvement.

> [When] the present small districts were laid out, ... the country was new, travel difficult, and communication slow. Farmers could not go very far to talk over school questions. In those days there was no rural free delivery. There were no telephones, no improved roads, nor automobiles....
>
> [Now] if Whitman County [Washington] as the school district were divided into five divisions for the election of the school

officers, the people could reach the center of any of those five divisions as easily as they used to reach the district school in the small local district.[9]

CONSOLIDATION OF SCHOOLS

It might be possible to argue, in view of today's educational theories, that the one-room district school was not as academically deficient as was commonly thought, or that the consolidation of schools was not an overwhelmingly positive step forward for rural education. The literature from the period 1893-1929, however, shows that both educational professionals and rural residents believed otherwise.

The idea of consolidating schools into larger units predated the major impact of the automobile in rural America, although the latter greatly accelerated the process by providing a solution to the transportation problem. One government expert claimed that by 1910 school consolidation had been accepted as sound educational policy throughout the United States.[10] In 1923, John M. Foote did a comparative study of one-room and consolidated schools. Although he was somewhat disappointed with the magnitude of the improvement, the results definitely did support earlier hypotheses about the educational advantages of centralization. Foote found that the consolidated school was superior in holding power and in grade, age, and subject achievement, and that these differences increased as pupils progressed through school.[11]

In addition to improvements in scholastic achievement, consolidated schools were credited with introducing large changes in the school system itself. For instance, because consolidated schools were financed by a broad tax base, support was likely to be relatively steady and equal to the number of pupils involved. Centralization also allowed a more economical use of faculty and administration, as well as facilities and equipment. Finally, the sheer size of the district mitigated against any local special-interest group controlling the public schools.[12]

Even when the advantages of the larger institution were apparent and the population was willing to pay the increased taxes, residents of the open country often hesitated because of the transportation problem. One observer of rural schools concluded that

> it is not enough to enlarge districts. Something must be done to overcome the barrier of distance. It is not sound policy to argue that we may have "Consolidation with or without Transportation," which, for example, is the title of a bulletin of the University of Texas, saying, "When only two or three schools are consolidated and when none of the children are placed thereby at great distance from the school, free transportation need not be provided." The traditional prejudice of country people in favor of a school near their homes should be respected unless provision is made for getting their children to school.[13]

Early experiments with transportation from rural areas to centralized schools generally involved horse-drawn wagons. Not until after World War I did the motor bus make any significant impact on country education. These early attempts revealed several previously unforeseen problems. For instance, in his annual report for 1912, the Indiana State Superintendent of Public Instruction noted, "When men of low ideals are in charge of transportation or when transportation is slow, or when distance is too great, then certain evils are at once seen, and just complaint is made against consolidated schools. These evils, however, are all remediable."[14]

The remedy was to come with the mechanization of the wagons. But this was to be a slow process, for as one Alabama school administrator observed, "Many superintendents have hesitated to recommend consolidation of schools to their boards, and the cause of their hesitation has been the uncertainty which surrounds the transportation side of the question. The superintendent who does not know the difference between a Ford truck and some other kind, or who does not know the transmission from the differential on any kind of truck, must have a liberal amount of nerve to put into operation ten or a dozen trucks to transport school children."[15]

Because of these transportation questions, the need for increased revenues, and a certain failure on the part of the rural population to see the pedagogical advantages of centralized schools, consolidation moved forward cautiously. In 1923, rural sociologist John M. Gillette reported that 76 percent of the nation's school buildings in communities of 2,500 or less were still one-room affairs.[16] By 1933, according to John H. Kolb and Edmund deS. Brunner, this figure had only fallen from 195,500 to 151,000. These figures may be misleading, because open-country districts often merged with enlarged high-school districts but maintained their own elementary schools.[17] But even so, consolidation affected a relatively small number of rural school children during the period of this study. Nevertheless, consolidation was to increase in importance; since discussion of centralization and its transportation problems was quite widespread from 1910 to 1930, it does merit consideration here.

TRANSPORTATION

Although in isolated cases passenger automobiles were used for school transport,[18] most of the vehicles employed were specially designed trucks or buses. These, in turn, were often credited with furthering the consolidation movement:

> When the area served by any one school had to be measured in terms of the walking strength of children, 3 miles in all directions from the schoolhouse was about the maximum limit. If horse-drawn vehicles were used, the limit could be extended to 6 or 7 miles. Under similar conditions with the same or less expenditure of time and strength on the part of the children, an auto bus can convey pupils from 15 to 20 miles. As a time-limit proposition, the automobile has multiplied by from 36 to 64 the possible area that may be served by one school. The better the road over which the auto busses must travel, the greater the area that may be served.

> Good roads make possible and often have a considerable effect in bringing about consolidation. An established consolidated school may serve to call attention to bad roads and lead in a movement for their betterment. Ease of communication makes for education, and education makes for ease of communication.[19]

Although consolidation technically had been feasible with horse-drawn wagons, the motor bus made it both practical and acceptable. In addition, a committee of Massachusetts educators found that, compared to horse-drawn vehicles, motorized ones carried "over twice as many children at one half the cost per pupil mile."[20] Finally, Professor Macy Campbell noted that the "time saved on the road means more time for the pupils at home.... The parents appreciate the time thus saved for the children's help in doing the chores about the farm, and the children form habits of work and develop initiative and sturdy qualities of character...."[21]

The motorization of school wagons may also have quelled the objections of many farm women to school transportation. According to the Department of Agriculture's 1914 *Yearbook*, the lengthy trip to a centralized school had come under attack because it "involves exposure which, in winter weather is, in the mother's eyes, too severe for young children, no matter how adequate the service of the school [horse] wagons may be. Moreover, many farm women fear the evil influence of towns and miscellaneous company upon their children. One Vermont woman complains specifically, for example, of the fact that in the school wagon her boys and girls must listen to unsupervised conversation for several hours each day."[22]

Professor Campbell's description of the ideal motor bus seems to answer these criticisms directly: "It should be well lighted; good lighting promotes good behavior. It should be roomy enough to permit the children to sit in orderly fashion without crowding; this also promotes good behavior.... The best arrangement for giving protection against inclement weather and yet admitting ample light is glass panels which may be closed tightly, like the body work of an inclosed automobile, on stormy days and opened on fine days."[23]

While the mechanical problems could be overcome easily, the conduct of pupils in such buses was more vexing. Montgomery County, Alabama, considered the situation serious enough to issue a series of rules governing the transportation of children. Included among these were the following items pertaining to discipline aboard school buses:

> 11. The principal will appoint a [student] captain for each truck. The captain's duty will be to assist driver in keeping order, see that all pupils are in truck, keep back door of truck closed, flag railroad crossings, and perform other duties directed by the principal.
> 12. There shall be no hanging on the steps, or any other part of the truck, while it is in motion.
> 13. There shall be no jumping on or off a truck while it is in motion.
> 14. Children who persistently refuse to conform to these rules or any other rule prescribed by the principal or by the County Board of Education, shall have taken away from them the privilege of riding in any of the trucks operated by the County Board of Education.[24]

Other school systems employed teachers or matrons to keep order in transit and to prevent lewd talk that might corrupt the younger students and girls.[25]

The greatest attention, however, was paid to the selection of drivers. Because they were ultimately responsible for both student safety and conduct on board, drivers were subject to constant observation and criticism. For instance, the Superintendent of Schools in Randolph County, Indiana, warned: "Only men of the highest moral worth should be employed as drivers. As much care should be exercised in the selection of a hack driver who has charge of the children to and from school as in the teacher who has charge of them while in school."[26] At one conference of administrators, an elaborate checklist was developed for overseeing school transportation. It recommended a speed limit of seventeen miles per hour and close surveillance of drivers to ensure adherence to that limit.[27]

The amount of attention paid to school transportation might have been justifiable if one believed, as did sociologist Thomas R. Miller, that "travel, even just to and from school, can be educational. If the problem is solved in the right way, pupils learn from their drivers, from the monitors, and from each other what is acceptable behavior in semi-public situations. This is just another type of contact with a larger social group than would be possible in the original district school, and because it is a larger social organization it has more problems."[28]

Still, some of this concern for discipline may have been unnecessary. Macy Campbell recalled that, before school buses, "when we walked home from the rural school in boyhood days we did not always cover the one mile as quickly as the motor bus covered the seven miles. Wading in the creek, teasing the girls with garter snakes, snowballing or fighting, often consumed.... much time.... "[29] Assuming that such horseplay is natural and necessary to some extent, it can be argued, as with so much else concerned with the automobile, that motor buses simply offered a new setting for very old practices.

EFFECTS OF MOTORIZATION

Educators had long realized that distance from school was a reason for poor attendance, which in turn usually led to unsatisfactory school work. A 1920 study of the factors controlling attendance in rural Maryland schools found that "although children living farther from school are farther behind for their ages and do inferior work, distance is only an indirect cause of retardation.... Children living greater distances attend fewer days, do inferior work and get farther behind, and then being both farther from school and farther behind in school, they lose still more time, do more inferior work, and still more often fail, and get even farther behind."[30]

Eleven years later, a comparative investigation of the attendance of transported and nontransported pupils found that rural children who were bused to school had significantly better attendance than those who were not.[31]

Thus the motorized school bus appears to have been at least indirectly responsible for cutting students' absence rates. It must share the credit for this with the better qualified teachers in consolidated schools, who probably made school more attractive. According to historian John B. Rae, such teachers were drawn to consolidated schools "partly because the teachers themselves owned automobiles and therefore did not have to fear being lost in the 'sticks' out of contact with their profession."[32] As the next chapter will discuss, improved health measures in the schools also contributed to the increased attendance. It should be acknowledged, however, that bus service, and the good roads it required, did little for the pupils who continued to walk to school, either by choice or because transportation was unavailable. "An improved road no doubt facilitates transportation, but it does not greatly help the attendance of children who walk," concluded one study of rural school attendance. "It is perhaps the length of exposure in going from home to school, rather than the effort of walking. A child would walk a given distance over a dirt road almost as quickly as over an improved road."[33]

It generally was believed that consolidated schools offered a higher level of education, so it is not surprising that one observer argued that

> efficient management of transportation is one of the most important duties of the board of education in a large school district. For this reason it is customary, even though a town of several hundred is contained in the district, to select a majority of the members of the board of education from the country. The farmers are usually better informed on road conditions and more conversant with the needs of the children who are being transported to school. It is wise to select for the board persons living in the various parts of the district, so that the board may have direct information on the state of the roads and on conditions of transportation throughout the district.[34]

Were such advice followed, the argument that the larger schools were breaking down the sense of community would be countered effectively. Rural sociologist Carl C. Taylor claimed that a consolidated school in itself was evidence that a larger, reintegrated, farm community had been established.[35] Similarly, Wilbert L. Anderson analyzed the social consequences of consolidation and concluded: "As soon as a public sentiment in favor of improved schools is developed and pride in the schools is justified, the community has a new social consciousness."[36]

Improved roads usually radiated from the center of the village or town, which therefore was often considered the logical place for a consolidated school.[37] The automobile and these roads had made village and town high schools readily available before consolidation really took hold,[38] and numbers of open-country residents therefore looked townward for educational leadership. Still, many who agreed with the concept of consolidation felt that the larger schools should be located outside the town. They argued against the moral evils of the town environment and the fact that the schools there educated away from the farm life.[39] These people favored placing the new schools in the open country and argued that they could serve as neighborhood meeting places. However, Dwight Sanderson, one of the leading rural sociologists of the day, took exception to the latter point, noting that "in the long run community life will flow to its natural centers and that the seeming success of such [school-based] social centers in the open country, unless the neighborhood be an isolated one, will tend to weaken the communities concerned."[40]

In the end, the argument was settled by a simple political fact of life. *Legal* consolidation involved merging open-country and town school districts, and thus the hinterland consistently was outnumbered and outvoted. Therefore, given the acceptance of a need to consolidate schools, it is logical that the overwhelming majority were placed in villages and towns.

In addition to improved attendance and increased town-country unity, centralization was responsible for better adminis-

This scene of pupils boarding a rural school bus could have been taken years earlier — or later. (*National Archives*)

Two rural educational institutions meet for their mutual benefit: the town library comes to the one room schoolhouse. (*National Archives*)

trative supervision of schools. More teachers could be visited in less time, and this in turn meant more effective in-service training and more competent instructors.[41]

Just as importantly, the majority of schools which remained isolated one-room institutions could now be adequately supervised. As a result, the provincialism that had characterized most rural schools was broken down. Supervision enabled teachers to develop a more professional attitude, because they were introduced to the latest in pedagogy. At the same time, the supervisor often served as a valuable link between school and community, explaining to each the needs and problems of the other.[42]

Before the introduction of the automobile into this type of work, Katherine M. Cook and Arthur C. Monahan reported that

> The average territory of the county superintendent is 1,672 square miles.... The rural-school term in the majority of ... States is so short (five to eight months) and the roads so bad that the county superintendent can not make many visits in the year.... In one-half of the States the prevailing number of visits per year to each teacher is one; in very few of the other half does it exceed two, the visits being one-half hour to two hours in length.[43]

This lack of supervision, combined with the difficulties of teaching ungraded classes with poor materials in an isolated environment, had been responsible for a high rate of teacher turnover in one-room schools. Consolidation and motorized supervision of open-country schools tended to ameliorate these conditions. A significant catalyst for this change was the growth of "in-service" education, which ran the gamut from assessment conferences involving a single teacher and supervisor to group extension courses offered by the state university.[44]

Using their own automobiles, teachers were able to attend professional training institutes; this was a truly revolutionary innovation. It made possible group activities such as that described below by a North Carolina rural supervisor:

> On two or three school days during the school term, the county superintendent and rural school supervisor bring the teachers from all the little schools affiliated with the group center school, to this demonstration school to see and study at first hand good teaching under normal conditions....
>
> The supervisor ... conducts in the afternoon a round table conference on the teaching they observed ..., leads them to discuss the vital things noted in the various lessons taught and ... works out and formulates with them from those discussions effective lesson plans or methods of teaching these various subjects.... And it seems quite reasonable to believe that even the weak teachers in this group have been rendered a far more effective service than would have been rendered them had the supervisor spent with each one of them an entire day in her own local school.[45]

The automobile itself helped to improve teacher efficiency. For instance, it could be used to visit parents in their homes.[46] The motor car enabled teachers of vocational subjects to supervise closely "the project," which usually involved some type of agricultural field work.[47] On the other hand, "the automobile has made it possible for many country school-teachers, 36.6 percent, to be exact, to live in one place and teach in another," reported Edmund deS. Brunner in 1927. "It was no unusual thing to see a Ford coupe parked in the country school yard. School administrators are wont to deplore this tendency, which weakens the tie between the teacher and her constituency."[48] Thus, once again, the impact of the automobile depended on how the individual chose to employ it.

The motor car could also be an educational tool in itself. As early as 1904, Albert L. Clough was lauding "The Educative Value of the Automobile":

> The exact and intimate knowledge obtainable by the taking apart, repairing and reassembling of machine parts cannot be equaled.... As the actual use of the machine continues, and one part after another is called to the owner's attention for inspection or repair, as it inevitably will be in time, he becomes absolutely

> conversant with the machine; ... in other words, he has received the elements of a good education as an engineer, which he might never have obtained had he not decided to drive an automobile .... He will not only have learned how things are done, but how to do things in the mechanical world, for the automobile school is one of manual training.[49]

In 1913, C. H. Claudy created the character of the "New Motorist" to explain the educational advantages of motor touring in the country:

> Historical spots which have always been names become facts when you study them with a car.... You've heard of Barbara Frietchie. You've heard of George Washington being a civil engineer. But did they ever mean anything to you? Were you ever in Frederick [Maryland] in your life, or have you ever seen Great Falls [on the Maryland-Virginia border] and the remains of the canal? Of course not. But you can't escape seeing both if you get a car, and your history will jump out of the past at you, when you do. You won't see George Washington as a little boy with a hatchet, or a statue in a boat dodging ice cakes after you've seen those canal remains.... Barbara won't be only a character in a poem after you've seen her town, her home, and heard from the lips of her townspeople the real story.[50]

These "extra-curricular" activities soon had their counterparts in new course offerings in the schools. By 1914, the public schools of Ohio had begun teaching the science of good roads.[51] More typical was a two-year course in automotive mechanics offered at Taylorville (Illinois) High School.[52] It also can be assumed that the elementary school curriculum began to deal with the history of the automobile; its relationship to other means of transportation, both past and present; and the importance of enforcing pedestrian and vehicle laws to guarantee road safety.

Obviously, the school was and is not the only institution concerned with educating the populace. The motor car greatly extended the range of libraries, agricultural extension projects, and economic cooperatives as well. The impact of the automobile on these activities will be discussed in the remainder of this chapter.

LIBRARY SERVICE*

Writing in a Farmers' Bulletin prepared for the United States Department of Agriculture in the late 1920s, Wayne C. Nason lamented the traditional lack of library services available to Americans living on farms. He noted that while there were libraries in some country villages and small towns, these usually had limited value for the farm family. In some cases, borrowing privileges were restricted to the residents of the particular municipality. It was argued that only those who supported the library through taxation should be allowed to use it. On occasion, these institutions would permit the farm population to patronize their facilities for a fee. (Such "generosity" most often followed the realization that bringing farmers into town generated income for local stores and services.)[53]

Even where the libraries were truly "free" ones, farmers found it both physically and psychologically difficult to use them. Library facilities were still a considerable distance from their farms; the libraries were open for few hours, which often varied from one week to the next; and trips into town were relatively rare in the age of the horse and buggy. This last item was a particular problem for women and children, who did not always accompany the men on trips, especially business ones.[54] Finally, since town people usually owned and controlled them, libraries were often viewed as alien institutions that did not cater to the needs of farm folk.[55]

*This section was originally published in a slightly different form as a note entitled "Reading, Roadsters, and Rural America," in *The Journal of Library History* 12 (Winter 1977):42-49, a publication of the University of Texas Press.

A study done by the American Library Association in the mid-twenties found that 86 percent of the rural population was not served by public libraries, whereas this figure was only 5 percent for city dwellers.[56] As a result, members of the farm community found themselves disadvantaged in comparison to their town or city cousins in matters related to books. An organizer for the New Jersey Public Library Commission argued that having only one town-centered library hurt such social and educational activities as study clubs, debating societies, reading circles, and the Grange. Even the public schools suffered from a lack of good literature with which to teach English and reading, having instead to rely solely on textbooks, many of which were dated.[57]

The first remedy for this problem sought to establish "deposit stations," or extension libraries, at those points where farm people were apt to gather. Thus, shelves and boxes of books appeared in or near country stores, post offices, tollgates, and rural churches, and in some private homes.[58] In Wayne County, Michigan, library centers were located at Pullen's Furniture Store, A. H. Griffin's Home, West's Grocery Store, the Dasher School, Loveland Drug Store, Bentley's General Store, the post office, the village hall, and McCulley's Laundry Service, among others.[59] "Many of these stations were so far from trolley or railway," observed an American Library Association pamphlet, "that it was necessary to use a (horse-drawn) Concord wagon to transport the boxes of books from the central library to the station.[60]

Such stations were fairly successful, since they were easily accessible from the farm by horse and were located in or near buildings that were centers of social intercourse. Books and magazines placed there were guaranteed a great amount of perusal by farmers, their wives, and their children. This was especially true when bookcases with glass (as opposed to opaque) doors were used. As one observer for the American Library Association noted, under such conditions there was the possibility that visitors might be attracted to a book title even when the "librarian" was not there.[61]

Still, circulation of books in the open country was limited by the relatively small selection available and the fact that the prospective borrower had to take the initiative under the deposit system. No trained librarian was present to encourage the reading habit, recommend particular volumes, or answer related questions.

As noted above, the physical difficulty of delivering books was often a serious obstacle. For instance, a report on the Brimfield (Massachusetts) Public Library noted that "it was a great problem to get the books to West Brimfield, as that section is not connected with the Center in any way. . . . The books are sent by stage to a Palmer grocery store, where they are carried by delivery team to West Brimfield. So the books travel out of town and back again, making a journey of twelve to thirteen miles to cover an actual distance of six miles."[62] As a result, the deposit station was often just that, rather than a true circulating library.

Into this world of limited rural library service came the motor car. As the farmer increasingly bypassed local institutions in his automobile to take advantage of the "superior" opportunities in a neighboring town or small city, the deposit station libraries suffered accordingly.

It might have been expected that the farmers would now patronize the town libraries, but this did not immediately happen. Municipal control and support continued to deter farmers. The greater mobility of open-country residents did little at first to destroy suspicions and hostilities toward town and city people, which had built up over a hundred years or more. Furthermore, the very existence of a separate library building could be forbidding. Farmers realized the benefits offered by the town libraries but were hesitant to visit an institution in which their rustic origins and ways might cause them some embarrassment. Finally, farmers had been conditioned, so to speak, to have no books or to consider them an integral part of some other social activity. For the time being, the library building remained a formidable town institution to be explored when one felt more up to it.

Realizing that it would take time for the farm family to feel at home in town, some librarians theorized that it might make sense to use the automobile to bring the books to the people, rather than vice versa. Thus, the very machine that had earlier been seen as a mortal threat to the deposit station movement temporarily became its savior.

According to Harriet C. Long of the American Library Association, librarians not only secured motor cars in which to visit country branches and deposit stations, but also modified them for their special purpose. "Where a roadster is used," claimed Mrs. Long, "it has been found a great advantage to remove the rear carrying compartment . . . and build in its place a larger carrying compartment with rear doors, which can convey boxes and packages to the branches and stations."[63] Not all supervisors, however, were convinced that their librarians needed such "custom-made" transportation. The former, observed one librarian from the California State Library system in 1919, "sometimes let their librarians show their skill and prowess in subjugating an ill-tempered, common-property machine. I know young women who, armed with a pair of broken pliers, have brought over mountain roads and after nightfall the wildest, most treacherous contraptions that any automobile manufacturer could turn out."[64] In time, however, supervisors realized the professional efficiency and financial economy of employing a first-rate machine.

Mobility enabled rural librarians to do more than merely ride herd on isolated book collections. The automobile also allowed them to influence the reading habits of rural America directly. A state library official noted that in a single day a librarian with a car might meet with school teachers in the morning, workers in a small-town factory at noon, and a mothers' club in the afternoon. Each time she would stress the benefits of book ownership and the need to select reading carefully.[65]

The motor car also provided a means to deliver books directly to the patron on the farm. In a sense, it put the deposit station on wheels, with the addition of a trained librarian. Although the first instance of such a bookmobile involved a horse-drawn wagon in 1905, the transformation to mechanical means was so swift that we may consider the real impact of this movement to have been caused by motorized service. The automobile provided more frequent deliveries than a horse-drawn wagon could, and its radius was larger as well.[66] Rural residents no longer had to choose their reading for an entire season at one visit, since service more often than every four months became possible.

Although some of the early "book wagons" were simply touring cars with books in the back seat, by the mid-twenties specially designed bookmobiles were being sold. For example, in Multnomah County, Oregon, the librarian reported: "A Graham truck was chosen with a specially made body fashioned to accomodate six persons and about five hundred books. The entrance is by the front door. Just back of the driver's seat is a small charging desk and in the rear of the car is another seat. Space for magazines is afforded at the top of the car along towards the front. On the inside of the car is a bulletin board which holds notices."[67] Similar vehicles were employed in Washington County, Maryland; Pacedale, Rhode Island; and Plainfield, Indiana, among other places.[68]

It should not be assumed, however, that county or state governments automatically approved motorization. A significant portion of the citizenry balked at the increased taxes that were needed to purchase such bookmobiles and pay the traveling librarians who accompanied them. For these people, the resulting improvement in book circulation was not worth the money.[69] Fortunately for those advocating rural bookmobiles, the opposition was never numerically large enough to block the motorization of library services.

The presence of these early bookmobiles, with the name of the local library emblazoned on their sides, probably contributed to the renewal of the reading habit in rural America during these years. The new means of transportation and its unique literary function brought knowledge of the county library to even the most remote farm.[70] As such, bookmobiles helped ameliorate the isolation that had so often accompanied life on the farm.

It was not the machine alone that made the bookmobile a success. Contemporary observers were quick to note that it was the trained librarian who accompanied such vehicles that made the difference. "Opinions differ as to the relative value of book-automobile factors," observed Wayne C. Nason in 1928. "A leading official of Jefferson County, Ala., in evaluating these factors and their influence on rural communities in that county, ranks the books two-tenths, the book-automobile one-tenth, and the county librarian seven-tenths."[71] Another observer noted that the person "who drives the automobile at once establishes a human relationship between the library and the farmer, a thing no deposit station can do."[72] Traveling allowed librarians to determine the preferences and needs of the farm family to a degree that had been impossible before the advent of the motor car. It also enabled them to spread the gospel of good reading habits in highly effective one-to-one conversations.[73] It was not unheard of for a traveling librarian to spend the night with a farm family, helping with the chores while she talked of the joys and advantages of reading.[74]

As a result of such service, the rural attitude toward libraries subtly changed. One visitor, on a tour of rural Minnesota with a "book-bus," wrote: "I fell to wondering why these rural patrons appeared to such advantage in the book-bus, and so devoid of personality when they approached the [town] library desk. It must be that books come to them on their own grounds and terms, and not those of the library. The warm personal interest of the bus librarians no doubt is the means of translating the cold written word to throbbing life to her patrons."[75]

Use of the bookmobile was not limited to visiting farmsteads. It was recognized early that this would be an excellent way to augment the then-meager school libraries. Bookmobiles could visit country schools every month or so, leaving both children's books to be read for pleasure and professional volumes and textbooks for the teacher to use in class. Professors Ralph A. Felton and Marjorie Beal of the New York State College of Agriculture described such a situation in their state:

> When the county librarian drives the book truck to a country school, the children and teacher flock out and choose the books they wish to read and to use in the classes. The schools enrich their present libraries with new titles for reading from the county library. The teacher requests special books, which will be sent out to her by parcel post. Enough books are left at each school to satisfy the needs until the county librarian drives in again in one or two months, when new books are left for old.[76]

Felton and Beal also noted two fringe benefits of the practices described above. First, the librarian often remained at the school to tell stories or to kindle an interest in a certain book or collection of books. Second, there developed a system whereby rural schools joined together to purchase books in quantity through the county librarian, thus realizing considerable economies over the previous method of individual purchases.[77]

Similar to this school-library cooperation was the rural librarian's alliance with agricultural extension agents, which gave her an opportunity to meet more adults. (The agents, at first, were more likely to have automobiles at their disposal.) One librarian for the California State Library observed as early as 1919 that when such agents went into rural areas they frequently took the county librarians with them. The librarian was often given the opportunity to discuss books with groups that had been assembled primarily to hear the latest word on scientific agriculture from Washington. Even when the librarian did not come along, the agent acted as a sort of para-librarian, carrying with him library books and technical volumes intended to help farmers raise or grow a better product.[78] Thus, by cooperating with other agencies that were concerned with the education of the farmer, the rural librarian was able to extend her sphere of influence.

Before concluding this section, it should be pointed out that although the automobile made traveling libraries and librarians possible, it eventually made them less necessary. The farmer and other open-country dwellers could now use their cars to travel to the town library regularly and avail themselves of the larger collection there. Yet, to the degree that farm people were unaccustomed to such an activity, the bookmobiles were a useful motivational instrument. They made borrowing books easier and more convenient than ever before. The bookmobile also performed the very real function of keeping up the habit when, for one reason or another, a trip to the town library was impossible.

EXTENSION AND COOPERATIVE WORK

In 1926, William A. Lloyd, of the Federal Extension Office, described the duties of the preautomobile county agent: "He traveled about his county by horse and buggy, on horseback, or even on foot. He left his home on Monday morning and returned again on Saturday night. During the week he followed the road, visiting and talking to farmers, inspecting demonstrations, and arranging for new ones. He lived with the farmers, staying overnight where night overtook him."[79]

The passage of the Smith-Lever Act in 1914 established a system of agricultural extension work to be run jointly by the Department of Agriculture and the land-grant colleges. County agricultural agents were therefore given substantial new federal aid. This largesse fortunately coincided with the mass introduction of the automobile into rural America. The motor car was adopted so eagerly by the agents that one agricultural professor felt compelled to warn, "The appearance, conduct and attitude of the county agent in making a farm visit is important. It will be well if his automobile is not too expensive, because this suggests an easy time and a good salary."[80]

Regardless of the automobile used, the agent was charged with showing how and why new techniques should be employed in agriculture and the home. One teaching strategy was to organize a motor tour of those farms which had adopted the new government methods. In the following excerpt from a Department of Agriculture circular, Grace E. Frysinger describes one such tour of home economics projects:

> Tours were taken either at points where sufficient progress in projects had been made to deem a tour desirable as a means of interesting others, or at the completion of a piece of work to observe results obtained.... The California home demonstration tour, which was conducted over a period of a week, began in the northern part of the State and ended in San Diego County in the southern part. This tour was outstanding as regards length of time and distance covered, and was so well planned and executed that every place scheduled was reached and left on time.[81]

Such tours grew out of the interest of government workers in reaching as many people as possible. Since the agents could not carry out a demonstration on every farm, the tours were arranged as the next best educational method. A variation on this idea, reported Bradford Knapp, was to invite residents living near a demonstration farm to hear a talk by the county agent and discuss how they might apply the lessons on their own farms. These sessions were termed "field meetings" or "field schools."[82] The automobile made attendance at such sessions easier. Farmers would have found it difficult to spare the time involved in such a trip with a horse-drawn vehicle, though demonstration work per se predates the full acceptance of the automobile in rural America.

The ability of farmers to gather easily for extension work demonstrations also augured well for cooperative economic and political associations. As rural sociologist John M. Gillette observed in 1923, such organization was difficult for farmers because "they are scattered, so that meetings to discuss matters to arrive at an understanding of conditions and to stimulate interest are infrequent."[83] Another student of rural America has claimed that "without the automobile, the development of cooperative marketing associations would have been impossible."[84]

This study's concern is not with whether these organizations served their intended economic and political functions, but rather with their effect on the community's social relations. At first, they seemed to solidify the neighborhood. As Warren H. Wilson noted, the farmer "does not join a cooperative that is too far from his home to drive. In spite of motor transit the cooperative still operates within the radius of the convenience of a horse-drawn vehicle. The reason is that these societies for buying, selling and manufacturing handle freight and in carrying produce on the farmer's roads the truck has not displaced the draft horse."[85] As the truck came into greater use, and as regional economic cooperatives began to replace communal ones, these groups were no longer protective of the local neighborhood.

Still, some claimed that economic cooperation would necessarily lead to cooperation in other areas as well. The Secretary of the American Institute of Cooperation wrote: "I know of many cooperative associations which annually set aside a part of their surplus earnings to be devoted to education work. This educational work oftentimes consists in supporting a lyceum course, or in bringing to the community noted speakers and sometimes noted artists."[86] When surveys were done of these types of activities, however, the results were much less impressive. In 1925 Benson Y. Landis found that financial contributions to social causes were nominal and usually made after a solicitation from a community organization, as opposed to planned, voluntary contributions.[87]

Furthermore, such cooperatives do not seem to have taken full advantage of the opportunity to provide recreational activities for their members. Landis discovered that only 11 percent of the associations sponsored recreational events and that three-quarters of these involved only one event per year — usually the annual association picnic or a social connected with the yearly business meeting.[88] Thus any social benefits accrued solely to the members at their meetings and were not shared with the community at large. Hence, unlike motorized demonstration tours and traveling libraries, cooperative activities did not alter the social fabric of the community to an extent that would have been impossible before the automobile.

CONCLUSION

Traditionally, education in the United States has been a local affair, and the quantity and quality available have varied from one community to another. For rural Americans at the turn of the century, this variation was most obvious in comparing educational opportunities in open-country and village schools with those in town and city institutions. Rightly or wrongly, most contemporary educators were convinced that the small size of open-country and village schools greatly limited the quality of rural education. Two systems of education had developed, and the separation between them was maintained largely because of the problems associated with transporting children by horse-and-buggy to schools outside their immediate neighborhood.

The development of the passenger motor vehicle, especially the school bus, enabled those who advocated larger school districts to implement consolidation plans that had long been proposed but effectively stalled by the transportation problem. The supposed academic and social benefits of consolidation meant little until its feasibility could be shown. Such feasibility went beyond logistics to include the protection and behavior of the children who would ride the buses.

By the early 1920s, most of the problems connected with motorized school transportation had been effectively solved. In a sense, the next decade became a longitudinal study of the effects of busing rural students to schools in more urban areas. This study showed increased attendance, better administrative supervision in the schools, and improvements in the in-service training and performance of teachers. Just as importantly, educational consolidation was a powerful force in restructuring rural community life. Part of a general townward trend, the consolidated school district allied open-country farmers with village and town merchants on a topic of mutual interest—the education of their children. Unlike recreation and religion, schooling was not a voluntary activity, and as such it was a unifying force that could not be ignored. Even those adults who did not have school-age children still had to pay the property taxes that supported public education.

Although the modifications of school administration and curriculum were significant, they were probably not as great as the changes in rural library service. No matter how isolated a family was, a local public school was provided, and after 1918, laws in all forty-eight states mandated attendance. Such was not the case with libraries. Potential borrowers had to seek out book collections, whether at deposit stations or in the larger towns. The reading habit was therefore difficult to cultivate, and the Sears catalog often took the place of more traditional literature.

The introduction of the automobile into rural America helped ameliorate this lack of library service in several ways. First, it allowed the librarian to visit open-country and village residents regularly and thereby increase interest in reading. Second, the motor car could be used to transport an entire collection of books and magazines to and from relatively isolated areas. Thus, many farmers for the first time had the advantage of choosing their reading from a wide selection of materials. Third, the longer, less time-consuming, more comfortable trips that the automobile afforded brought the larger town and even city libraries within the range of open-country dwellers. To the extent that traveling librarians and motorized book wagons increased the desire of individual rural families to read, such people were likely to avail themselves of the superior collections available in more urban areas.

Extension work underwent much the same transformation as rural library service. Agricultural agents quickly siezed upon the motor car as a device to obtain greater exposure within the community. More individual farms could be visited and advice dispensed than by any other means of transportation. Just as importantly, the widespread ownership of the automobile in rural America enabled farmers who wanted to attend group demonstrations, tours, or field meetings to minimize the time they spent away from the farm.

The automobile also made geographically larger cooperative economic and political associations more feasible. However, such cooperative endeavors do not seem to have had the social impact that might have been predicted. Only a very small percentage of cooperatives were forces in enlarging or disintegrating a community's social fabric.

Yet, on balance, the effect of motorization on rural educational institutions must be judged to have been profound. Schools and libraries underwent changes of such permanence that they are still manifest today. Although the impact on extension and cooperative work was probably less significant, the economic and political changes that the automobile facilitated complemented the corresponding social changes that arose from the modified structure of the public schools and libraries.

VII. Health and the Environment*

Unlike the hesitant majority of the American populace, health authorities were quick to seize upon the automobile as a solution to their transportation problems. Obviously, physicians using the early automobiles were subject to the same travails as lay drivers. Yet the automobile offered the doctor certain advantages that did not apply to the general population. Dr. F. M. Crain of Redfield, South Dakota, wrote in 1906:

> An automobile is capable of doing the work of three good driving teams, and the driver can accomplish three times the amount of work, with more ease and comfort, than with horses. The auto enables the physician to spend more time in his office, that can be profitably employed in studying or recreation, the value of which can not be computed in dollars and cents....
>
> A machine that is capable of running continually for an indefinite period certainly commends itself to the busy physician.

* Portions of this chapter were originally published in a slightly different form as an article entitled "The Influence of the Automobile on Rural Health Care, 1900-29," *Journal of the History of Medicine and Allied Sciences* 28 (October 1973): 319-35.

> In country practice, where physicians were often times compelled to make from 50 to 100 miles a day, the horse can never compete with an automobile in the hands of an intelligent operator.[1]

In 1901 another doctor gave *Horseless Age* what must be one of the first accounts of motorized ambulance service. The trip to the nearest hospital, which normally required two days to go and return, was accomplished in an hour and a half by automobile.[2]

Others noted that the well-kept car started instantly, whereas the horse always required preparations.[3] Since time saved frequently meant lives saved, this development had far-reaching health benefits. One practitioner observed that with the automobile one did not have to worry about "raw winds, cold rains, sleet and snow ... [which] make you pity the poor horse, you never shorten your call because the horse is standing, overheated, in a cold rain, nor go to the window to see if he is tired of waiting for you and gone to the barn. ..."[4]

Not all motives for adopting the motor car were so altruistic. One physician admited that in addition to the above benefits, he "saw visions of a $20,000 practice annually in consequence of purchasing an automobile. I could visit my patrons with more speed, and oftener; I would be the first physician on the spot in all cases of injury or poisoning. I should be the envy of all horse owners and the pet of all the charming young women in the country around."[5]

Journey by automobile also was easier on the physician himself. Traveling by horse and buggy was so time-consuming and tiring that the rural practitioner was often forced to sleep in the buggy seat.[6] Weariness brought on by excessive travel was sometimes cause for poor medical treatment. Dr. Arthur E. Hertzler remembered one such incident that fortunately did not have severe repercussions:

> My patient on this occasion was a small boy with an abscess in his neck. Obviously it needed opening. I placed my instrument bag on the table and proceeded to inspect its contents. I went to sleep while doing so—it must have been but momentarily; I closed my bag and

> went back to town .... When I awoke the next morning I remembered that I had not opened that abscess. I hastened back to do the necessary operation. The family thought that after looking in my bag I found I lacked the necessary instruments and had gone back to town after them. They did not realize that I had gone to sleep.[7]

The *potential* for geographically wider health care created by the automobile was accepted as *fact* by the general public. As one suburban doctor observed, "there are many people living in the suburbs today that would not have moved out there until they discovered that they could get a doctor in an emergency just as quickly as in the city."[8] Similarly, a doctor in a Connecticut farming community noted that "the automobile and the telephone have *set people's minds at rest.* They don't send for me in the middle of the night the way they used to. If it is only a slight matter they wait until morning. If a little more serious, they telephone. Only in emergencies do they ask me to come to the house at night. In the past they wanted me to come anyway, in case there might be critical developments; but now they know I can get there in no time if needed, and they do not worry."[9]

This confidence was based on a comparison of medicine in horse-and-buggy days with that of the automobile period. The widespread use of the motor car virtually wiped out practices such as the following described by Dr. Hertzler: "I remember a lacerated hand treated by amputation, and a simple compound fracture of the tibia like-wise amputated, and in the mid-thigh at that.... The reason for such radical measures was that because of suppuration the surgeon, usually called from a distance, found amputation the most practical measure. There was no one present to care for the wound. The experience was that if amputation was not done death from infection would most likely follow...."[10] By 1920, surgeons could be summoned by telephone from town and brought to the scene of the accident or illness by motor vehicle, or the patient could be rushed by ambulance to the new rural hospitals.

Fatigue from horse-and-buggy trips was not unique to the medical profession; it was experienced by all elements of society. Not surprisingly, one of the early claims in favor of the automobile was that riding in one was beneficial to health. United States Senator Royal S. Copeland, the former Health Commissioner of New York City, observed in the July 1922 issue of *Motor:*

> Not only does the driver get the full benefit of open road and fresh air, but he gets actual physical exercise in a form best calculated to repair the damages wrought by our modern existence. The slight physical effort needed in moving the steering wheel reacts on the muscles of the arms and abdomen. Most of us get enough exercise in the walking necessary, even to the most confined life, to keep the leg muscles fairly fit. It is from the waist upward that flabbiness usually sets in. The slight, but purposeful effort demanded in swinging the steering wheel, reacts exactly where we need it most.[11]

Early in the century, automobile trips were often considered treatments for specific diseases, especially tuberculosis.[12] A Ford limerick that appeared around 1910 shows the popularity of the idea that the motor car provided health benefits.

> There was a fat man from Fall River
> Who said as he drove his Ford flivver,
> "This bumping and jolting
> To me is revolting!
> It's hell! but it's good for the liver."[13]

The automobile was also capable of ministering to mental health needs, or so thought *Horseless Age* in 1903:

> Automobile rides have been recommended by eminent medical authorities as a cure for nervousness. Nervous persons should, of

course, not drive themselves, and the speed should be kept moderate, as high speeds are a strain on the nerves of both driver and passenger ...

In general an automobile ride at normal speed on fair roads and in good weather has a refreshing and exhilarating influence and has been observed to restore interest in life in despondent people. The effect on normal and healthy persons is often that of rejuvenation of spirits, and automobiling is about the only form of enlivening the spirits known which is not followed by reaction.[14]

The alleged relationship between health and the motor car probably reached its zenith in the mid-twenties, with the publication by the *Delaware Health News* of the following item comparing the care of the automobile with that of the human body:

TABLE 2

EFFICIENCY CHART

Good gas	Good food
Clean spark plugs	Clean teeth
Clean headlights	Good eyes
Tuning and adjusting	Outdoor exercise
Full air pressure	Good posture
No carbon	No constipation
Keep clean and oiled	Frequent baths and plenty of sleep
Good mixture	Balanced ration — vegetables, fruits, etc.
Don't choke engine	Chew food thoroughly
Humming motor	Cheerfulness
Keep radiator filled	Drink plenty of water
Good brakes	Self control and self reliance
A hot spark	Ambition
Strong axles and frame	Stamina
Well balanced mechanism	Even temper
Rolls easy	Plays well
Good hill climber	Hard worker
A tiny speck in the current breaker can kill the engine	A tiny germ may cause fatal illness

Source: "Efficiency Chart," *Journal of Rural Education* 4 (November 1924): 137.

Even repair work was sometimes seen as beneficial to health. A physician in Bath, Maine, reported in 1906: "I care for the machine myself. This I find a great pleasure, and as a mental and physical diversion it is of much value."[15]

Finally, some advocates claimed that the motor car would make for a more leisurely lifestyle and that this would have health benefits for the entire family. One 1929 suburban writer for *American Home* magazine observed: "The doctors tell us that digestion is easier if there can be a short period of relaxation directly after eating. Then what could be more healthful as well as helpful, than for mother to drive the folk to their trains, or their offices and their schools—thus making more time in which to eat breakfast."[16]

Some doctors, however, were not as enthusiastic. Dr. Charles P. Sylvester set out early in the century to measure scientifically the effect of motoring on the human body:

> I recorded my pulse on several of my first and fast long drives, being careful not to inflate my tires or to crank my machine before starting. The result was always an increase of about six in the number of beats per minute, with an increase in the tension....
>
> Increased exercise might have been the cause, but in my mind it was due to a chauffeur's responsibilities regarding the police, public and passengers, order reversed.... This may be a form of auto-intoxication which we should bear in mind in examining our patients.[17]

Others who prescribed automobiling for certain maladies offered specific cautions for taking this "medicine":

> The traumatism of the conjuctiva in motoring is very severe and one should always wear goggles. Particles of dust and dirt are constantly getting into the eyes, even with goggles on, and I advise to have constantly on hand some 1 percent solution of cocain and a saturated solution of boric acid. I also prescribe after a long motor run to douch the nose and throat with some mild antiseptic, thus obviating any infection which might be in the dust which has accumulated in the nostrils, nose, and throat.[18]

The disagreement over whether or not the motor car was beneficial to health was reflected to some extent in automobile advertisements. Car manufacturers generally pointed to the alleged benefits, while those making automobile accessories attempted to capitalize on real or imagined liabilities. In 1911 the Parry Automobile Company of Indianapolis proclaimed in an ad, "Away in a Parry! The sun warms you, the air cleans you."[19] It may be assumed that the last statement was in reference to the supposed rejuvenating effect of an automobile ride on a diseased pulmonary system. In a full-page 1920 advertisement in *Motor Age,* Overland Sedan boasted that its new Triplex springs allowed passengers to "rest as you ride. You miss the usual road fatigue."[20] Nevertheless, such references were quite exceptional. Early car makers were primarily concerned with proving the dependability of their products and with outdoing the competition in what was then a high-risk business. There was little of the industry-wide advertising that might have found the theme of health advantageous.

The success of the accessory manufacturer, on the other hand, depended on his ability to produce devices applicable to all makes of automobiles. Since the majority of cars produced before 1920 were not enclosed, there was a ready market for paraphernalia designed to protect a person while driving. Advertisements for such items often appealed to people's concern with good health. For instance, the Scott Muffler Company of Portsmouth, Ohio, noted in one of their ads: "MANY PEOPLE are troubled with bronchial and throat afflictions during the cold weather, and remain indoors the greater part of the winter. If a Scott Muffler is worn when going out, those susceptible to zero weather will find that the Scott Muffler MAKES ZERO WEATHER PLEASANT."[21] This ad was illustrated with several pictures of people out for a winter drive in their autos, and there can be little question as to which market it sought. Similarly, an advertisement urging the use of Truffault-Hartford shock absorbers carried a doctor's warning of the dangers of driving without them: "The passengers as well as the drivers should pay especial attention to the muscular support of the abdominal viscera .., since the jolting of the vehicle over ruts and obstructions in the road tends to produce prolapse of the stomach, kidney, intestines, and liver if the spinal and abdominal muscles are not kept at a proper balance of contraction."[22]

Obviously, automobile accidents were a hazard to health. Between 1910 and 1929, deaths from automobile accidents increased by 1,344 percent. "The tremendous increase in fatal automobile accidents is due to the fact that the period 1910-1929 is a period of automobile development," wrote Edgar Sydenstricker in a monograph prepared for the President's Committee on Social Trends, "but even since automobiles came into general use a steady increase in automobile deaths has occurred."[23] The motor car was responsible for 1.8 deaths per 100,000 people in 1910, 6.4 in 1915; 12.1 in 1920; 19.1 in 1925; and 26.0 in 1929.[24]

Still, this threat, if indeed it was a threat, must be viewed in perspective. Two students of automobile history maintain that "even at its dangerous worst, the automobile, proportionately, never was as great a killer as the horse. In 1909, for example, 3,850 lost their lives in accidents involving horses and horse-drawn vehicles. The horse was not driven more than five hundred miles a year. On a mileage basis, compared with the automobile's average run of ten thousand miles a year, the horse was twice as deadly as the automobile."[25]

Though the horse may have been proportionately deadlier than the motor car, there is no question that the latter was responsbile for the violent deaths of thousands who otherwise would have lived. It is therefore fitting that the coming of the automobile changed funeral arrangements. In his novel *The Farm,* Louis Bromfield laments the disappearance of the livery stable and the vehicles it had housed:

> With it have gone those wonderful, dark, smelly conveyances known as cabs which conveyed the citizenry with dignity to and from funerals and weddings. Gone with them is much of the dignity which belongs to death. When Johnny was a small child there was always great excitement in the house when one of those dark,

> upholstered cabs arrived at the front door and the family set out for the station to visit Greataunt Esther or Greataunt Susan. Something of the mystery of death clung to those pompous old hacks, accumulating a little more with each successive funeral. They smelled faintly of death just as they smelled faintly of ammonia. They were exciting.[26]

Rural Sociologist Albert Blumenthal adds that in a Rocky Mountain town of 1,410 traditionally almost "everyone went to the funeral—the status being determined by the means of conveyance. Those with the finer teams were next to the hearse, and there were many gradations between them and those riding horseback at the end of the procession." By 1932, funerals were not the townwide occasions they had once been, and "in place of a hierarchy of horse-drawn vehicles and horses there are correspondingly degrees of automobile values from a costly Lincoln at the head to a rattling and balky Model-T Ford at the tail end."[27]

There was a certain dignity in being driven to one's final resting place in an ornate carriage driven by a fine team. Samuel Eliot Morison probably is correct when he concludes that "until the 1930's it was thought indecorous for a corpse to be hustled to the grave in a motor hearse."[28]

CHANGES IN PRIVATE MEDICAL PRACTICE

Many changes in rural health care were initiated more by the action of the patients than by the physicians themselves. Lewis Mayers and Leonard V. Harrison in their classic 1924 study *The Distribution of Physicians in the United States* observed that, as a result of the coming of the motor car, country doctors faced severe competition for the first time. A practitioner could no longer count on monopolizing a given territory simply on the basis of proximity. Not surprisingly, rural residents lost little time in taking advantage of this opportunity. After all, the local doctor's professional mistakes and failures as well as his personal life were a regular topic of discussion, and it was not unusual to find a significant part of the local population dissatisfied with him, but unable to go elsewhere when horse transportation was the only option.[29]

It was the more isolated rural doctor who suffered the most from this new competition. Village practitioners lost out to town ones, who in turn saw their patients attracted to the small cities. Mayers and Harrison observed that

> in the era of the horse-and-buggy, a distance of even five miles rendered the competition of the town doctor in ordinary practice a negligible factor. With the acquisition of automobiles by the rural dwellers and town doctors, village practitioners located ten, fifteen and even twenty miles from town were exposed to a competition with the town physician which was peculiarly damaging both to their incomes and to their morale. This competition affected every branch of medical practice, but it came to be particularly severe in the matter of nonemergent [*sic*] visits to the physician's office, in which the rural dweller could now patronize the town physician without extra expense as an incident to the occasional visit to town.[30]

Although this rivalry may have been anathema to the village doctor, at least one observer has pointed out that it probably helped to keep rural medical standards high.[31]

Partially as a result of the competition, there was a marked movement of rural doctors into larger towns of 5,000 to 10,000 people after World War I.[32] In fact, according to statistics collected by Dr. William A. Pusey and published in the *Journal of the American Medical Association,* one-third of the towns having populations of 1,000 or less which had doctors in 1914 were without them in 1927.[33] In addition, according to the rural sociologist Edmund deS. Brunner, "the long hours, arduous trips at all hours, low economic returns, increasing tendency on the part of rural folk to employ urban specialists, absence of laboratory facilities, and the desire for urban educational and social advantages were all given as causes of this movement."[34]

Unfortunately, as a result of this migration, medical care actually may have become less efficient than in the preautomobile period. Thus, Samuel Hopkins Adams, in a series of articles written for the *Ladies' Home Journal,* observed:

> To any consideration of present conditions the automobile is, next to the doctor himself, the most important contributory element. Where the horse-and-buggy rounds of pre-gasoline days could cover half a dozen country calls in a day, the agile little motor car completes twenty or thirty. Hence the theory is that even though the rural shingle be removed to the city, Sawbones, M.D., can still take care of his patients better than his rural grandfather could....
>
> Cheerful though the theory be and highly reassuring to its proponents, it leaves one stubborn and prevalent fact out of reckoning—weather; also one stubborn and once prevalent animal—the doctor's horse. The universality and convenience of the automobile have relegated the medical equine to the dodo class; the species is fast becoming extinct; but when roads are knee-deep in mud or neck-deep in snow, we dwellers on countryside roads miss that noble nag and his trick of getting through somehow, sometime, when need calls.[35]

Furthermore, it was predominantly the wealthier rural dwellers who could afford to drive to town to see the doctor or the "specialist." As a result, the open-country physician found his practice limited to the less affluent. In addition, as one contemporary observer noted, "his expenses are increasing. He must maintain not only an automobile, but a horse and buggy for use when the roads are bad in the winter."[36]

The "average" farm family had always had difficulty affording the customary mileage charge assessed by country doctors. Now, the nearest physician was farther away. Accompanying this new distribution of doctors were increases in fees and demands for immediate payment. "In part this tendency is chargeable," explained Mayers and Harrison, "to the greater economic pressure on the rural physician himself . . . making it increasingly imperative that he receive payment for his time-consuming and expensive drives into the country; in part, it is to be explained by the greater independence of the physician, and particularly of the town physician, now that he is no longer restricted as formerly in his practice to a severely limited area and clientele."[37] For the poorer rural resident, who had always been hesitant to summon the doctor except in cases of life and death, these developments probably effectively decreased the availability of health care.

An indirect result of higher prices and less direct contact with the family doctor was an apparent increase in the number of chiropractors and osteopaths in country communities. Dr. James A. Hayne, State Health Officer of South Carolina, felt that the scattering of medical practitioners discouraged the patient, who therefore went to an "irregular" doctor. "A patient sees the consultant," said Dr. Hayne, "then he goes to the dentist, the dentist finds an abscess; he goes to the x-ray man and the x-ray man finds everything he can see in the plate which is most anything, and so he goes the rounds and ends with a deflated pocketbook and no faith in the medical profession."[38]

This change in the availability of the village doctor made health-related transactions much more formal and less intimate. As such, it may have retarded somewhat the field of preventative medicine in rural areas. Thus, Samuel Hopkins Adams observed of the country doctor:

> Not only is he the curator and healer of his community — the auto-borne city specialist may be that if he can get there in time — he is also its ever-watchful guardian, as the city man never can be . . . .
>
> We may take it for granted that the city man will report epidemic diseases among his country patients, as the law requires; but what will he know of the evil underlying conditions that breed and disseminate disease? That is not his business; he is not paid for that when he comes rushing out to visit a sick man and goes rushing on to visit another. . . .

> But the country physician, knowing his people as well as his profession, is eternally on the job of watchfulness and protection if he is the right kind of man for the job.[39]

RURAL HOSPITALS

Except for cases involving surgery, the hospital was a little-used medical extravagance in rural America before 1900. Most patients could ill afford hospitalization; all but a few of these institutions were located in the cities; and, most importantly, the types of medical examinations given at the time could as easily be administered at the patient's home. In addition, as Dr. Arthur E. Hertzler points out, rural Americans developed a fear of hospitals because

> the conveyances in that day were such that most country patients were a long way from a hospital.... If the roads were bad the distance was lengthened. By the time the family gathered and sat as a jury on the doctor's judgment that an operation was needed, many other precious hours elapsed. Because of the delay the mortality of operations, therefore, was necessarily very high. When fatalities occurred, the hospital, being the last link of the chain, became, at least subconsciously, the culprit — the ultimate cause of death.[40]

As medical knowledge expanded in the twentieth century, the advantages of having hospitals in the country became clearer and more persuasive. Happily, this coincided with the widespread introduction of the motor car into rural America. "Since travel in an automobile or an ambulance is now possible in rural sections," wrote rural sociologist Charles R. Hoffer, "the chief limitation of inter-community support for [local rural] hospitals appears to be the lack of a cooperative attitude and technique on the part of people living in different communities."[41]

Attempts to bring about such cooperation stressed the benefits of building rural hospitals rather than relying on distant urban institutions. A bulletin published by the Department of

Agriculture, entitled *Rural Hospitals*, emphasized that such facilities would: (1) assure personal attention, by maintaining the traditional neighborhood relationships; (2) eliminate the complications that often arose in transporting emergency cases to distant hospitals; (3) allow for outpatient care of convalescent patients; (4) be less expensive, since they would not need such intricate equipment or such expensive buildings as the city hospitals; and (5) provide educational and preventive lessons for the community.[42]

In addition, such hospitals were seen as a way to keep established physicians in the more rural areas and to attract recent medical school graduates. Specialists and surgeons required hospitals, laboratories, and clinics in which to work. As long as these were available only in urban areas, it was absurd to expect such practitioners to work in the country.[43] The introduction of the automobile meant that such doctors need not live in the immediate neighborhood of such institutions to practice in them.

As a result of such thinking and the availability of improved roads, many rural hospitals were established during this period. A surgeon in Cambridge, New York, described a typical one: "The hospital itself is located in a village of about a thousand inhabitants. Within a dozen miles there are perhaps a dozen villages and towns, varying in size from a few hundred to a few thousand, with in between a more or less thickly settled farming district devoted mostly to dairying.... The greatest number of people come and go from the hospital in automobiles, and the range of an automobile drive is a usual measure of the line of contact of the hospital."[44]

In time, rural people began to frequent local hospitals for relatively minor ailments, which too often in the past had been left untreated and had become harbingers of more serious diseases. "Patients were much more willing to go to a hospital near their friends, under the care of a doctor known to them, than to go long distances to a city to be placed under the charge of a strange doctor and in strange surroundings," claimed Dr. Arthur E. Hertzler in his 1928 autobiography.[45] Earlier recourse to hospital treatment increased the recovery rate, which in turn helped to diminish the farmers' fear of such institutions.[46]

Thanks to the motor car, a rural hospital could boast of a consulting staff "made up of men of note in their respective specialties of medicine, surgery, urology, obstetrics and radiology, living at distances of from forty to two hundred miles, and coming to the hospital either at regular intervals of weeks or months, or whenever there is a patient who needs their attention," observed Dr. Denver M. Vickers.[47] Obviously, such travel would have been difficult or impossible with a horse and buggy.

Some rural hospitals were private ventures started by one or more local physicians. The motives behind such establishments came under careful scrutiny by the medical profession during this period. Mayers and Harrison, while recognizing that private local hospitals allowed for economies of scale, especially in time and cost, cautioned that "partly offsetting this gain [for the patient] would be the expense of an ambulance service, a type of transportation relatively more costly than that employed by the physician in making his visits."[48] More severe was the condemnation of Dr. Frank Billings: "Many private practitioners whose chief practice a few years ago consisted of domiciliary visitation now refuse to give this real obligation to the public and compel their patients who are too ill to visit the office to go to the hospital."[49]

This problem was aggravated by the distribution of automobiles among the rural population. Mayers and Harrison felt that "as far as visitation by the physician is concerned, the use of the automobile may now [1924] be regarded as virtually universal during the good roads season." However, they continued, "so far as the visit of the patient to the physician's office is concerned, the use of the automobile is by no means so common."[50] This is an important point, for it indicates that automobile ownership was more common among physicians than among the general populace. This meant that it was always easier for the doctor to visit the patient than vice versa, though not necessarily more efficient medically.

Unfortunately local hospitals, whether public or private, were not established in every rural village and town. Although such institutions were usually within commuting distance, many were located in neighboring towns. As a result, Mayers and Harrison observed, patients sometimes found themselves taken out of the care of their family doctor, either because he lived too far away to commute regularly, even with a motor car, or because the hospital only allowed staff doctors to practice within it.[51]

Because of these problems, the goal of rural hospitals — to keep local practitioners and patients satisfied with nonurban health facilities — may have been achieved in only a limited number of cases. In fact, as rural sociologist Newell L. Sims observed, "motor transportation and improved highways have put increasing numbers of country people within easier reach of city hospitals. This tends to weaken interest in the growth of local institutions."[52] The rural hospital, then, seems to have had varying impacts on rural America, depending on such factors as the condition of the roads, geographical placement of rural and urban hospitals, and the initiative and training of local physicians.

PUBLIC HEALTH SERVICES

Because the practitioner almost always had greater mobility than the patient, various methods were used during this period to put health service on wheels. Proponents of these plans were anxious to bring the expertise of specialists, such as surgeons, oculists, and dentists, out into the country. One 1924 investigation into the health of rural children reported on a typical clinic made possible by transportation advances: "North Carolina has inaugurated a plan of free dental clinics. The work is done by dentists who travel by automobile into rural communities and give free dental treatment to children between the ages of six and thirteen. These dentists are employed by the State Board of Health and have their itineraries arranged by the county health authorities. The clinic is financed by public funds."[53] Such treatment was a vast improvement over the previous method, whereby traveling nurses notified parents of defects. It was found that the earlier method had led to treatment in only 1 percent of the cases.[54]

Part and parcel of the traveling clinic movement were demands for universal and effective medical inspection of school children. A Farmers' Bulletin of 1926 observed that most cities had mandatory school medical inspection whereas only eleven states required such coverage for rural schools.[55] An earlier statistical summary of public health work had condemned the fact that only 30 percent of rural communities had some form of school health supervision, and approximately 60 percent of all school children attended rural schools.[56] It was hoped that more widespread use of school nurses, along with clinics for preschool children, would "stimulate the home to better health," in the words of Dwight Sanderson.[57]

In addition, the need for more visiting home nurses was emphasized. Although these nurses had been active since at least 1896,[58] they were practically unknown in rural areas before 1914. At that time the American Red Cross instituted its Town and Country Nursing Service, which helped supervise the practice of trained public-health nurses. Their numbers remained small, however, through World War I.[59] The movement of large numbers of rural doctors to more urban localities created a demand for visiting nurses, and the mass acceptance of the motor car provided the means to supply them. Therefore, the number of rural visiting nurses significantly increased.

The problem of "irregular" doctors, created by the demise of the neighborhood physician, has been mentioned previously. Not surprisingly, disreputable traveling practitioners surfaced along with state-approved visiting nurses and doctors. One student of this phenomenon observed that "itinerant quacks" were attracting large numbers of patients. The automobile enabled these "doctors" to stay well ahead of any irate citizens they left behind. Typical of this situation were groups of "rupture experts" who toured eastern rural areas in 1922.[60]

Finally, health professionals did not use the automobile simply to fill voids in rural medical practice. It was also used in various in-service instructional programs aimed at improving the quality of medical care provided by physicians who either could not leave their patients or could not afford to study at established institutions or clinics. F. Dennette Adams reported on one such program in the South: "Classes were organized on two circuits of six centers each, with an instructor from outside the state assigned to each circuit. The instructors rotated about their respective circuits, meeting each group once a week and giving each a lecture and clinical demonstration."[61] These programs therefore brought postgraduate medical training to the rural doctor.

THE ENVIRONMENT

Present-day ecologists point to the automobile as a significant contributor to our modern pollution problems. The literature for the period 1893-1929 shows that, although there were precedents for our current difficulties, the automobile also contributed to a cleaner environment. Our initial concern, however, will be the automobile's negative effects on the environment.

Floyd Clymer has observed that most of the early cars "spat oil, fire, smoke, and smell, and, to a person who disliked greasy machinery and had been brought up to expect the shiny elegance and perfection of the horse carriage, they were revolting."[62] They were also quite noisy. One disgruntled owner remarked sarcastically that his "machine had a sweet, purring sound, like a roadroller loaded with scrap-iron crossing a cobblestone bridge, when in motion; and when at rest the motor made a noise like fire-crackers under a dish-pan."[63]

As early as 1901, one New Jersey country doctor offered "a word regarding [automobile] noise: This at times is very annoying, and on one or two occasions has been quite detrimental in its influence on patients with nervous disorders."[64] Yet the previous year, a reporter for the *Detroit News-Tribune* described the sound of a motor car as "a long, quick, mellow gurgling sound, not harsh, nor unmusical, not distressing; a note that falls with pleasure on the ear."[65] The levels of noise produced by various types of automobiles apparently differed as much then as they do now.

One obvious source of noise pollution was the engine's exhaust system. However, *Motor World* magazine warned in 1903 that "to strive to remedy the trouble at the exhaust end is to run the risk of encountering a boomerang. No one can avoid the conclusion that the exploded charge must find ready egress if back pressure is not to result. No matter how ingenious the construction of the muffler may be, it will almost certainly be regarded with suspicion. Loss of power will not be readily put up with; if there must be a choice of evils ninety-nine out of a hundred users will choose the noise."[66]

Motor World's constituency, however, was minute in comparison to the number of people who did not own automobiles at this time, and so by 1908 most states had laws requiring some type of exhaust filter. Typical was Part II, Section 7 of the New Jersey state highway law: "Every motor vehicle must have devices to prevent excessive noise, annoying smoke and the escape of gas and steam, as well as the falling out of embers or residue from the fuel."[67] Such laws, combined with improvements in engine design and body workmanship, decreased the noise level considerably. In fact, by 1915, one observer could conclude that "some years ago an automobile was a noisy and ill-smelling machine and was possessed of various other attributes which have long since been overcome."[68]

One school of thought even felt that the replacement of the horse would actually reduce the noise level. Clyde B. Davis recalled that "the clopping hooves and the steel tires of the express wagons and drays made a dreadful noise on the bricks [of the town streets], especially going to and coming from the Southwest Limited [a local train] after nine o'clock at night when all decent people should be in bed."[69] Still, the internal combustion engine continued to be relatively noisy in the usual quiet of rural America.

A seemingly greater problem was caused by the interaction between the motor car and unimproved country roads, as described by social historian Bellamy Partridge: "With its greater speed and its broader, softer tires, it [the automobile] threw up suffocating clouds of highway dust such as the oldest inhabitants had never dreamed of even in the driest of seasons. And not only that, but the vehicle that raised the dust was so rapid in its movements that it left its dust far behind, to be coped with by slower-moving traffic."[70]

In 1910 a writer for *Scientific American* directly connected the dust menace with human and animal health: "The effect of the huge clouds of dust upon health must be very great, as most forms of disease are transmitted by this germ-laden dust.... Its effect upon some classes of live stock is most severe, cattle and horses in particular being susceptible to the germs of tuberculosis carried by the dust. The automobile cannot be held responsible for these forms of damage, but it has undoubtedly intensified them."[71]

The only solution to this problem, short of banning the automobile or drastically regulating its speed, was to pave or improve the roads. Unfortunately, road improvements did not keep pace with the development of the automobile during this period. In the mid-1920s the federal government estimated that only 12 percent of the public roads were surfaced, and that half of those were covered only with sand, clay, gravel or water-bound macadam. Surfaced roads were principally located near or between large population centers, so the figures for rural areas (which were not compiled) were probably much lower.[72]

Closely akin to the dust problem was that of gasoline fumes. Chapter 1 notes how the "smell" of the car often upset horses, both literally and figuratively, in the early days of motoring. The medical profession also looked askance at automotive exhaust fumes. In 1912 a writer for *Country Life in America* reported:

> Physicians are now announcing that the opaque smoke exhausted from the rear of some automobiles is not only nauseating, but that large quantities of it are actually dangerous to the health of the community. Whatever of truth there may be in the reports of these investigators, the fact remains that these vapors are annoying and disagreeable in the extreme, and even an automobile owner himself will admit that he would almost rather take his fellow-owner's "dust" than to be forced to breathe his smoky exhaust.
>
> And so, many of the City Fathers are humanizing the automobile by prohibiting it, along with mankind in general, from smoking in certain public places.[73]

Billboards. The problem of the defacement of the highway right-of-way with advertisements has deep roots in our country. One student of patent-medicine advertising in America concluded that, as early as the Revolutionay period, Americans were advertising various nostrums "in broadsides and handbills and on the exposed surfaces of rocks, rills, woods, and templed hills."[74]

Despite attempts to promote the notion that farmers who allowed commercial signs on their property were advertising their own lack of success,[75] advertisers had little trouble securing desired locations. In fact, one official of the company that produced "Burma-Shave" cream, which was advertised in the famous "serial signs," claimed that farmers took pride in the signs and often repaired any damage to them.[76]

According to one advertising historian, the automotive age created "a rolling audience of thousands along country roads that formerly had seen only the occasional farmer going to town. The 'circ' that grew with the spread of the automobile gave outdoor display a new importance to both local and national advertisers."[77]

One H. M. Lewis of the Lewis Battery Service of Pawhuska, Oklahoma, spelled out his message on a local hillside in 1923, using whitewashed stones to create letters forty-five feet high. "It is said," commented *Motor Age*, "that on a clear day the sign can be read at seven miles."[78]

In the end, it was not the farmer that brought about regulation of this eye pollution. Rather, it was a combination of pressure from civic organizations translated into law and self-regulation by the advertising industry itself. By 1917, seven states had laws

An Excelsior, Minnesota roadside of the early 1920s before and after an environmental clean-up. (*National Archives*)

An Iowa patient travels to the county hospital by motorized ambulance in 1925. (*National Archives*)

restricting the free use of highway right-of-ways for private advertising. New York's law, passed in 1911, was typical: "A person who in any manner paints, puts or affixes any business or commercial advertisement on or to any stone, tree, fence, stump, pole, mile-board, mile-stone, danger-sign, danger-signal, guide-sign, guide-post, bill-board, building or other structure within the limits of a public highway is guilty of a misdemeanor. Any advertisement in or upon a public highway in violation of the provisions of this subdivision may be taken down, removed or destroyed by any one."[79]

The Automobile Club of America and other groups responsible for such legislation took it to heart. *Horseless Age* noted, only half in jest: "Already many of the signs advertising Punq's Pink Pills for Pallid People, Fusser's Fireproof Biscuits, Oops Medeer's Antiseptic Shoe Laces, etc., decorating the trees and posts along the public highways have been removed. Legends to the effect that Skate non-skidding tires run 15,000 miles without a puncture and also that such-and-such a brand of oil is best for your cylinders, your back and your hair, will no longer be seen staring motorists in the goggles as they speed along the highways."[80]

Nonetheless, legal and illegal signs continued to mar the roadside. The law could do little to a private citizen who allowed a placard to be erected on his property, provided it did not create a safety problem. In response to continuing protests, however, the Outdoor Advertising Association was formed in 1925 and adopted a code forbidding signs that destroyed scenic beauty, were erected in purely residential areas, or created traffic hazards.[81] Just how effective this code was is difficult to tell. Certainly individual provisions of it were open to varying interpretations and degrees of enforcement. Yet, according to one advertising historian, this self-regulation did much to defuse anti-billboard agitation.[82]

Cleaner Surroundings. The automobile, however, was not totally detrimental to the environment. In several instances, health conditions improved with the passing of the horse. As early as 1896, *Scientific American* correctly prophesied that, with the coming ascendancy of the horseless carriage, "the stable pit filled with the defiled bedding of our obedient and faithful four-legged servant would be known no more to our senses. The contagia bred in its midst and scattered in the dry dust of the summer air, to find their way within our sleeping and sitting rooms, would be only the remembered signs of a past and primitive civilization."[83] Similarly, one 1902 letter to *Horseless Age* insisted: "The horse is largely responsible for the dust nuisance. With four pestles reducing the road material to dust and other impurities from the horse waiting to be carried into the houses by wind, who will not hail the day with pleasure when the automobile will control streets and every street will be a perfect street without wear or tear?"[84] In 1925 a citizen of Rochelle, Indiana, optimistically noted, "Gone are the fifty loads of manure garnered from four hundred feet of our best business street ... during Mayor Wilbur McHenry's spring house cleaning of 1902."[85]

The associated improvement of town streets and farm roads also had health advantages. In 1914 the State Board of Health of Oklahoma noted that clearing weeds and trash from the shoulder of roads eradicated an area that tended to retain moisture and made an ideal breeding ground for disease-carrying insects. Secondly, well-kept ditches along roads were often the only means of draining stagnant pools on farm property. Finally, the then-common practice of oiling roads had been shown to be an effective deterrent to the growth of insect larvae, especially mosquitoes.[86]

However, although such roads benefited the health of local residents, they also enabled swarms of tourists to enter rural areas for the first time, as discussed in chapter 4. A doctor writing in a 1924 issue of the *American Journal of Public Health* hypothesized that these travelers were potential disease carriers: "Disease control always has been inseparable from travel. The great plagues have moved from place to place as infected people moved. Until recently control measures of proven value could be used quite effectively to prevent the introduction of infectious diseases into new territory, but with universal automobile traffic new measures and methods must be devised and applied in daily public health practice. . . ."[87] Many states took measures to minimize the risk of infection. Pennsylvania, for example, instituted a system in which health inspectors roamed the state testing the water of roadside streams.[88] Where travelers stopped only at established camping grounds, control was greatly simplified. In Iowa, the state board of health assumed responsibility for keeping automobile tourist camps sanitary. Detailed regulations were issued, providing for safe water; fly-proof rest rooms; clean, metallic garbage cans; and a caretaker to keep the grounds free of refuse.[89]

Camping areas were not cleaner after the motor tourists came than before. However, where health regulations were strictly enforced, the environment was altered but not adversely affected. More importantly, the emphasis on disease control and preventive measures was perceived by the native population and thus carried over into aspects of their day-to-day lives.

CONCLUSION

Probably no other occupational group adopted the automobile with so little debate as did rural physicians. For them, it was obviously an invention whose time had come, and they quickly made the motor car part of their practices. However, most doctors probably didn't realize the profound effect that motorization would have on the organization of the rural medical profession, especially hospital services.

The ability to speedily deliver better medical treatment did much to improve the health of the farmer and village resident. Even though physicians often joined the general townward migration, the motor car effectively kept them as close to their patients as in the horse-and-buggy period. Just as importantly, improved transportation gave patients access to the superior medical facilities in more urban areas. Since such improved health care raised the recovery rate from illness and disease, many rural people became less hesitant about seeking out professional advice and care when they felt sick, thus further enhancing the health of the country population.

One has only to look at the health claims made for automobile driving and riding to see the motor car's importance in the medical thinking of the day. Some of these claims might be justified by the fact that their automobiles enabled city residents to get some fresh air, but it is difficult to understand why the rural population and its physicians were so impressed. After all, a ride in a horse and buggy provided the same health benefits with none of the evils (dust, exhaust, mechanical difficulties, etc.) of the automobile. Nonetheless, no rural-urban differences of opinion regarding the benefits of motoring appear to have arisen.

It should be noted, though, that the motor car made health care less accessible for a significant minority of rural dwellers. They had relied heavily on local practitioners who were neighbors and who charged minimal fees for their services. These people gave little thought to the quality of the treatment or how it compared to that of the physician in the next village. As health care became more centralized in the larger towns and rural hospitals, poorer rural residents and those who were extremely isolated found themselves worse off than they had been before the automobile era.

In summary, three aspects of the motor car's influence on rural health care should be emphasized. First, the quality of medical care available to rural Americans improved. Although medical coverage may have varied more from one area to the next, there can be little question that "the best" was within range of anyone with an automobile. Second, medical practice became more complex for country dwellers. In part, this was caused by advances in the field. More important, the automobile brought the specialist, the hospital, and the public-health officer out of urban areas and into the country. No longer did one deal solely with the village's general practitioner. Third, the improved medical service that resulted was impersonal. The missionary spirit that had permeated much of rural health care before the acceptance of the motor car disappeared. The rural patient was no longer part of the doctor's larger social life, but rather someone who was seen only in a professional capacity.

In recent years, increasing attention has been given to preventive medicine. One aspect of this movement has been an attempt to restrict the sources of environmental pollution. Interestingly, the introduction of the motor car into rural America gave rise to discussions of many of the same issues that are prominent today.

As a new application of technology, the automobile was scrutinized carefully to ascertain its impact on the environment. Both problems and benefits were discovered. The motor car itself was a polluter, even more then than now. Its exhaust was unhealthy to breathe, it created much more noise than a horse and buggy, and its tires threw dust and road debris into the air. Even so, the exhaust of the automobile might be considered clean when compared to the presence of horse manure. The high noise level could be controlled by improved technology. And the increasing acceptance of the motor car created an overwhelming demand for improved roads, which quickly diminished the dust problem.

Even more difficult to evaluate, because of its psychological aspects, was the "pollution" caused by changes in rural advertising practices and country touring. Farmers and residents of small villages and towns had happily survived for a long time with a minimum of both, but the increased presence of billboards and motor tourists gave life in the open country a more modern, commercialized appearance. Whether such developments were good or bad depends largely on one's view of the social and economic needs of rural America at the time.

VIII. Conclusion

"For the first time in world history," historian George E. Mowry has written in regard to the motor car, "mass man became the master of a complicated piece of power machinery by which he could annihilate distance."[1] One key to the social impact of the automobile on rural America between 1893 and 1929 stems from this idea: a major instrument of change was made available to the average country citizen to do with as he or she pleased. Although the early years of motoring were controlled by the affluent, the introduction of Ford's Model T and other inexpensive makes democratized the motor car by lowering its price. It was so widely adopted that by 1929 ownership of an automobile was considered less an extravagance than a necessity.

Once the economic and social usefulness of the motor car had been demonstrated, and its superiority to the horse seemingly proven, most of the early hostility toward it in rural regions disappeared. Much of this antagonism had been irrational, based on the universal tendency to blame outside forces for seemingly insoluble internal problems. Viewing the motor car as evil incarnate, the rural dweller was released from his or her own moral restrictions in doing battle with it. The results of this approach were adequately illustrated in the first part of chapter 1.

However, as the advantages of motorization began to outweigh the unpleasant aspects, the motor car came to be viewed more as a godsend than as a devil wagon. It was then relatively easy for rural people to accept the new invention and cease agitation against it, because so much of the initial hostility had been so unreasonable.

To understand why rural institutions and values changed as they did, it is as necessary to know how the automobile was adopted as why it was accepted. The motor car was not introduced by government fiat, nor did the town council vote funds for its acquisition. Purchase was an individual act, and this condition more than anything else may help to explain early opposition to the automobile and the failure of some neighborhood institutions to adapt to it. None of the changes for which it has been blamed or given credit were predetermined. The social change that transpired was the result of the sum total of millions of individual social actions. The motor car was, after all, an inanimate object. Whether it split up families or brought them closer together, helped or hindered rural health care, and fostered or fragmented religion in the country was up to the men, women, boys, and girls who drove cars.

In fact, it is possible to conclude that the changes were so sudden (well within one generation) and so far beyond the control of the individual, that it became impossible for any one group of people to stop the collective revolution that they themselves were individually putting in motion. If one owned a car but did not believe in Sunday driving, there was no way to prevent one's neighbor who did. The very breakdown of isolation fostered by the automobile made it increasingly difficult to control actions by bringing familial and/or community pressure to bear. The larger the effective unit of living became, the easier it was to adopt the anonymity of the big town or city.

It logically follows that the automobile was accepted most quickly in those aspects of rural life that traditionally had been loosely structured. Thus, there was little opposition to the motor car's effect on medicine, but severe criticism of its innovations in the religious sphere. As Robert and Helen Lynd have noted, the motor car met its fiercest opposition in those aspects of life that evoke strong emotions. It was easier to adopt the machine per se than to adapt it to existing values and institutions.[2]

When the automobile did begin to affect the institutions of rural America, the immediate impact was shock and disarray. Yet, because these institutions were an important part of rural American life, there were always movements to re-create what had been destroyed. Obviously, such movements had to take into account the instrument that had caused the chaos. Hence, the new structure that evolved was always different from the old insofar as the automobile had affected that particular institution.

Nonetheless, certain similarities were discernible in all the institutions of the "new" rural America. For one, everything was more complex. No longer did one choose friends, leisure activities, or the family doctor merely on the basis of proximity. The new associations included people from geographically separate units, and interest rather than location became the primary tie among them. As John H. Kolb and Edmund deS. Brunner concluded in 1935, "rural society is becoming less dependent upon locality and organic relationships and is freer to employ voluntary and contractural forms."[3] Time ceased to be the barrier it had once been.

The introduction of wider choice into rural living had both positive and negative effects. Indeed, the automobile, like all inventions or innovations, was a force neither solely for good or for ill, but rather a combination of the two. On the positive side, it helped introduce what many believed to be a better quality of goods, services, and people. In some respects, this improvement was simply a question of numbers. With more goods and people available, it should have been easier to find the right shoe, church, or marital partner. On the other hand, the offerings were often beyond the control of any one community, and were, therefore, dependent on self-regulation for control. For roadside dance establishments, such discipline did not exist; for YMCA/YWCA activities it did.

Although the groups that appealed to specialized interests tended to break up traditional family- and neighborhood-based activities, they in turn led to new types of association. The country store may have been eliminated as a social and educational center, but the traveling librarian and the agricultural extension worker were able to work and motor together to improve the lot of the farmer. By diminishing isolation, the automobile helped create a spirit of cooperation among farmers as well. Such cooperation, Professor John Gillette theorized at the First National Country Life Conference in 1919, "furnished the basis for undermining the individualism of the farmer. The more intelligent farmers have turned from viewing themselves as alone responsible for their own success and toward an interest in joint undertakings."[4] Just how successful this new cooperative attitude would be was largely determined by the automobile's effect on the community.

Writing in a 1966 issue of the *Journal of American History*, Burl Noggle hypothesized that the "emphasis on tensions in the decade [of the twenties] — brought on by a conflict between an older, rural, Anglo-Protestant America and a newer, urban, and cosmopolitan one — may well be the most revealing and comprehensive concept that historians of the 1920s have recently brought to the period."[5] Noggle's conclusions seem to be equally valid for the early years of the century, in terms of the automobile's social impact on rural America. Much early rural hostility to the motor car was based on its urban ownership. The motor car's later availability to the masses largely eliminated this antagonism, but it could not end the continuing rural suspicion of the urban way of life. The nation's disparate social elements may have blended together, but the finished product bore a closer resemblance to its city cousin than its country parent.

Urban values were able to take hold to the extent they did largely because rural America was unprepared for the assault.

Because the family and the local neighborhood were unable to deal effectively with the challenge, larger and larger units of control were attempted, and all of these were abetted by the automobile. Ironically, such actions created a more urban way of life, because these enlarged rural communities began to encroach on and, eventually, to be pulled into the orbit of city life. Wayne E. Fuller has noted how proponents of rural free delivery hoped that the service would provide enough outside contact that people would be content to remain on the farms. Paradoxically, the rural values that they had hoped to retain were in part the product of isolation. By introducing RFD, the federal government ran the risk of opening channels of communication that might weaken these values and lure the farmer away from the country to the city.[6]

Although the automobile helped to create new and reintegrated rural communities, these lacked the "unique" institutions of the past, because the isolation on which these institutions had been based was no longer possible. Those who boasted of a decrease in urban migration had to balance their joy with the realization that their limited success had been achieved by urbanizing the social institutions and values they wished to preserve. It is no wonder that women and children, who had been most isolated in the horse-and-buggy community, experienced the greatest changes in attitude. They were suddenly exposed to a world of conflict, change, and insecurity, rather than harmony, stability, and protection.

Yet, one must guard against the tendency to see only good in the past and only evil in the present. The Reverend Wilbert L. Anderson characterized the preautomobile era as "an age of sects, intolerant from lack of acquaintance. The simplicity of life, and the uniformity of conditions, and the supremacy of a few ideals alone prevented the disruption of society."[7] Because motorization brought urban and rural people together, it is not surprising that their tolerance and respect for each other grew through closer acquaintance. We have emphasized throughout how rural America became "citified." It is therefore important to note, as

Roderick D. McKenzie put it, that "if the suburban and country districts are urbanized the city is in a degree ruralized. Its people more and more go outside the corporate limits to live, to spend their vacations and find recreation."[8] Thus, there was an enlightenment in social relationships and experiences on both sides. Rural people became less fearful of being uncouth with the more sophisticated urban populace. City dwellers, for their part, began to admire the virtues and practices of the rural existence once again.

While this intermingling of rural and urban interests was taking place, there was a new recognition of the nature and value of the uniquely rural aspects of society. "This rural social self-discovery," wrote Professor Gillette in 1919, "has involved the discovery of the function of rural society relative to the larger society, their mutual dependence, and has brought to rural peoples a new appreciation of their dignity and worth to humanity."[9] Thus, rural America did not completely lose its identity. Those institutions and ideas survived that were basically sound and easily adaptable.

Caught in the middle of this rapprochement was the small rural town, a social and economic victim. Rather than mourn its passing, rural America seemed to realize that its *raison d'etre* had disappeared along with horse transportation. With it went an open country — town friction that had helped no one and had tended to perpetuate inefficiency in many aspects of social life.

Much of the transformation of rural life was underway before the acceptance of the motor car. For instance, mail-order houses were hurting the trade of small towns well before the automobile had its full impact. Similarly, many weaknesses in rural life that had been deliberately hidden for years were illuminated, but not created, by the motor car. Neither rural church attendance nor moral standards were as high as country people, and for that matter, urban dwellers, pictured them. Furthermore, many of the changes that upset rural America were long overdue. The United States was no longer a nation of small, self-sufficient farmers. The administratively inefficient crossroads schools, for example, probably should have been consolidated into larger units earlier.

Yet as Walter Burr has observed, a major reason for the decay of the old rural community was that population had fallen below the point necessary for efficient economic and social cooperation. "It may be assumed," he argued, "that for proper exchange of ideas and ideals, and proper support in time, money, and energy for local institutions, a certain efficient minimum of people would be required."[10] The new, enlarged community made possible by motorization allowed for these numbers and consequently successfully adapted many rural values and institutions to a more urban world.

Rural America's early reaction to the automobile contained a curious combination of wonder and damnation. Even while the latter seemed more prominent, an almost imperceptible groundwork was being laid to bring the wonder out into the open country. The rural dweller knew that his or her life was not perfect and realized that the motor car offered solutions to many of the problems he or she faced. In fact, there was a certain interaction among the various effects of motorization, as there is with all new inventions and innovations, which seemed to make the automobile the key to a better future. Thus, the desire for consolidated schools required improved transportation, which in turn created a demand for the motor bus, necessitating improved highways; these roads could be used by owners of automobiles to travel to the newly consolidated churches, to visit the town physician, or to motor into the city for a show.

Less understood, however, was the fact that temporary periods of flux would accompany such changes—for example, times when some forms of leisure would be eliminated, and others would become more available. Even more disturbing was the fact that certain services, such as rural hospitals, would be made possible just as they were being made less necessary by the new accessibility of their urban counterparts.

During the resulting transition periods, it was more difficult than ever for adults to teach familial and societal values to the young for the life ahead, or to follow them themselves, because no one really knew what they were or would be. Some correctly prophesied the future, and others did not; some wanted to keep the status quo regardless, and others favored change at any cost; and the majority, when they had any opinion at all, favored some type of compromise. But these are all verities that we should have expected to find.

What had really changed was the *structure* of rural social life. So vast was the transition that, in 1929, the person who did not own a car was at a definite disadvantage in rural America. Fewer support facilities were available for his or her way of life. There was a smaller number of blacksmiths and livery stables, the railroad ran less frequently, and some things that might have been better accomplished by horse power, such as getting the doctor through a three-foot snow drift, were less likely to be attempted.

Part and parcel of this development was the removal of various service people and facilities to the larger population centers. While they obviously moved cityward to improve themselves, they did so at the expense of personalized service. The missionary spirit that had permeated much of church work, teaching, and health care declined. There was no assurance that the doctor, teacher, or minister viewed rural residents in any thing other than a professional context. Farmers or small-town dwellers were not part of his or her larger life, but rather people who were seen only on a professional basis. Tragically, the practitioners who remained in the open country experienced a loss of prestige as their professional ability was increasingly compared with that of their urban counterparts, and they often found themselves ministering to the most backward of the country dwellers.

Finally, the structure of the rural community and the family was changed by the introduction of goods and services that had previously been restricted to urban areas. Thus, "door-to-door" service, which had formerly existed only for RFD, spread to other institutions. Not only were visiting nurses and county agricultural agents in evidence, but so were YMCA/YWCA representatives and market delivery trucks.

The real loser in the early automobile era was neither the rural family nor the rural community. The Lynds in their classic study of American culture may have provided the answer: "In 1924 a Bible class teacher in a Middletown school concluded her teaching of the Creation: 'And now, children, is there any of these animals that God created that man could have got along without?' One after another of the animals from goat to mosquito was mentioned and for some reason rejected; finally, 'The Horse!' said one boy triumphantly, and the rest of the class agreed."[11]

Notes

NOTES TO *I. THE COMING OF THE AUTOMOBILE*

1. Cited in Rudolph E. Anderson, *The Story of the American Automobile: Highlights and Sidelights* (Washington, D.C.: Public Affairs Press, 1950), p. 104.
2. Ralph N. Hill, *The Mad Doctor's Drive: Being An Account of the 1st Auto Trip Across the United States of America, San Francisco to New York, 1903, or, Sixty-Three Days on a Winton Motor Carriage* (Brattleboro, Vt.: Stephen Greene Press, 1964), p. 13.
3. Lloyd R. Morris, *Not So Long Ago* (New York: Random House, 1949), p. 272.
4. L. E. French, "A White Mountain Tour," *Horseless Age* 14 (1904): 338.
5. Hiram P. Maxim, *Horseless Carriage Days* (New York: Harper & Brothers, 1937), pp. 85-86.
6. Interview in the *Detroit News-Tribune,* February 4, 1900, cited in Allan Nevins, *Ford: The Times, the Man, the Company* (New York: Charles Scribner's Sons, 1954), p. 182.
7. Cited in George O. Draper, "Advice from a Horse Driver," *Horseless Age* 14 (1904): 609.
8. Frederick Lewis Allen, *The Big Change: America Transforms Itself, 1900-1950* (New York: Harper & Brothers, 1952), pp. 122-23.
9. Bellamy Partridge, *Fill 'er Up!: The Story of Fifty Years of Motoring* (New York: McGraw-Hill Book Company, 1952), pp. 44-45.
10. Merrill Denison, *The Power to Go,* American Industries Series (Garden City, N.Y.: Doubleday & Company, 1956), p. 206.
11. Cited in "Rights of Motor Vehicles," *Scientific American,* supplement. January 26, 1901, p. 20967.

12. Ibid., and "Some Leading Automobile Suits," *Horseless Age* 10 (1902): 512.
13. Charles M. Harger, "The Automobile in Western Country Towns," *World Today* 13 (1907): 1279.
14. Reproduced in Floyd Clymer, *Treasury of Early American Automobiles, 1877-1925* (New York: Bonanza Books, 1950), p. 62.
15. Harger, "Automobile in Western Country Towns," p. 1279.
16. Sterling North, *Plowing on Sunday* (New York: Macmillan Company, 1934), pp. 27-28.
17. Harold B. Chase, *Auto-biography: Recollections of A Pioneer Motorist, 1896-1911* (New York: Pageant Press, 1955), pp. 101-3. The monetary aspect of such experiences was occasionally more civilized. Thus, Mrs. T. H. R. noted in 1904, "We stopped, went back and offered to pay the owner, who said 'I won't take it; if you are honest enough to speak about it, I do not want any pay'. But we insisted on his taking half a dollar for his chicken. This being a part of the country where autos are not very often seen, we did not want to give the impression that we were reckless drivers and had no thought for the rights of others." (Mrs. T. H. R., "A Day's Auto Outing in New England," *Horseless Age* 13[1904]:554.)
18. W. P. Flint, "The Automobile and Wild Life," *Science* 63, n.s. (1926): 427.
19. Dayton Stoner, "Toll of the Automobile," *Science* 61, n.s. (1925): 57; Dayton Stoner, "Automobiles and Animal Mortality," *Science* 69, n.s., (1929): 670; and Flint, "The Automobile and Wild Life," pp. 426-27.
20. Stoner, "Toll of the Automobile," p. 57.
21. Stoner, "Automobiles and Animal Mortality," p. 671.
22. John G. Speed, "Modern Chariot," *Cosmopolitan*, June 1900, p. 148.
23. Chase, *Auto-biography*, p. 135.
24. John Scott-Montagu, "Automobile Legislation: A Criticism and Review," *North American Review* 179 (August 1904): 176.
25. Stephen Longstreet, *The Boy in the Model T: A Journey in the Just Gone Past* (New York: Simon and Schuster, 1956), pp. 57-59.
26. E[dward] R. Eastman, *These Changing Times: A Story of Farm Progress during the First Quarter of the Twentieth Century,* with a foreword by L. H. Bailey (New York: Macmillan Company, 1927), p. 227.
27. Ethel Sturtevant, "Living Off the Land," *Harper's Monthly Magazine* 154 (March 1927): 526. It should be emphasized that the conditions described here for the 1920s date back to the introduction of the automobile. In fact, by 1920 the situation had been ameliorated to some extent. Improved roads and automobiles made possible overnight motor trips, and the demand from these created a fairly elaborate network of tourist camps, parks, hotels, and other facilities catering to the needs of the automobile vagabond. It was no longer absolutely necessary to impose on the farmer. For a more detailed discussion of this phenomenon, see chapter 4.
28. C. B. Glasscock. *The Gasoline Age: The Story of the Men Who Made It* (Indianapolis: Bobbs-Merrill Company, 1937), pp. 72-73.
29. Partridge, *Fill 'er Up!,* pp. 102-3. Some New England *resort* areas, such as Nantucket, Massachusetts, and Mt. Desert Island, Maine, continued to exclude

motor traffic until well into the second decade of the century. This was undoubtedly because the wealthy residents there wished to maintain the "exclusiveness" of these summer retreats and is therefore an exceptional situation. ("Mount Desert Now Open to Automobiles," *Horseless Age* 25 (1915): 558, and "Nantucket's Losing Fight against the Motor-Car," *Literary Digest,* April 30, 1921, p. 51).

30. Floyd Clymer, *Those Wonderful Old Automobiles* (New York: Bonanza Books, 1953), p. 39.

31. Ibid., p. 30.

32. Morris, *Not So Long Ago*, p. 271.

33. Cited in "Iowa Repeals Ruling for Nervous Horses," *Automotive Industries* 52 (1925): 885.

34. "Automobile Legislation in the United States," *Horseless Age* 10 (1902): 509.

35. "Connecticut," in *Automobile Laws of the New England States, New York, New Jersey, and Pennsylvania,* ed. Arthur C. Wyman, Legislative Reference Bulletin No. 2 (Providence: E. L. Freeman Company, State Printers for the Legislative Reference Bureau of the Rhode Island State Library, 1908), pp. 45-46.

36. Richard H. Lee, "Serving the Motorist — The Work of The National Motorists' Association," in "The Automobile: Its Province and Its Problems," ed. Clyde L. King, *Annals of the American Academy of Political and Social Science* 116 (November 1924): 267.

37. Partridge, *Fill 'er Up!,* pp. 43-44.

38. Cited in H. D. Wright, "The Whipper Whipped," letter to the editor of *Horseless Age* 16 (1905): 298.

39. "Auto Shooting in South Carolina," *Horseless Age* 15 (1905): 323.

40. "The Return of the Glidden Tourists," *Horseless Age* 16 (1905): 152.

41. Reginald M. Cleveland and S. T. Williamson, *The Road Is Yours: The Story of the Automobile and the Men Behind It* (New York: Greystone Press, 1951), p. 114.

42. Bellamy Partridge, *Excuse My Dust* (New York: McGraw-Hill Book Company, Whittlesey House, 1943), p. 338.

43. "New Jersey," in Wyman, ed., *Automobile Laws,* p. 53.

44. "New York," in Wyman, ed., *Automobile Laws,* pp. 49-50.

45. Partridge, *Fill 'er Up!,* p. 111.

46. Longstreet, *Boy in the Model T,* p. 283.

47. Cleveland and Williamson, *The Road is Yours,* p. 114.

48. C. H. Claudy, "Some Practical Points on Motor Touring," *Country Life in America* 19 (1911): 248.

49. Partridge, *Excuse My Dust,* p. 280.

50. Ibid., pp. 185-86.

51. James J. Flink *America Adopts the Automobile, 1895-1910* (Cambridge, Mass.: MIT Press, 1970), pp. 68-69. It is difficult, however, to accept this author's conclusion that "little popular prejudice toward the motor vehicle was evident either in absolute terms or compared with earlier responses to innovation in transportation, particularly the bicycle and the self-propelled trolley car." (Ibid., p. 34)

52. Louise Closser Hale, *We Discover the Old Dominion* (New York: Dodd, Mead, and Company, Publishers, 1916), pp. 344-47.
53. Partridge, *Excuse My Dust,* pp. 70-71.
54. Denison, *The Power To Go,* p. 153.
55. L. Saviers, "A Michigan Outing," *Horseless Age* 13 (1904): 502.
56. Cited in David L. Cohn, *Combustion on Wheels: An Informal History of the Automobile Age* (Boston: Houghton Mifflin Company, 1944), pp. 137-38.
57. C. O. Morris, "The Truth about the Automobile," *Country Life in America,* 15 (1909): 259.
58. Reproduced in Clymer, *Those Wonderful Old Automobiles,* p. 16.
59. Walter Langford, "What the Motor Vehicle is Doing for the Farmer," *Scientific American,* January 15, 1910, p. 50.
60. Morris, "The Truth about the Automobile," p. 260.
61. National Automobile Chamber of Commerce, *Facts and Figures of the Automobile Industry: 1926 Edition* (New York), p. 27.
62. Cited in "American Farmers Potential Market for 8,500,000 Cars in Ten Years," *Automotive Industries* 42 (1920): 1199.
63. Untitled poem attributed to "F. H." in Charles J. Finger, *Adventure under Sapphire Skies* (New York: William Morrow & Company, 1931), pp. 262-63.
64. Gerald Carson, *The Old Country Store* (New York: Oxford University Press, 1954), p. 200.
65. Hale, *We Discover the Old Dominion,* pp. 163-64.
66. James West [Carl Withers], *Plainville, U.S.A.* (New York: Columbia Univesity Press, 1945), p. 211.
67. *Horseless Age* 5 (1900): 5, advertisement.
68. Reproduced in Q. David Bowers, ed., *Early American Car Advertisements* (New York: Bonanza Books, 1966), p. 126.
69. Frank Presbrey, *The History and Development of Advertising* (Garden City, N.Y.: Doubleday & Company, 1929), p. 560.
70. Advertisement reproduced in Clymer, *Treasury of Early American Automobiles*, p. 104.
71. *Rural New Yorker* 71 (1912): 577, advertisement.
72. Nevins, *Ford*, p. 385.
73. Clymer, *Those Wonderful Old Automobiles*, pp. 82, 164.
74. Kathleen A. Smallzreid and Dorothy J. Roberts, *More than You Promise: A Business at Work in Society* (New York: Harper & Brothers, 1942), p. 142.
75. Cited by Clymer, *Treasury of Early American Automobiles,* p. 12.
76. Boris Emmet and John E. Jeuck, *Catalogues and Counters: A History of Sears, Roebuck and Company* (Chicago: University of Chicago Press, 1950), pp. 220-22.
77. Floyd Clymer, *Henry's Wonderful Model T, 1908-1927* (New York: Bonanza Books, 1955), p. 20.
78. "Farmers and Roads," *Motor Age,* February 9, 1911, p. 10.
79. "Automobiles Conspicuous at State Fair," *Horseless Age* 30 (1912): 354.
80. "From the Four Winds," *Motor Age,* December 4, 1913, p. 46.
81. Norman G. Shidle, "*The Small Town* — That's Where Biggest Automobile Market Lies," *Automotive Industries* 54 (1926): 397.

82. "Automobile Notes," *Scientific American,* January 15, 1910, p. 64.
83. Madison R. Phillips, "The Motor Car on the Farm," *Country Life in America* 19 (1911): 258.
84. Ernest L. Ferguson, "The Rural Motor Vehicle: What Gasoline Means in Agriculture," *Scientific American,* February 10, 1912, p. 133.
85. Langford, "What the Motor Vehicle Is Doing for the Farmer," p. 50, and Theodore M.R. Von Kéler, "The Farmer and the Motor Car," *Collier's,* supplement, January 9, 1915, p. 34.
86. Clymer, *Henry's Wonderful Model T,* pp. 164-65.
87. Edward C. Crossman, "The Gasoline Horse in the West," *Scientific American,* January 5, 1918, p. 45.
88. Charles E. Sorensen, *My Forty Years with Ford* (New York: W.W. Norton & Company, 1956), p. 241.
89. Clymer, *Henry's Wonderful Model T,* p. 11, and C. O Morris, "The Farmer and the Automobile," *Country Life in America* 15 (1909): 636.
90. Morris, "The Farmer and the Automobile," p. 636.
91. Ellis, P. Butler, "The Adventures of a Suburbanite. V: My Domesticated Automobile," *Country Life in America* 17 (1910): 419.
92. John M. Gillette, *Rural Sociology* (New York: Macmillan Company, 1923), p. 241.
93. Cohn, *Combustion on Wheels,* p. 151, and William A. Grimes, *Financing Automobile Sales: By the Time-Payment Plan* (Chicago: A. W. Shaw Company, 1926), p. 95.
94. J. C. Long, "Passing of the Hick," *Outlook* 126 (1910): 427.
95. John B. Rae, *The American Automobile: A Brief History,* Chicago History of American Civilization (Chicago: University of Chicago Press, 1965), p. 197.
96. Harvey W. Peck, "Civilization on Wheels," *Social Forces* (December 1928): 303, 307.
97. Cited in Smallzreid and Roberts, *More than You Promise,* p. 226.
98. "How Many More Motor Cars Have We Room For?" *Literary Digest,* October 7, 1922, p. 62.
99. "How Many American People Can Afford Automobiles?" *Current Opinion* 72 (February 1922): 264.
100. Cited in National Automobile Chamber of Commerce, *Facts and Figures of the Automobile Industry: 1925 Edition* (New York), p. 41.
101. Cited in National Automobile Chamber of Commerce, *Facts and Figures of the Automobile Industry: 1929 Edition* (New York), p. 4.
102. Grimes, *Financing Automobile Sales,* p. 6.
103. Lambert G. Sullivan, "Getting Your Story Across," *Motor Age,* June 10, 1920, p. 8.
104. "Farmer Buying Power Much Higher than It Was in 1914," *Automotive Industries* 48 (1923): 21.
105. James R. Howard, "'Automobiles Increase Agricultural Production,'" *Automotive Industries* 47 (1922): 112.
106. North, *Plowing on Sunday,* p. 100.
107. Charles M. Harger, "Automobiles for Country Use," *Independent* 70 (1911): 1208.

108. Ferguson, "The Rural Motor Vehicle," p. 133.
109. "Educating the Farmer-Motorist," *Motor Age,* March 18, 1915, p. 12.
110. Nevins, *Ford,* p. 493.
111. Cited in National Automobile Chamber of Commerce, *Facts and Figures of the Automobile Industry: 1929 Edition,* p. 82.
112. Charles R. Hoffer, *Services of Rural Trade Centers in Distribution of Farm Supplies,* Bulletin No. 249 (St. Paul: University of Minnesota Agricultural Experiment Station, 1928), p. 4.
113. Cited in National Automobile Chamber of Commerce, *Facts and Figures of the Automobile Industry: 1929 Edition,* p. 82.
114. It is important to note that these figures are for Minnesota only. In 1923, it was reported by the United States Department of Agriculture (Bulletin No. 1214) that in Livingston County, New York, the average farm family spent $2,012 annually, of which $86 or 4 percent was for repair and operation of a motor vehicle. (Cited in "Farmer Spends $65 Year in Owning Car," *Automotive Industries* 49 (1923): 1071, and National Automobile Chamber of Commerce, *Facts and Figures of the Automobile Industry: 1925 Edition,* p. 19.) Unfortunately, a follow-up survey was not done. One can only assume that regional differences account for this discrepancy between the New York and Minnesota findings. Upstate New York was more heavily settled, and thus the cost of parts and service may have been lower. This seems to be supported by another United States Department of Agriculture Bulletin (No. 1466) issued in 1926, which shows expenditures for motor vehicles as averaging $108 per family in New England and $119 for those living in the North Central states. (Cited in National Automobile Chamber of Commerce, *Facts and Figures of the Automobile Industry: 1927 Edition,* [New York], p. 37.)
115. J. F. Steiner, "Recreation and Leisure Time Activities," in President's Research Committee on Social Trends, *Recent Social Trends in the United States,* with a foreword by Herbert Hoover (New York: McGraw-Hill Book Company, 1933), p. 950.
116. Richard Rodgers and Oscar Hammerstein II, *Oklahoma!* (New York: Random House, 1942), p. 9.
117. George E. Mowry, *The Urban Nation, 1920-1960,* Vol. 6 of *The Making of America,* ed. David Donald, 6 vols., (New York: Hill and Wang, 1965), p. 12.
118. Longstreet, *Boy in the Model T,* p. 105.
119. Anderson, *Story of the American Automobile,* pp. 97-98.
120. Frank Donovan, *Wheels for a Nation* (New York: Thomas Y. Crowell Company, 1965), p. 110.
121. Bradley to M. L. Berger, April 7, 1971.
122. Clymer, *Henry's Wonderful Model T,* p. 16.
123. Lee Strout White [E. B. White], "Farewell, My Lovely!" *The New Yorker,* May 16, 1936, p. 22. Recall the earlier discussion of assigning animal qualities to the inanimate machine.
124. Nevins, *Ford,* p. 403.
125. Hollister Moore, "Marketing Data," *Automotive Industries* 62 (1930): 268. These figures need not imply the absolute number of dealerships, but rather the relative commitment of various companies to the rural market.

However, since Ford dominated the market absolutely as well, it can be assumed that the actual number of Ford dealers vis-à-vis all others was proportionally *larger* than these percentages would indicate.

126. Moore, "Marketing Data," p. 268.

127. John Keats, *The Insolent Chariots* (Philadelphia: J.B. Lippincott Company, 1958), p. 25-26.

128. George Milburn, *Catalogue* (New York: Harcourt, Brace and Company, 1936), p. 219.

129. "Ford Parts for All Garages," *Motor Age,* January 2, 1919, p. 15.

130. Chase, *Auto-biography,* pp. 93-94.

131. C[lare] E. Griffin, *The Life History of Automobiles,* Michigan Business Studies, Vol. 1, No. 1 (Ann Arbor, Mich.: Bureau of Business Research, Graduate School of Business Administation, University of Michigan, 1926), p. 35.

132. Homer Croy, *R.F.D. No. 3* (New York: Harper & Brothers, 1924), p. 2.

133. Phillips, "The Motor Car on the Farm," p. 258.

134. Cited in National Automobile Chamber of Commerce, *Facts and Figures of the Automobile Industry* (New York, 1922), p. 19.

135. Cited in R[oderick] D. McKenzie, *The Metropolitan Community,* Recent Social Trends Monographs (New York: McGraw-Hill Book Company, 1933), p. 271.

136. National Automobile Chamber of Commerce, *Facts and Figures of the Automobile Industry: 1930 Edition,* (New York), p. 16.

137. "The Modern Car and Its Work," *Rural New Yorker,* 83 (1924): 906.

138. Cited in "Automobiles on Farms Almost Equal Telephone in Numbers," *Automotive Industries* 47 (1922): 276.

139. Obviously, to the extent that some farms had three or more automobiles, these figures would be decreased. The number of farms with three or more cars, however, was probably low.

140. Cited in Edmund deS. Brunner and J[ohn] H. Kolb, *Rural Social Trends* (New York: McGraw-Hill Book Company, 1933), p. 63. These percentages are for the nation as a whole. Many of the farming states of the Great Plains showed much higher figures. A survey of farm families in four districts of Iowa, undertaken by the United States Department of Agriculture, revealed that almost 93 percent had motor cars. The tenant families achieved the impressive figure of 89 percent. (Cited in National Automobile Chamber of Commerce, *Facts and Figures of the Automobile Industry: 1925 Edition,* p. 91.) In addition, some discrepancies exist in the available *national* figures, apparently because of various definitional and survey problems. As a result, information furnished by the federal government has been used where possible. However, census data characteristically suffers from survey omissions, and thus these figures may be low. On the other hand, those of the National Automobile Chamber of Commerce, with a vested interest in the success of the motor car, may be assumed to be high. As often happens, the truth probably lies somewhat in between.

141. "Hawkeye Speeds Up; Buys a Buggy," *Motor Age,* February 23, 1922, p. 30.

NOTES TO *II. THE FARM FAMILY*

1. E[dward] R. Eastman, *These Changing Times: A Story of Farm Progress during the First Quarter of the Twentieth Century,* with a foreword by L. H. Bailey (New York: Macmillan Company, 1927), p. 7.
2. Cited by George Soule, *Prosperity Decade: From War to Depression, 1917-1929,* Vol. 8 of *The Economic History of the United States,* ed. Henry David et al., 9 vols. (New York: Rinehart & Company, 1946-47), p. 250.
3. U.S. Department of Agriculture, *The Farm Women's Problems,* by Florence E. Ward, Department Circular No. 148 (Washington, D.C.: Government Printing Office, 1920), p. 12.
4. Theodore M. R. von Keler, "The Farmer and the Motor Car," *Collier's* supplement, January 9, 1915, p. 34.
5. Eastman, *These Changing Times,* p. 8.
6. Charles R. Hoffer, *Introduction to Rural Sociology* (New York: Richard R. Smith, Inc., 1930), p. 43.
7. Warren H. Wilson, *The Evolution of the Country Community,* 2nd ed., rev. (Boston: Pilgrim Press, 1923), p. 117.
8. Horace B. Hawthorn, *The Sociology of Rural Life* (New York: Century Co., 1926), p. 420.
9. Charles J. Galpin, *Rural Life* (New York: Century Co., 1918), pp. 18-19, 39-40.
10. Roy H. Holmes, "The Passing of the Farmer," *Atlantic Monthly* 110 (October 1912): 521.
11. Cited in U.S. Department of Agriculture, Office of the Secretary, *Social and Labor Needs of Farm Women,* Report No. 103 (Washington, D. C.: Government Printing Office, 1915), p. 50. The coming of the automobile allowed salesmen to go out "into the field," and yet return home or to a town hotel at night. Unfortunately for farm women, farmers later invited their town friends with motor cars to "come out and spend the day; bring your wife and family." Frequently, these were as unannounced to the women of the farmstead as the old salesman had been. (Ibid., p. 52.)
12. Ibid., p. 40.
13. See chapters 5 and 6 for a detailed explanation of this point.
14. Ernest R. Groves, *The Rural Mind and Social Welfare,* with a foreword by Kenyon L. Butterfield (Chicago: University of Chicago Press, 1922), p. 88.
15. Ernest L. Ferguson, "The Rural Motor Vehicle: What Gasoline Means in Agriculture," *Scientific American,* February 10, 1912, p. 133.
16. James M. Williams, *The Expansion of Rural Life: The Social Psychology of Rural Development* (New York: F. S. Crofts & Co., 1931), p. 154.
17. Robert S. Lynd and Helen Merrell Lynd, *Middletown: A Study in Modern American Culture,* A Harvest Book (New York: Harcourt, Brace, & World, 1929), p. 153n. While Muncie, Indiana, was clearly a small city at the time of the Lynds' study, there is little reason to doubt that such conditions also existed in rural localities.
18. Malcolm M. Willey and Stuart A. Rice, *Communication Agencies and Social Life,* Recent Social Trends Monographs (New York: McGraw-Hill Book Company, 1933), p. 57.

19. Pitirim A. Sorokin, Carle C. Zimmerman, and Charles J. Galpin, eds., *A Systematic Source Book in Rural Sociology,* 3 vols. (Minneapolis: University of Minnesota Press, 1930-32), vol. 3, p. 642.
20. Ibid.
21. John M. McKee, "The Automobile and American Agriculture," in *The Automobile — Its Province and Problems,* ed. Clyde L. King, *Annals of the American Academy of Political and Social Science* 116 (November 1924): 13.
22. Lynd and Lynd. *Middletown,* p. 177.
23. G. Walter Fiske, "The Development of Rural Leadership," in *The Sociology of Rural Life,* ed. Scott E. W. Bedford, *Publications of the American Sociological Society* 11 (March 1917): 56-57.
24. "The Motor-Car and Country Life," *Craftsman,* May 1911, p. 227.
25. David L. Cohn, *Combustion on Wheels: An Informal History of the Automobile Age* (Boston: Houghton Mifflin Company, 1944), p. 200.
26. George W. Anderson, "Roads — Motor and Rail," *Atlantic Monthly* 135 (March 1925): 400. Obviously, such comparisons did not calculate the wear and capital depreciation of the automobile.
27. Dwight Sanderson, *The Farmer and His Community,* The Farmer's Bookshelf (New York: Harcourt, Brace, and Company, 1922), p. 157.
28. Hawthorn, *The Sociology of Rural Life,* pp. 187-88.
29. Cited by Frank E. Brimmer, "The Nickel-and-Dime Stores of Nomadic America," *Magazine of Business,* (August 1927), p. 152.
30. Walter Burr, *Small Towns: An Estimate of Their Trade and Culture* (New York: MacMillan Company, 1929), p. 43.
31. Lynd and Lynd, *Middletown,* p. 260.
32. H.V. Van Norman, "Rural Conveniences," in *Country Life,* ed. J.P. Lichtenberger, *Annals of the American Academy of Political and Social Sciences* 40 (March 1912): 166.
33. H[arvey] W. Peck, "The Influence of Agricultural Machinery and the Automobile on Farming Operations," *Quarterly Journal of Economics* 41 (May 1927): 540.
34. Sorokin, Zimmerman, and Galpin, eds., *Systematic Source Book,* pp. 141-42.
35. Sanderson, *The Farmer and His Community,* pp. 15-16.
36. Frederick Lewis Allen, *The Big Change: America Transforms Itself, 1900-1950* (New York: Harper & Brothers, 1952), p. 113.
37. C. H. Claudy, "The Woman and Her Car," *Country Life in America* 23 (1913): 42.
38. L. B. Pierce, "The Ohio Farm Woman's Car," *Rural New Yorker* 78 (1919): 1804.
39. H. L. Barber, *Story of the Automobile: Its History and Development from 1760 to 1917, With an Analysis of the Standing and Prospects of the Automobile Industry* (Chicago: A.J. Munson & Co., 1917), p. 160.
40. Cited in Franklin M. Reck, *A Car Traveling People: How the Automobile Has Changed the Life of Americans — A Study of Social Effects* (Detroit: Automobile Manufacturers Association, 1945), p. 8.
41. Cited in National Automobile Chamber of Commerce, *Facts and Figures of the Automobile Industry: 1926 Edition,* (New York), p. 78.

42. "Is this Eggsactly Right?," *Motor Age,* December 28, 1916, p. 15.
43. Elizabeth Janeway, *The Early Days of Automobiles,* A Landmark Book (New York: Random House, 1956), p. 165.
44. State of New York, Crime Commission, Sub-Commission on Causes and Effects of Crime, *A Study of Delinquency in Two Rural Counties,* Legislative Document No. 94 (Albany, N.Y.: J. B. Lyon Company, Printers, 1927), p. 410.
45. Newell L. Sims, *Elements of Rural Sociology,* Crowell's Social Science Series (New York: Thomas Y. Crowell Company, 1928), p. 382.
46. Reck, *A Car Traveling People,* p. 19.
47. Mary Meek Atkeson, *The Woman on the Farm* (New York: Century Co., 1924), p. 13. This point will be discussed in regard to morality in chapter 5.
48. Carl C. Taylor, *Rural Sociology: In Its Economic, Historical, and Psychological Aspects,* rev. ed. (New York: Harper & Brothers Publishers, 1933), p. 299.
49. Lynd and Lynd, *Middletown,* p. 257.
50. Ibid.
51. Albert Blumenthal, *Small-Town Stuff,* University of Chicago Sociological Series (Chicago: University of Chicago Press, 1932), p. 261.
52. Cited by Frank Donovan, *Wheels for a Nation* (New York: Thomas Y. Crowell Company, 1965), p. 8.
53. Robert Bruce, "Place of the Automobile," *Outing* 37 (October 1900): 68-69.
54. C. B. Glasscock, *The Gasoline Age: The Story of the Men Who Made It* (Indianapolis: Bobbs-Merrill Company Publishers, 1937), p. 133.
55. Peck, "The Influence of Agricultural Machinery," p. 540.
56. Marsh K. Powers, "The Forgotten Fireside," *Outlook* 130 (1922): 608.
57. Judson C. Welliver, "The Automobile in our County," *Collier's,* January 8, 1916, p. 72.
58. Reginald M. Cleveland and S. T. Williamson, *The Road Is Yours: The Story of the Automobile and the Men Behind It* (New York: Greystone Press, 1951), p. 18.
59. Williams, *The Expansion of Rural Life,* p. 154.
60. Donovan, *Wheels for A Nation,* p. 160.
61. David L. Hatch, "Changes in the Structure and Function of a Rural New England Community since 1900," (Ph.D. diss., Harvard University, 1948), pp. 280-81.
62. W. E. Duckwall, "Why the Car Driver 'Moves On,' " *Rural New Yorker* 76 (1917): 188.
63. M. B. D., "From New York to West Virginia," *Rural New Yorker* 82 (1923): 44.
64. A. P. Hitchcock, "The Joys of Being a Farmer," *Country Life in America* 20 (July 1, 1911): 50.
65. Eastman, *These Changing Times,* p. 196.
66. Charles M. Harger, "Automobiles for Country Use," *Independent* 70 (1911): 1208.
67. See, for instance, Thomas D. Clark's description of changing feminine

styles in his *Pills, Petticoats, and Plows: The Southern Country Store* (Norman, Okla.: University of Oklahoma Press, 1964), pp. 169-70.
68. Christy Borth, "He 'Liberated the Women,'" *Think* 12 (December 1946): 30 [National Automotive Jubilee edition].
69. Boris Emmet and John E. Jeuck, *Catalogues and Counters: A History of Sears, Roebuck & Company* (Chicago: University of Chicago Press, 1950), p. 323.
70. Clark, *Pills, Petticoats, and Plows,* pp. 170-71.

NOTES TO *III. THE RURAL COMMUNITY*

1. Harlan P. Douglass, *The Little Town: Especially in Its Rural Relationships,* rev. ed. (New York: Macmillan Company, 1927), p. 76.
2. Ibid., p. 77.
3. C. M. Babcock, "The Highway and the Small Town," in *Small City and Town: A Conference on Community Relations,* ed. Roland S. Vaile (Minneapolis: University of Minnesota Press, 1930), p. 107.
4. Charles J. Galpin, *The Social Anatomy of a Rural Community,* Research Bulletin No. 34 (Madison, Wisc.: University of Wisconsin Agricultural Experiment Station, 1914), p. 25.
5. Edmund deS. Brunner, Gwendolyn S. Hughes, and Marjorie Patten, *American Agricultural Villages,* American Village Studies of the Institute of Religious and Social Research (New York: George H. Doran Company, 1927), p. 98.
6. Lewis Atherton, *Main Street on the Middle Border* (Bloomington, Ind.: Indiana University Press, 1954), p. 64.
7. Horace B. Hawthorn, *The Sociology of Rural Life* (New York: Century Co., 1926), p. 174.
8. R[oderick] D. McKenzie, *The Metropolitan Community,* Recent Social Trends Monographs (New York: McGraw-Hill Book Company, 1933), p. 83.
9. Ibid., p. 6.
10. Wayne E. Fuller, *RFD: The Changing Face of Rural America* (Bloomington, Ind.: Indiana University Press, 1964), pp. 148-49, 154-55.
11. "Motor Mail Is Planned," *Motor Age,* January 10, 1918, p. 20, and "From the Four Winds," *Motor Age,* September 10, 1908, p. 28. In regard to the date of the last citation, it should be noted that individual rural carriers often adopted the automobile prior to the *official* Post Office Department decision to do so.
12. Warren H. Wilson, "Social Life in the Country," in *Country Life,* ed. J. P. Lichtenberger, *Annals of the American Academy of Political and Social Science* 40 (March 1912): 128.
13. Harvey W. Peck, "The Economic Status of Agriculture," *Journal of Political Economy* 34 (October 1926): 636.

14. Edward A. Ross, "Folk Depletion as A Cause of Rural Decline," in *The Sociology of Rural Life,* ed. Scott E. W. Bedford, *Publications of the American Sociological Society* 11 (March 1917): 27.
15. See, for instance, his introduction to U.S., Congress, Senate, *Report of the Country Life Commission: Special Message from the President of the United States Transmitting the Report of the Country Life Commission,* S. Doc. 705, 60th Cong., 2d Sess., 1909, pp. 3-9.
16. Cited by Samuel R. McKelvie, "What the Movies Mean to the Farmer," in *The Motion Picture in Its Economic and Social Aspects,* ed. Clyde L. King and Frank A. Tichenor, *Annals of the American Academy of Political and Social Science* 128 (November 1926): 132.
17. Judson C. Welliver, "The Automobile in our County," *Collier's,* January 8, 1916, p. 74.
18. John North Willys, interviewed in Henry I. Dodge, "Transportation and the Cost of Living," *Country Gentleman,* February 22, 1919, p. 24.
19. Ibid., pp. 24, 26.
20. Ibid.
21. Charles R. Hoffer, *Introduction to Rural Sociology* (New York: Richard R. Smith, Inc., 1930), p. 17.
22. Carl C. Taylor, *Rural Sociology: In Its Economic, Historical, and Psychological Aspects,* rev. ed. (New York: Harper & Brothers Publishers, 1933), p. 6.
23. George Soule, *Prosperity Decade: From War to Depression, 1917-1929,* vol. 8 of *The Economic History of the United States,* ed. Henry David, et al., 9 vols. (New York: Rinehart & Company, 1946-47), p. 211, and C. Luther Fry, *American Villagers* (New York: George H. Doran Company, 1926), p. 44.
24. Soule, *Prosperity Decade,* p. 11.
25. Edmund deS. Brunner and J[ohn] H. Kolb, *Rural Social Trends,* Recent Social Trends Monographs (New York: McGraw-Hill Book Company, 1933), p. 16.
26. Roy H. Holmes, "The Passing of the Farmer," *Atlantic Monthly* 110 (October 1912): 523.
27. Fry, *American Villagers,* p. 42.
28. J[ohn] H. Kolb, *Service Institutions for Town and Country,* Research Bulletin No. 66 (Madison, Wisc.: University of Wisconsin Agricultural Experiment Station, 1925), p. 59.
29. Eugene A. Clancy, "The Car and the Country House," *Harper's Weekly,* May 6, 1911, p. 30.
30. Harlan P. Douglass, *The Suburban Trend* (New York: Century Co., 1925), pp. 6-7.
31. Douglass, *The Suburban Trend,* pp. 263-64.
32. "One More Revolution," *Independent* 55 (1903): 1163.
33. M. Worth Colwell, "The Worst Roads in America," *Outing* 51 (November 1907): 247.
34. Sinclair Lewis, *Free Air* (New York: Harcourt, Brace and Howe, 1919), p. 4.

35. Lloyd R. Morris, *Not So Long Ago* (New York: Random House, 1949), pp. 242-43.
36. U.S. Department of Agriculture, Office of the Secretary, *Social and Labor Needs of Farm Women,* Report No. 103 (Washington, D.C.: Government Printing Office, 1915), p. 73, and Hoffer, *Introduction to Rural Sociology,* p. 393.
37. Cited in U.S. Department of Agriculture, Office of the Secretary, *Social and Labor Needs of Farm Women,* p. 74.
38. "Roads — Good and Bad: How They Came to Be and What They Mean to the User," *Scientific American,* January 5, 1918, p. 12.
39. John M. Gillette, *Rural Sociology* (New York: Macmillan Company, 1923), p. 330.
40. Theodore Saloutous and John D. Hicks, *Twentieth-Century Populism: Agricultural Discontent in the Middle West, 1900-1939,* A Bison Book (Lincoln, Nebr.: University of Nebraska Press, 1951), pp. 225-26.
41. Floyd Clymer, *Treasury of Early American Automobiles, 1877-1925* (New York: Bonanza Books, 1950), p. 6.
42. Mary Doane Shelby, "An Open Letter to Secretary Houston," in *Readings in Rural Sociology,* ed. John Phelan (New York: Macmillan Company, 1920), pp. 321-22.
43. Llewellyn MacGarr, *The Rural Community* (New York: Macmillan Company, 1924), p. 135. Consolidated schools are discussed in more detail in the chapter on education.
44. Although it was probably foreseen by few, the passenger automobile and bus were to deal a serious blow to rail passenger traffic. Many railroads abandoned their branch lines, and the interurban trolley disappeared. As a result, communities that had thrived simply because the railroad ran through town came upon hard times. (Frank Donovan, *Wheels for A Nation* [New York: Thomas Y. Crowell Company, 1965], p. 161.)
45. Homer Croy, *West of the Water Tower* (New York: Harper & Brothers Publishers, 1923), pp. 358-59.
46. Clyde B. Davis, *The Age of Indiscretion* (Philadelphia: J. B. Lippincott Company, 1950), p. 90.
47. This, however, was not conclusively shown until studies were done in the mid-1920s, such as Gillette's *Rural Sociology,* see p. 331.
48. H[arvey] W. Peck, "The Influence of Agricultural Machinery and the Automobile on Farming Operations," *Quarterly Journal of Economics* 41 (May 1927): 537-38.
49. Archer B. Hulbert, "The Future of Road-making in America," in *The Future of Road-making in America: A Symposium,* ed. Archer B. Hulbert, vol. 15 of *Historic Highways of America,* ed. Archer B. Hulbert, 16 vols. (Cleveland: Arthur H. Clark Company, 1902-5), p. 23.
50. Harvey W. Peck, "Civilization on Wheels," *Social Forces* 7 (December 1928): 306.
51. Logan W. Page, "How Small Communities May Have Good Roads: The Value of Whole-Hearted Co-Operation," *Scientific American,* January 2, 1915, p. 14.

52. Allan Nevins, *Ford: The Times, the Man, the Company* (New York: Charles Scribner's Sons, 1954), p. 483.
53. E[dward] R. Eastman, *These Changing Times: A Story of Farm Progress during the First Quarter of the Twentieth Century*, with a foreword by L. H. Bailey (New York: Macmillan Company, 1927), p. 125.
54. Clarence Heer, "Taxation and Public Finance," in Report of the President's Research Committee on Social Trends, *Recent Social Trends in the United States,* with a foreword by Herbert Hoover, 1-vol. ed. (New York: McGraw-Hill Book Company, 1933), pp. 1360-61.
55. Gillette, *Rural Sociology*, p. 326.
56. Cited in Gerald Carson, *The Old Country Store* (New York: Oxford University Press, 1954), p. 281.
57. Otto Dorner, "Good Roads and State Aid," *Forum* 26 (February 1899): 668.
58. Martin Dodge, "Government Cooperation in Object-Lesson Road Work," in *The Future of Road-making in America*, ed. Hulbert, pp. 70-72.
59. James F. Menehan, cited in Walter Burr, *Rural Organization* (New York: Macmillan Company, 1921), pp. 136-37.
60. James J. Flink, *America Adopts the Automobile, 1895-1910* (Cambridge, Mass.: MIT Press, 1970), p. 212.
61. Bruce Smith, *Rural Crime Control* (New York: Institute of Public Administration, Columbia University, 1933), p. vi.
62. Cited in Gilman M. Ostrander, *American Civilization in the First Machine Age, 1890-1940* (New York: Harper & Row, Publishers, 1970), p. 50.
63. Cited in David L. Cohn, *Combustion on Wheels: An Informal History of the Automobile Age* (Boston: Houghton Mifflin Company, 1944), p. 180.
64. David L. Hatch, "Changes in the Structure and Function of a Rural New England Community since 1900" (Ph.D. diss., Harvard University, 1948), pp. 278-79.
65. "From the Four Winds," *Motor Age*, October 28, 1908, p. 36.
66. Quintan Wood and Charles P. Cushing, "The Return of the Bad Men: The Rural West Arms to Repel City Bank Raiders," *Country Gentleman*, June 1926, p. 8.
67. Louise van Voorhis Armstrong, *Good Roads: A Play in One Act* (New York: Samuel French, 1929), act 1, sc. 1.
68. C. R. Henderson, "Rural Police," in *Readings in Rural Sociology*, ed. Phelan, p. 304.
69. Hoffer, *Introduction to Rural Sociology*, pp. 156-57.
70. "Motor Posse Runs Down a Murderer in Nebraska," *Motor Age*, October 8, 1914, p. 15.
71. Smith, *Rural Crime Control*, pp. 160-61.
72. Cohn, *Combustion on Wheels*, pp. 197-98.
73. Walter Burr, *Small Towns: An Estimate of Their Trade and Culture* (New York: Macmillan Company, 1929), p. 262.
74. U.S. Department of Labor, Children's Bureau, Dependent, Defective, and Delinquent Classes, *Juvenile Delinquency in Rural New York*, by Kate H. Claghorn, Series No. 4, Bureau Publication No. 32 (Washington, D. C.: Government Printing Office, 1918), p. 46.

NOTES TO *IV. LEISURE*

1. Warren H. Wilson, *The Evolution of the Country Community*, 2nd ed., rev. (Boston: Pilgrim Press, 1923), pp. 231-32.
2. Harlan P. Douglass, *The Little Town: Especially in Its Rural Relationships*, rev. ed. (New York: Macmillan Company, 1927), p. 127.
3. Ernest R. Groves, *The Rural Mind and Social Welfare*, with a foreword by Kenyon L. Butterfield (Chicago: University of Chicago Press, 1922), pp. 148-49.
4. Warren H. Wilson, "Social Life in the Country," in *Country Life*, ed. J. P. Lichtenberger, *Annals of the American Academy of Political and Social Science* 40 (March, 1912): 122.
5. Wilson, *Evolution of the Country Community*, pp. 119, 122-23.
6. Edmund deS. Brunner, *Village Communities*, American Village Studies of the Institute of Social and Religious Research (New York: George H. Doran Company, 1927), p. 91.
7. L. J. Hanifan, *The Community Center*, Teacher Training Series, ed. W. W. Charters (Boston: Silver, Burdett & Company, 1920), p. 59.
8. J. O. Rankin, *Reading Matter in Nebraska Farm Homes*, Bulletin No. 180 (Lincoln, Nebr.: University of Nebraska Agricultural Experiment Station, 1922).
9. Edwin P. Chase, "Forty Years of Main Street," *Iowa Journal of History and Politics* 24 (July 1936): 238-39.
10. Carl C. Taylor, *Rural Sociology: In Its Economic, Historical, and Psychological Aspects,* rev. ed. (New York: Harper & Brothers, Publishers, 1933), p. 507.
11. Dwight Sanderson, *The Farmer and His Community*, The Farmer's Bookshelf (New York: Harcourt, Brace and Company, 1922), p. 153.
12. Mary Meek Atkeson, *The Woman on the Farm* (New York: Century Co., 1924), p. 140.
13. Truman S. Vance, "Why Young Men Leave the Farms," *Independent* 70 (1911): 555.
14. J[esse] F. Steiner, "Recreation and Leisure Time Activities," in Report of the President's Research Committee on Social Trends, *Recent Social Trends in the United States*, with a foreword by Herbert Hoover, 1-vol. ed. (New York: McGraw-Hill Book Company, 1933), p. 944.
15. Charles R. Hoffer, *Introduction to Rural Sociology* (New York: Richard R. Smith, Inc., 1930), pp. 198-99.
16. Cited in Edmund deS. Brunner, Gwendolyn S. Hughes, and Marjorie Patten, *American Agricultural Villages*, American Village Studies of the Institute of Social and Religious Research (New York: George H. Doran Company, 1927), p. 214.
17. Wayne C. Neely, *The Agricultural Fair*, Columbia University Studies in the History of American Agriculture (New York: Columbia University Press, 1935), vol. 2, pp. 258-59.
18. Ibid., pp. 258-60.
19. Ibid., pp. 115-16.
20. Albert Blumenthal, *Small-Town Stuff*, University of Chicago Sociological Series (Chicago: University of Chicago Press, 1932), p. 253.

21. John R. McMahon, "Our Jazz-Spotted Middle West: Small Towns and Rural Districts Need Clean-Up as well as Chicago and Kansas City," *Ladies' Home Journal*, February 1922, p. 38.
22. New York State Crime Commission, Report of the Sub-Commission on Causes and Effects of Crime, *A Study of Delinquency in Two Rural Counties*, Legislative Document No. 94 (Albany, N.Y.: J. B. Lyon Company, Printers, 1927), pp. 408-9.
23. Charles M. Wilson, "The Country Store Survives," *Outlook and Independent* 157 (1931): 143.
24. Charles R. Hoffer, *Services of Rural Trade Centers in Distribution of Farm Supplies*, Bulletin No. 249 (St. Paul: University of Minnesota Agricultural Experiment Station, 1928), p. 11.
25. George Milburn, "Catalogues and Culture," *Good Housekeeping*, (April 1946) pp. 183-84.
26. Cited in Charles M. Harger, "The Country Store," *Atlantic Monthly* 95 (January 1905): 96.
27. J[ohn] H. Kolb and Edmund deS. Brunner, "Rural Life," in Report of the President's Research Committee on Social Trends, *Recent Social Trends in the United States*, p. 536.
28. See, for instance, Paul D. Converse, "Retail Business in the Small Town," in *Small City and Town: A Conference on Community Relations*, ed. Roland S. Vaile (Minneapolis: University of Minnesota Press, 1930), pp. 43-48, and University of Nebraska, Committee on Business Research of the College of Business Administration, *The Influence of Automobiles and Good Roads on Retail Trade Centers*, Nebraska Studies in Business, No. 18 (Lincoln, Nebr.: Extension Division of the University of Nebraska, 1927).
29. Cited by J[ohn] H. Kolb and Edmund deS. Brunner, *A Study of Rural Society: Its Organization and Changes* (Boston: Houghton Mifflin Company, 1935), p. 496.
30. Ibid., p. 495.
31. Gerald Carson, *The Old Country Store* (New York: Oxford University Press, 1954), p. 276.
32. Frank Farrington, *More Talks by the Old Storekeeper* (Chicago: Byxbee Publishing Company, 1912), pp. 112-13.
33. University of Illinois, College of Commerce and Business Administration, Bureau of Business Research, *The Automobile and the Village Merchant: The Influence of Automobiles and Paved Roads on the Business of Illinois Village Merchants*, Bulletin No. 19 (Urbana, Ill.: University of Illinois, 1928), p. 36.
34. Theodore M. R. Von Kéler, "Suburban Changes and the Automobile," *Collier's*, January 8, 1916, pp. 60, 62.
35. Carson, *The Old Country Store*, pp. 284-85.
36. Kolb and Brunner, "Rural Life," p. 521.
37. Kolb and Brunner, *A Study of Rural Society*, p. 500.
38. This seems to have been more common among farmers than villagers. (Kolb and Brunner, *A Study of Rural Society*, p. 497.) It was probably a question of proximity for town dwellers. For the farmers, once in the car, it was just as easy to bypass the less efficient smaller town as to trade there.

39. University of Nebraska, Committee on Business Research of the College of Business Administration, *Influence of Automobiles and Good Roads*, p. 18.
40. David L. Cohn, *Combustion on Wheels: An Informal History of the Automobile Age* (Boston: Houghton Mifflin Company, 1944), pp. 183-84.
41. Neely, *The Agricultural Fair*, p. 260.
42. Samuel R. McKelvie, "What the Movies Mean to the Farmer," in *The Motion Picture in Its Economic and Social Aspects*, ed. Clyde L. King and Frank A. Tichenor, *Annals of the American Academy of Political and Social Science* 128 (November 1926): 131.
43. Ibid. By the late 1920s, however, this function may have been in eclipse. The townward trend discussed in chapter 3 had, on the whole, a detrimental effect on the village picture show. Unable to compete with their larger rivals, the neighborhood theatres took to showing old films and ones of questionable virtue. (T. A. Coleman, "Communication and Transportation," in *A Decade of Rural Progress*, ed. Benson Y. Landis and Nat T. Frame [Chicago: University of Chicago Press, for the American Country Life Association, 1928], p. 90.)
44. Lewis Atherton, *Main Street on the Middle Border* (Bloomington, Ind.: Indiana University Press, 1954), p. 320.
45. Horace B. Hawthorn, *The Sociology of Rural Life* (New York: Century Co., 1926), p. 381.
46. See, for example, Hawthorn, *The Sociology of Rural Life*, p. 422, and Edmund deS. Brunner, *The Growth of a Science: A Half-Century of Rural Sociological Research in the United States* (New York: Harper & Brothers, Publishers, 1957), pp. 16-17.
47. Hawthorn, *The Sociology of Rural Life*, p. 422.
48. Kolb and Brunner, "Rural Life," p. 522.
49. Hawthorn, *The Sociology of Rural Life*, pp. 178-79.
50. Kolb and Brunner, *A Study of Rural Society*, p. 526.
51. Cohn, *Combustion on Wheels*, pp. 178-79.
52. Elmer Davis, "The American at Leisure," in *America as Americans See It*, ed. Fred J. Ringel (New York: Harcourt, Brace and Company, 1932), pp. 211-12.
53. Bellamy Partridge, *Fill 'er Up!: The Story of Fifty Years of Motoring* (New York: McGraw-Hill Book Company, 1952), pp. 72-73.
54. Cited in Lincoln Highway Association, *The Lincoln Highway: The Story of A Crusade that Made Transportation History* (New York: Dodd, Mead & Company, 1935), pp. 4-5.
55. Frank Farrington in *Motor Life*, cited in "Some Snares and Delusions of Country Roads," *Literary Digest*, September 11, 1920, p. 101.
56. In earlier efforts, bicycle enthusiasts had been successful in erecting some signs, but that fad had ended by the turn of the century. (Charles Merz, *And Then Came Ford* [Garden City, N.Y.: Doubleday, Doran & Company, 1929], pp. 63-64.
57. Louise Closser Hale, *We Discover the Old Dominion* (New York: Dodd, Mead, & Company, Publishers, 1916), p. 161.
58. Dorothy Canfield, "Tourists Accommodated," *Country Gentleman*, June 1927, p. 82.

59. John Amid, "The New Game of Touring," *Country Gentleman*, July 25, 1925, p. 44.
60. Frank Presbrey, "Opening Up the 'Back Country,'" *Collier's*, January 15, 1910, p. 17. These establishments should not be confused with the summer resort hotels, which probably lost business as a result of the motor car. Their clientele could now commute back and forth between their own summer cottages and their town homes. (Frederick L. Allen, *The Big Change: America Transforms Itself, 1900-1950* [New York: Harper & Brothers Publishers, 1952], p. 127.)
61. Malcolm M. Willey and Stuart A. Rice, "The Agencies of Communication," in Report of the President's Research Committee on Social Trends, *Recent Social Trends in the United States*, p. 188.
62. Merrill Denison, *The Power to Go*, American Industries Series (Garden City, N.Y.: Doubleday & Company, Inc., 1956), p. 16, and figure from *Motor Camper and Tourist*, cited in National Automobile Chamber of Commerce, *Facts and Figures of the Automobile Industry: 1926 Edition*, (New York), p. 26.
63. M.B.D., "Tourists' Cabins on the Farm," *Rural New Yorker*, 89(1930):908.
64. Canfield, "Tourist Accommodated," p. 82.
65. Cohn, *Combustion on Wheels*, p. 216.
66. L. F. Kneipp, "Camping Sites in Public Parks and Forests," in *The Automobile: Its Province and Its Problems*, ed. Clyde L. King, *Annals of the American Academy of Political and Social Science*, 116 (November 1924): 63. This problem is discussed in more detail in the chapter on health.
67. Frank E. Brimmer, "The Nickel-and-Dime Stores of Nomadic America," *Magazine of Business*, August 1927, pp. 151-52.
68. Ibid., p. 152.
69. Ibid.
70. Willey and Rice, "The Agencies of Communication," pp. 187-88.
71. Hoffer, *Introduction to Rural Sociology*, p. 127.

NOTES TO *V. RELIGION*

1. Lewis Atherton, *Main Street on the Middle Border* (Bloomington, Ind.: Indiana University Press, 1954), p. 257.
2. E[dward] R. Eastman, *These Changing Times: A Story of Farm Progress during the First Quarter of the Twentieth Century*, with a foreword by L. H. Bailey (New York: Macmillan Company, 1927), p. 176.
3. Paul L. Vogt. *A Rural Survey in Southwestern Ohio*, Miami University Bulletin, Series 11, No. 8 (Oxford, Ohio: Miami University, 1913), p. 34.
4. Dwight Sanderson, *The Farmer and His Community*, The Farmer's Bookshelf (New York: Harcourt, Brace and Company, 1922), p. 123.
5. Walter Burr, *Small Towns: An Estimate of Their Trade and Culture* (New York: Macmillan Company, 1929), pp. 250-51.

6. U.S., Congress, Senate, *Report of the Country Life Commission: Message from the President of the United States Transmitting the Report of the Country Life Commission,* S. Doc. 705, 60th Cong., 2d sess., 1909, p. 61.
7. H[arlan] Paul Douglass and Edmund deS. Brunner, *The Protestant Church as a Social Institution* (New York: Harper and Brothers, for the Institute of Social and Religious Research, 1935), p. 85.
8. H. N. Morse and Edmund deS. Brunner, *The Town and Country Church in the United States: As Illustrated by Data from One Hundred Seventy-Nine Counties and by Intensive Studies of Twenty-Five* (New York: George H. Doran Company, 1923), pp. 56-57, and Douglass and Brunner, *The Protestant Church as a Social Institution,* pp. 40-41. Absolutely, however, country, village, and town churches all gained membership from 1920 to 1930; all except the country churches had done so from 1910 to 1920. (Edmund deS. Brunner and J[ohn] H. Kolb, *Rural Social Trends,* Recent Social Trends Monographs [New York: McGraw-Hill Book Company, 1933], p. 354.)
9. J[ohn] H. Kolb and Edmund deS. Brunner, *A Study of Rural Society: Its Organization and Changes* (Boston: Houghton Mifflin Company, 1935), pp. 465-66.
10. Arthur J. Vidich and Joseph Bensman, *Small Town in Mass Society: Class, Power and Religion in a Rural Community* (Princeton, N.J.: Princeton University Press, 1958), p. 231.
11. Warren H. Wilson, "What the Automobile Has Done To and for the Country Church," in *The Automobile: Its Province and Its Problems,* ed. Clyde L. King, *Annals of the American Academy of Political and Social Science,* 116 (November 1924): 85-86.
12. Kolb and Brunner, *A Study of Rural Society,* p. 465.
13. David Morgan, "As a Veteran Rural Pastor Sees It," *Christian Century* 42(1925):58. Morgan's observation that tenants "have no automobiles" is not supported by the available statistical data, cited in chapter 1 above.
14. Wilson, "What the Automobile Has Done to and for the Country Church," p. 83.
15. David L. Cohn, *Combustion on Wheels: An Informal History of the Automobile Age* (Boston: Houghton Mifflin Company, 1944), p. 191.
16. "From the Four Winds," *Motor Age,* August 3, 1916, p. 50.
17. Alva W. Taylor, "Moving the Country up to Town," *Christian Century* 40(1923):178.
18. Walter Burr in the *New York Christian Advocate,* cited in "Gas Chariots and Dead Churches," *Literary Digest,* February 28, 1925, p. 32.
19. O. R. Geyer, "Motorizing the Rural Church," *Scientific American,* May 14, 1921, pp. 385-87, 397.
20. Earl C. May, "My Town and the Motor Car," *Collier's,* January 3, 1925, p. 18.
21. Atherton, *Main Street on the Middle Border,* pp. 79-80.
22. Allen D. Albert, "The Social Influence of the Automobile," *Scribner's Magazine* 71 (June 1922): 687.
23. Cited by Robert S. Lynd and Helen Merrell Lynd, *Middletown: A Study in Modern American Culture*, A Harvest Book (New York: Harcourt, Brace & World, 1929), p. 260.

24. This "vastly improved regular attendance of Catholics living in the country at church services. For the most part Catholic churches ... [were] situated in the towns. . . ." (Edwin V. O'Hara, "The Catholic Experience," in *A Decade of Rural Progress*, ed. Benson Y. Landis and Nat T. Frame [Chicago: University of Chicago Press, for the American Country Life Association, 1928], p. 62.) It should be remembered, however, that Catholics were a definite minority in rural America.
25. Kolb and Brunner, *A Study of Rural Society*, p. 470.
26. Wilson, "What the Automobile Has Done to and for the Country Church," p. 85.
27. Ruth Suckow, *Country People* (New York: Alfred A. Knopf, 1924), pp. 97-98.
28. Atherton, *Main Street on the Middle Border*, p. 259.
29. Bellamy Partridge, *Excuse My Dust* (New York: Whittlesey House of McGraw-Hill Book Company, 1943), p. 134.
30. Louise Closser Hale, *We Discover the Old Dominion* (New York: Dodd, Mead, & Company, Publishers, 1916), pp. 335-36.
31. Harry T. Stock, "Over the Gasoline Trail," *Christian Century*, 45 (1928): 1073.
32. "Motor Cars and Sunday Observance," *Watchman-Examiner* 10 (1922): 519.
33. "After the Motor Car 'Got Religion,'" *Motor Age*, October 30, 1919, p. 40.
34. See, for example, Newell L. Sims, *Elements of Rural Sociology*, Crowell's Social Science Series (New York: Thomas Y. Crowell Company, Publishers, 1928), p. 338; John M. Gillette, *Rural Sociology* (New York: Macmillan Company, 1923), p. 440; and Sanderson, *The Farmer and His Community*, p. 126.
35. Cohn, *Combustion on Wheels*, p. 194.
36. Cited in Eastman, *These Changing Times*, p. 189.
37. John H. Mueller, "The Automobile: A Sociological Study" (Ph.D. diss., University of Chicago, 1928), p. 171.
38. Gilman M. Ostrander, *American Civilization in the First Machine Age, 1890-1940* (New York: Harper & Row, Publishers, 1970), p. 45.
39. Frederick L. Allen, *Only Yesterday: An Informal History of the Nineteen-Twenties* (New York: Harper & Brothers Publishers, 1931), pp. 88-89.
40. H.T.P., "The Return of the Horse," *Bookman* 13 (July 1901): 427. In the same vein, the Dunkards, a German Baptist sect, forbade its members to drive motor cars because they made the user feel "high minded, superior and puffed up." In addition, they felt that automotive use was contrary to the lessons of the Bible. (Cited in "Dunkards Wrestle with the Motor Car Problem," *Motor Age*, June 18, 1914, p. 13.)
41. Edward A. Ross, "Folk Depletion as A Cause of Rural Decline," in *The Sociology of Rural Life,* ed. Scott E. W. Bedford, *Publications of the American Sociological Society* 11 (March 1917): 23-24.
42. Frederick L. Allen, *The Big Change: America Transforms Itself, 1900-1950* (New York: Harper & Brothers Publishers, 1952), p. 123.

43. John Keats, *The Insolent Chariots* (Philadelphia: J. B. Lippincott Company, 1958), p. 70.
44. Albert Blumenthal, *Small-Town Stuff*, University of Chicago Sociological Series (Chicago: University of Chicago Press, 1932), p. 251.
45. Eastman, *These Changing Times*, p. 207.
46. Lynd and Lynd, *Middletown*, pp. 137-38.
47. Blumenthal, *Small-Town Stuff*, p. 256.
48. Cited in National Automobile Chamber of Commerce, *Facts and Figures of the Automobile Industry: 1930 Edition* (New York), p. 8.
49. Cited in Automobile Manufacturers Association, *Automobiles of America*, A Savoyard Book, 2nd ed., rev. (Detroit: Wayne State University Press, 1968), p. 70, and Floyd Clymer, *Treasury of Early American Automobiles, 1877-1925* (New York: Bonanza Books, 1950), p. 105.
50. Floyd Clymer, *Henry's Wonderful Model T, 1908-1927* (New York: Bonanza Books, 1955), p. 27.
51. Cited in Blumenthal, *Small-Town Stuff*, p. 246.
52. See, for instance, Thomas D. Clark's description of changing feminine styles in his *Pills, Petticoats and Plows: The Southern Country Store* (Norman, Okla.: University of Oklahoma Press, 1964), pp. 169-70.
53. Cited in Merrill Denison, *The Power to Go*, American Industries Series (Garden City, N.Y.: Doubleday & Company, 1956), p. 185.
54. Christy Borth, "He 'Liberated the Women,'" *Think* 12 (December 1946): 30 [National Automotive Jubilee Edition].
55. Lynd and Lynd, *Middletown*, p. 258.
56. Cited in Atherton, *Main Street on the Middle Border*, p. 273.
57. Cohn, *Combustion on Wheels*, pp. 224-25.
58. Atherton, *Main Street on the Middle Border*, pp. 39-40.
59. Stewart H. Holbrook, *Murder Out Yonder: An Informal Study of Certain Classic Crimes in Back-Country America* (New York: Macmillan Company, 1941), p. 69.
60. Chet Shafer, "The Old Livery Stable," *Saturday Evening Post*, February 5, 1927, p. 158.
61. Cited by Hermann N. Morse, "Report of the Committee on Communications and Transportation on Activities of National Religious Organizations," in American Country Life Association, *Religion in Country Life: Proceedings of the Seventh National Country Life Conference, Columbus, Ohio, 1924* (Chicago, 1925), p. 194.
62. J[esse] F. Steiner, "Recreation and Leisure Time Activities," in Report of President's Research Committee on Social Trends, *Recent Social Trends in the United States*, with a foreword by Herbert Hoover, 1-vol. ed. (New York: McGraw-Hill Book Company, 1933), p. 945.
63. Joseph K. Hart, "The Automobile in the Middle Ages," *Survey* 54 (1925): 497.

NOTES TO *VI. EDUCATION*

1. Carl C. Taylor, *Rural Sociology: In Its Economic, Historical, and Psychological Aspects*, rev. ed. (New York: Harper & Brothers, Publishers, 1933), p. 404.
2. Ibid., and Report of the President's Research Committee on Social Trends, *Recent Social Trends in the United States*, with a foreword by Herbert Hoover, 1-vol. ed. (New York: McGraw-Hill Book Company, 1933), p. xxxix.
3. E[dward] R. Eastman, *These Changing Times: A Story of Farm Progress during the First Quarter of the Twentieth Century*, with a foreword by L. H. Bailey (New York: Macmillan Company, 1927), pp. 140-41.
4. Dwight Sanderson, *The Farmer and His Community*, The Farmer's Bookshelf (New York: Harcourt, Brace and Company, 1922), p. 91.
5. Edmund deS. Brunner, *Village Communities*, American Village Studies of the Institute of Social and Religious Research (New York: George H. Doran Company, 1927), p. 34.
6. Ray P. Snyder, cited in Eastman, *These Changing Times*, pp. 134-35.
7. Walter Burr, *Rural Organization* (New York: Macmillan Company, 1921), pp. 144-45.
8. Ernest Burnham, *Two Types of Rural Schools: With Some Facts Showing Economic and Social Conditions* (New York: Teachers College, Columbia University, 1912), p. 65.
9. C. W. Stone, "Do We Want the County as the School District?," *Journal of Rural Education* 2 (March 1923): 311, 313.
10. U.S. Department of the Interior, Bureau of Education, *Consolidation of Schools and Transportation of Pupils*, by J[ames] F. Abel, Bulletin No. 41 (Washington, D.C.: Government Printing Office, 1923), p. 17.
11. John M. Foote, "A Comparative Study of Instruction in Consolidated and One-Teacher Schools," *Journal of Rural Education* 2 (April 1923): 350-51.
12. Theodore Macklin, W. E. Grimes, and J[ohn] H. Kolb, *Making the Most of Agriculture* (Boston: Ginn and Company, 1927), pp. 460-61.
13. George H. Reavis, *Factors Controlling Attendance in Rural Schools* (New York: Teachers College, Columbia University, 1920), pp. 21-22.
14. Cited in U.S. Department of the Interior, Bureau of Education, *Consolidation of Rural Schools and Transportation of Pupils at Public Expense*, by A[rthur] C. Monahan, Bulletin No. 30 (Washington, D.C.: Government Printing Office, 1914), p. 44.
15. T. L. Head, Jr., "Transportation of School Children in Montgomery County, Alabama," *Journal of Rural Education* 2 (December-January 1922-23): 160.
16. John M. Gillette, *Rural Sociology* (New York: Macmillan Company, 1923), p. 405.
17. J[ohn] H. Kolb and Edmund deS. Brunner, "Rural Life," in President's Research Committee on Social Trends, *Recent Social Trends in the United States*, with a foreword by Herbert Hoover, 1-vol. ed. (New York: McGraw-Hill Book Company, 1933), p. 507.
18. See, for example, Joseph A. Baer, "Transportation of Pupils in Cuyhoga

County, Ohio," *Journal of Rural Education* 5 (September-October 1925): 16.
19. U.S. Department of the Interior, Bureau of Education, *Consolidation of Schools*, p. 35.
20. "Transportation Problems in Massachusetts," *Journal of Rural Education* 5 (September-October 1925): 24.
21. Macy Campbell, *Rural Life at the Crossroads* (Boston: Ginn and Company, 1927), p. 398.
22. Edward B. Mitchell, "The American Farm Woman as She Sees Herself," in U.S. Department of Agriculture, *Yearbook, 1914* (Washington, D.C.: Government Printing Office, 1915), pp. 315-316.
23. Campbell, *Rural Life at the Crossroads*, p. 396.
24. T. L. Head, Jr., "Transportation of School Children in Montgomery County, Alabama," p. 165.
25. "Transportation Problems in Massachusetts," pp. 25-26, and U.S. Department of Agriculture, Office of the Secretary, *Educational Needs of Farm Women*, Report No. 105 (Washington, D.C.: Government Printing Office, 1915), p. 11.
26. Cited in Ellwood P. Cubberly and Edward C. Elliott, eds., *State and County School Administration*, vol. 2: *Sourcebook* (New York: Macmillan Company, 1915), p. 271.
27. Cited in "Everyday Questions on Transportation of Pupils," *Journal of Rural Education* 5 (September-October 1925): 21.
28. Thomas R. Miller, "Some Social Implications of the Central Rural Schools of New York State" (Ph.D. diss., Syracuse University, 1938), p. 198.
29. Campbell, *Rural Life at the Crossroads*, p. 413.
30. Reavis, *Factors Controlling Attendance*, pp. 13-14.
31. U.S. Department of the Interior, Office of Education, *Availability of Public School Education in Rural Communities*, by W[alter] H. Gaummitz, Bulletin No. 34 (Washington, D.C.: Government Printing Office, 1930), p. 30.
32. John B. Rae, *The American Automobile: A Brief History*, Chicago History of American Civilization (Chicago: University of Chicago Press, 1965), pp. 196-97.
33. Reavis, *Factors Controlling Attendance*, p. 14.
34. Campbell, *Rural Life at the Crossroads*, p. 410.
35. Taylor, *Rural Sociology*, p. 569.
36. Wilbert L. Anderson, *The Country Town: A Study of Rural Evolution*, with an introduction by Josiah Strong (New York: Baker & Taylor Co., 1906), p. 253.
37. Sanderson, *The Farmer and His Community*, p. 92.
38. J[ohn] H. Kolb and Edmund deS. Brunner, *A Study of Rural Society: Its Organization and Changes* (Boston: Houghton Mifflin Company, 1935), p. 396.
39. Campbell, *Rural Life at the Crossroads*, pp. 347-48.
40. Sanderson, *The Farmer and His Community*, p. 93.
41. U.S. Department of the Interior, Bureau of Education *Consolidation of Schools*, pp. 39-40.
42. Edgar W. Knight, "Fundamental Needs of the Country School," in *The*

Country Life of the Nation, ed. Wilson Gee (Chapel Hill: University of North Carolina Press, 1930), pp. 143-44.

43. U.S. Department of the Interior, Bureau of Education, *Rural School Supervision*, by Katherine M. Cook and A[rthur] C. Monahan, Bulletin No. 48 [1916] (Washington, D.C.: Government Printing Office, 1917), pp. 31-32.

44. E. W. Ireland, "Supervising the One Teacher School," *Journal of Rural Education* 3 (May-June 1924): 415-16.

45. Hattie S. Parrott, "Rural School Supervision in North Carolina," *Journal of Rural Education* 5 (January-February 1926): 223-24.

46. John W. Studebaker, "The Automobile and Rural Education," *Think* 12 (December 1946): 29 [National Automobile Jubilee Edition].

47. LeRoy A. King, "Consolidation of Schools and Pupil Transportation — The Use of the Automobile in Education," in *The Automobile: Its Province and Its Problems*, ed. Clyde L. King, *Annals of the American Academy of Political and Social Science* 116 (November 1924): 79.

48. Brunner, *Village Communities*, pp. 52-53.

49. Albert L. Clough, "The Educative Value of the Automobile," *Horseless Age* 13 (1904): 424.

50. C. H. Claudy, "Building Character with a Motor Car," *Country Life in America* 24 (August 1913): 82.

51. "From the Four Winds," *Motor Age*, March 26, 1914, p. 37.

52. "High School Adds 2-Year Automotive Course," *Motor Age*, February 15, 1923, p. 28.

53. U.S. Department of Agriculture, *Rural Libraries*, by Wayne C. Nason, Farmers' Bulletin No. 1559 (Washington, D.C.: Government Printing Office, 1928), p. 8.

54. Ibid., pp. 8-9. After the introduction of rural free delivery in 1896, books were available from libraries by parcel post. While this undoubtedly increased circulation, especially during periods of bad weather, it required a knowledge of particular volumes and their availability through the town library, and many farmers did not have this knowledge. (American Library Association, *Book Wagons: The County Library with Rural Book Delivery* [Chicago: American Library Association, 1922], p. 6.)

55. U.S. Department of Agriculture, *Rural Libraries*, p. 9.

56. Cited in J[ohn] H. Kolb and Edmund deS. Brunner, *A Study of Rural Society*, p. 448.

57. Sarah Askew, "Library Work in the Open Country," in *New Possibilities in Education*, ed. Ambrose L. Suhrie, *Annals of the American Academy of Political and Social Science* 67 (September 1916): 257.

58. Harriet C. Long, *County Library Service* (Chicago: American Library Association, 1925), p. 102.

59. Photograph of circular produced by the Wayne County (Michigan) Library, reproduced in Joseph L. Wheeler, *The Library and the Community: Increased Book Service through Library Publicity Based on Community Studies* (Chicago: American Library Association, 1924), p. 382.

60. American Library Association, *Book Wagons*, p. 4.

61. Long, *County Library Service*, p. 103.

62. Mary Anna Tarbell, *A Village Library in Massachusetts: The Story of Its Upbuilding*, Library Tract No. 8 (Boston: American Library Association Publishing Board, 1905), p. 9.
63. Long, *County Library Service*, pp. 164-65.
64. Milton J. Ferguson, "Getting Books to Farmers in California," *Bulletin of the American Library Association* 13 (July 1919): 139.
65. Askew, "Library Work," pp. 259-60.
66. Evelyn E. Tilton, "The Library in the Rural School," *Journal of Rural Education* 4 (December 1924): 167, and Llewellyn MacGarr, *The Rural Community* (New York: Macmillan Company, 1922), p. 214.
67. Anne M. Mulherson, "Rural Library Service to Multnomah County, Oregon," *Journal of Rural Education* 4 (April 1925): 374. It is interesting to note that "the first book cars were painted darker colors and did not have glass doors, so they usually were taken for the 'dead wagon' as the popular phrase went and often urged to pass on from the door where they had stopped." (Katherine Tappert, "The Automobile and the Traveling Library: The Book Wagon Service," in *The Automobile: Its Province and Its Problems*, ed. Clyde L. King, *Annals of the American Academy of Political and Social Science* 116 [November 1924]: 66.)
68. MacGarr, *Rural Community*, pp. 214, 216.
69. Wheeler, *Library and Community*, p. 383.
70. Ferguson, "Getting Books to Farmers," p. 139.
71. Nason, *Rural Libraries*, pp. 45-46.
72. Dalton Wylie, "Taking the Library to the People," *Country Life in America* 23 (March 1913): 66.
73. Askew, "Library Work," p. 259.
74. See, for example, the description of one Miss Hopkins of Sussex County, Delaware, in American Library Association, *Book Wagons*, p. 269.
75. Irma M. Walker, "The Book Peddler Glorified," *Public Libraries* 25 (February 1920): 61. Similarly, Tappert refers to librarians knowing "the psychology of the borrowers." (Tappert, "The Automobile and the Traveling Library," p. 68.)
76. Ralph A. Felton and Marjorie Beal, *The Library of the Open Road*, Cornell Extension Bulletin No. 188 (Ithaca, N.Y.: New York State College of Agriculture at Cornell University, cooperating with the Library Extension Division of the New York State Department of Education, 1929), pp. 30, 32.
77. Ibid., p. 32.
78. Ferguson, "Getting Books to Farmers," p. 139.
79. U.S. Department of Agriculture, *County Agricultural Agent Work under the Smith-Lever Act, 1914-1924*, by William A. Lloyd, Miscellaneous Circular No. 59 (Washington, D.C.: Government Printing Office, 1926), p. 5.
80. M[aurice] C. Burritt, *The County Agent and the Farm Bureau*, The Farmer's Bookshelf (New York: Harcourt, Brace and Company, 1922), pp. 118-19.
81. U.S. Department of Agriculture, *Home Demonstration Work, 1922*, by Grace E. Frysinger, Department Circular No. 314 (Washington, D.C.: Government Printing Office, 1924), p. 20.

82. Bradford Knapp, "Education through Farm Demonstration," in *New Possibilities in Education*, ed. Ambrose L. Suhrie, *Annals of the American Academy of Political and Social Science* 67 (September 1916): 231.
83. Gillette, *Rural Sociology*, p. 344.
84. Eastman, *These Changing Times*, p. 9.
85. Warren H. Wilson, *The Evolution of the Country Community*, 2nd ed., rev. (Boston: Pilgrim Press, 1923), pp. 110-11.
86. Charles W. Holman, "The Social Goal of the Cooperative," in *Farm Income and Farm Life: A Symposium on the Relation of the Social and Economic Factors in Rural Progress*, ed. Dwight Sanderson (Chicago: University of Chicago Press, for the American Country Life Association, 1927), p. 245.
87. Benson Y. Landis, *Social Aspects of Farmers' Cooperative Marketing*, Federal Council of Churches of Christ in America, Department of Research and Education Bulletin No. 4 (Chicago: University of Chicago Press, for the Department of Research and Education, Federal Council of Churches of Christ in America, 1925), pp. 14-15.
88. Ibid., p. 14.

NOTES TO *VII. HEALTH AND THE ENVIRONMENT*

1. F. M. Crain, "The Auto as A Physician's Vehicle," in "Automobiles for Physicians' Use," *Journal of the American Medical Association* 46 (1906): 1172.
2. Dr. H. L. S., "The Automobile in My Business," *Horseless Age* 7 (1901): 23.
3. See, for example, M. G. Sloan, "An Iowa Experience," and A. A. Bondurant, "The Question of Roads," in "Automobiles for Physicians' Use," *Journal of the American Medical Association* 46 (1906): 1180.
4. Harry S. Kiskadden, "The Objections to the Use of the Horse," in "Automobiles for Physicians' Use," *Journal of the American Medical Association* 46 (1906): 1203.
5. Dr. H. L. S., "The Automobile in My Business," p. 21.
6. Arthur E. Hertzler, *The Horse and Buggy Doctor* (New York: Harper & Brothers, 1938), p. 65.
7. Ibid., pp. 71-72.
8. Theodore M. R. Von Kéler, "Suburban Changes and the Automobile," *Collier's*, January 8, 1916, p. 62.
9. Cited in John C. Long, "The Motor's Part in Public Health," in *The Automobile: Its Province and Its Problems*, ed. Clyde L. King, *Annals of the American Academy of Political Science* 116 (November 1924): 20-21.
10. Hertzler, *The Horse and Buggy Doctor*, p. 7.
11. Cited in Long, "The Motor's Part in Public Health," p. 19.
12. See, for instance, "Automobile Rides as A Consumption Cure," *Horseless Age* 13 (1904): 522.

13. Cited in David L. Cohn, *Combustion on Wheels: An Informal History of the Automobile Age* (Boston: Houghton Mifflin Company, 1944), p. 137. Recall in this regard the derivation of the term "flivver" discussed in chapter 1.
14. "The Healthfulness of Automobiling," *Horseless Age* 12 (1903): 420.
15. Langdon T. Snipe, "The Automobile in Maine," in "Automobiles for Physicians' Use," *Journal of the American Medical Association* 46 (1906): 1178.
16. Phoebe Cole, "The Auto Solves Some Household Problems," *American Home* 2 (June 1929): 345.
17. Charles P. Sylvester, "Statistics on Auto, Horse and Pulse," in "Automobiles for Physicians' Use," *Journal of the American Medical Association* 46 (1906): 1185.
18. Joseph A. Robertson, "From the Standpoint of the Large Machine," in "Automobiles for Physicians' Use," *Journal of the American Medical Association* 46 (1906): 1196.
19. Floyd Clymer, *Treasury of Early American Automobiles, 1877-1925* (New York: Bonanza Books, 1950), p. 102.
20. *Motor Age*, May 20, 1920, back cover, advertisement.
21. Reproduced in Clymer, *Treasury of Early American Automobiles*, p. 79.
22. *Motor Age*, September 14, 1911, p. 87, advertisement.
23. Edgar Sydenstricker, *Health and Environment*, Recent Social Trends Monographs (New York: McGraw-Hill Book Company, 1933), p. 167.
24. Ibid. These figures do not include deaths from collisions involving automobiles and railroad trains and automobiles and streetcars. They also fail to differentiate between rural and urban fatalities. On this latter point, those statistics that are available are inconclusive. A 1912 investigation in Massachusetts found that fewer accidents occurred on country roads than on town and city streets for the years 1908-1911. More important, the discrepancy increased with each succeeding year. ("Accidents in Bay State Probed by Investigators," *Motor Age*, [April 25, 1912], p. 23.) On the other hand, a 1925 survey by the National Automobile Chamber of Commerce revealed an increase of 23 percent in rural motor deaths as opposed to 10 percent for the country as a whole. ("Much Higher Rate for Increase in Rural Motor Fatalities than in Cities," *Motor Age*, August 26, 1926, p. 40.) Even if both sets of figures are correct, responsibility for the apparent deterioration in rural road safety remains unclear.
25. Reginald M. Cleveland and S. T. Williamson, *The Road Is Yours: The Story of the Automobile and the Men Behind It* (New York: Greystone Press, 1951), p. 70.
26. Louis Bromfield, *The Farm*, Harper's Modern Classics, ed. Winfield H. Rogers (New York: Harper & Brothers, Publishers, 1933), p. 220.
27. Albert Blumenthal, *Small-Town Stuff*, University of Chicago Sociological Series (Chicago: University of Chicago Press, 1932), pp. 374-75.
28. Samuel Eliot Morison, *The Oxford History of the American People* (New York: Oxford University Press, 1965), p. 891.
29. Lewis Mayers and Leonard V. Harrison, *The Distribution of Physicians in the United States* (New York: General Education Board, 1924), pp. 10-11.
30. Ibid., pp. 12-13.

31. Long, "The Motor's Part in Public Health," p. 20.
32. W. S. Rankin, "Rural Medical and Hospital Services," *American Journal of Public Health* 17 (January 1927): 18.
33. William A. Pusey, "The Disappearance of Doctors from Small Towns: Irregulars in Small Towns," *Journal of the American Medical Association* 88 (1927): 505.
34. Edmund deS. Brunner, *Village Communities*, American Village Studies of the Institute of Social and Religious Research (New York: George H. Doran Company, 1927), p. 65.
35. Samuel H. Adams, "The Vanishing Country Doctor," *Ladies' Home Journal*, October 1923, p. 180.
36. N. P. Colwell, cited in Harry H. Moore, *American Medicine and the People's Health: An Outline with Statistical Data on the Organization of Medicine in the United States with Special Reference to the Adjustment of Medical Service to Social and Economic Change* (New York: D. Appleton and Company, 1927), pp. 515-16.
37. Mayers and Harrison, *The Distribution of Physicians,* pp. 87-88.
38. Cited in Moore, *American Medicine and the People's Health*, pp. 138-39.
39. Samuel H. Adams, "Medically Helpless," *Ladies' Home Journal*, February 1924, p. 150.
40. Hertzler, *The Horse and Buggy Doctor*, pp. 251-52.
41. Charles R. Hoffer, *Introduction to Rural Sociology* (New York: Richard R. Smith, Inc., 1930), p. 113.
42. U.S. Department of Agriculture, *Rural Hospitals*, by Wayne C. Nason, Farmer's Bulletin No. 1485 (Washington, D.C.; Government Printing Office, 1926), pp. 9-10.
43. J[ohn] H. Kolb, *Service Institutions for Town and Country*, Research Bulletin No. 66 (Madison, Wisc.: University of Wisconsin Agricultural Experiment Station, 1925), p. 49.
44. Denver M. Vickers, "One Method of Bringing Metropolitan Service to Country Communities," *Transactions of the American Hospital Association* 26 (1924): 50-51.
45. Hertzler, *The Horse and Buggy Doctor*, p. 255.
46. Ibid.
47. Vickers, "One Method of Bringing Metropolitan Service to Country Communities," pp. 51-52.
48. Mayers and Harrison, *The Distribution of Physicians*, p. 119.
49. Cited by Adams, "Medically Helpless," p. 150. Although Dr. Billings is referring in this instance to Chicago, Adams assures the reader of his article that "it is quite as true of much country practice." (Ibid., p. 150.)
50. Mayers and Harrison, *The Distribution of Physicians*, p. 80.
51. Ibid., p. 35.
52. Newell L. Sims, *Elements of Rural Sociology*, Crowell's Social Science Series (New York: Thomas Y. Crowell Company, Publishers, 1928), p. 426.
53. A. D. Mueller, "The Health of Rural School Children," *Journal of Rural Education* 4 (November 1924): 110.
54. Harry H. Moore, *Public Health in the United States: An Outline with Statistical Data* (New York: Harper & Brothers Publishers, 1923), p. 253.

55. U.S. Department of Agriculture, *Rural Hospitals*, p. 8.
56. Moore, *Public Health in the United States*, p. 252.
57. Dwight Sanderson, *The Farmer and His Community*, The Farmer's Bookshelf (New York: Harcourt, Brace and Company, 1922), p. 99.
58. Annie M. Brainard, *The Evolution of Public Health Nursing* (Philadelphia: W. B. Saunders Company, 1922), p. 297.
59. Sanderson, *The Farmer and His Community*, p. 146.
60. Moore, *Public Health in the United States*, pp. 178-79.
61. F. Dennette Adams, "The North Carolina Extension Plan: An Experiment in Postgraduate Medical Teaching," *Journal of the American Medical Association* 80 (1923): 1717.
62. Clymer, *Treasury of Early American Automobiles*, p. 5.
63. Ellis P. Butler, "The Adventures of a Suburbanite, V: My Domesticated Automobile," *Country Life in America* 17 (February 1910): 417.
64. Cited in "From Physicians East and West," *Horseless Age* 7 (February 6, 1901): 27.
65. Cited in Allan Nevins, *Ford: The Times, the Man, the Company* (New York: Charles Scribner's Sons, 1954), p. 182.
66. Cited in "Reduction of Noise in Automobiles," *Scientific American*, April 11, 1903, p. 262.
67. "New Jersey" in Arthur C. Wyman, ed., *Automobile Laws of the New England States, New York, New Jersey, and Pennsylvania*, Legislative Reference Bulletin No. 2 (Providence: E. L. Freeman, Company, State Printers for the Legislative Reference Bureau of the Rhode Island State Library, 1908), p. 94.
68. Herbert H. Harrison, "Automobiles as A Social Factor," *American Homes & Gardens*, July 1915, p. 241.
69. Clyde B. Davis, *The Age of Indiscretion* (Philadelphia: J. B. Lippincott Company, 1950), p. 89.
70. Bellamy Partridge, *Excuse My Dust* (New York: McGraw-Hill Book Company, Whittlesey House, 1943), p. 144.
71. Logan W. Page, "The Motor Car and the Road: The Destructive Effect of High Speed," *Scientific American*, January 15, 1910, p. 46.
72. Cited by Mayers and Harrison, *The Distribution of Physicians*, pp. 80-81.
73. Harold W. Slauson, "The Automobile and the Smoke Nuisance," *Country Life in America* 21 (April 15, 1912): 48.
74. James H. Young, *The Toadstool Millionaires: A Social History of Patent Medicines in America before Federal Regulation* (Princeton, N.J.: Princeton University Press, 1961), p. 112.
75. E[rnest] S. Turner, *The Shocking History of Advertising!* (London: Michael Joseph Ltd., 1952), p. 259.
76. Cited in Frank Rowsome, Jr., *The Verse by the Side of the Road: The Story of the Burma-Shave Signs and Jingles* (Brattleboro, Vt.: Stephen Greene Press, 1965), p. 42. This needs to be qualified by two facts. First, although Burma-Shave erected their first signs in 1925, the typical jingle did not appear until 1929. (Ibid., p. 14.) Second, because of the success of the jingles, the Burma-Shave signs may have elicited a special type of affection that earlier advertising signs on rural property did not.

77. Frank Presbrey, *The History and Development of Advertising* (Garden City, N.Y.: Doubleday & Company, 1929), p. 503.
78. "Motor Age's Picture Pages of Automotive Interest," *Motor Age*, May 17, 1923, p. 27.
79. Cited in "Post No Bills Here," *Motor Age*, March 15, 1917, p. 32.
80. "Outlawed Signs Being Torn Down," *Horseless Age* 28 (1911): 360.
81. Presbrey, *History and Development of Advertising*, p. 504.
82. Ibid.
83. "Horseless Carriages and Sanitation," *Scientific American*, January 18, 1896, p. 36.
84. J. C. F., "The Passing of the Horse," *Horseless Age* 10 (1902): 218.
85. Earl C. May, "My Town and the Motor Car," *Collier's*, January 3, 1925, p. 17.
86. "Good Roads and Good Health are Allied Benefits," *Motor Age*, April 6, 1914, p. 15.
87. A. J. Chesley, "The Automobile as A Public Health Hazard," *American Journal of Public Health* 14 (November 1924): 918.
88. Long, "The Motor's Part in Public Health," p. 19.
89. "State Assumes Sanitary Control of Tourists Camps," *Motor Age*, July 20, 1922, p. 39.

NOTES TO *VIII. CONCLUSION*

1. George E. Mowry, *The Urban Nation, 1920-1960*, vol. 6 of *The Making of America*, ed. David Donald, 6 vols. (New York: Hill and Wang, 1965-68), p. 17.
2. Robert S. Lynd and Helen Merrell Lynd, *Middletown: A Study in Modern American Culture*, A Harvest Book (New York: Harcourt, Brace & World, Inc., 1929), pp. 499-500.
3. J[ohn] H. Kolb and Edmund deS. Brunner, *A Study of Rural Society: Its Organization and Changes* (Boston: Houghton Mifflin Company, 1935), p. 577.
4. John M. Gillette, "The Social Effects of Improved Communication in Country Life," in National Country Life Association, *Proceedings of the First National Country Life Conference, Baltimore, 1919,* (Ithaca, N.Y.), p. 148.
5. Burl Noggle, "The Twenties: A New Historiographical Frontier," *Journal of American History* 53 (September 1966): 307.
6. Wayne E. Fuller, *RFD: The Changing Face of Rural America* (Bloomington, Ind.: Indiana University Press, 1964), pp. 282-83.
7. Wilbert L. Anderson, *The Country Town: A Study of Rural Evolution*, with an introduction by Josiah Strong (New York: Baker & Taylor Co., 1906), pp. 209-10.
8. R[oderick] D. McKenzie, "The Rise of Metropolitan Communities," in Report of the President's Research Committee on Social Trends, *Recent Social Trends in the United States*, with an introduction by Herbert Hoover, 1-vol. ed. (New York: McGraw-Hill Book Company, 1933), p. 444.

9. Gillette, "Social Effects of Improved Communication," pp. 147-48.
10. Walter Burr, *Small Towns: An Estimate of Their Trade and Culture* (New York: Macmillan Company, 1929), p. 96.
11. Lynd and Lynd, *Middletown*, p. 251.

Bibliography

ARTICLES

"Accidents in Bay State Probed by Investigators." *Motor Age*, April 25, 1912, pp. 23-24.

Adams, F. Dennette. "The North Carolina Extension Plan: An Experiment in Postgraduate Medical Teaching." *Journal of the American Medical Association* 80 (1923): 1714-17.

Adams, Samuel H. "Medically Helpless." *Ladies' Home Journal*, February 1924, p. 31.

_____. "The Vanishing Country Doctor." *Ladies' Home Journal*, October 1923, p. 23.

"After the Motor Car 'Got Religion.'" *Motor Age*, October 30, 1919, pp. 39-40.

Albert, Allen D. "The Social Influence of the Automobile." *Scribner's Magazine* 71 (1922): 685-88.

"American Farmers Potential Market for 8,500,000 Cars in Ten Years." *Automotive Industries* 42 (1920): 1199.

Amid, John. "The New Game of Touring." *Country Gentleman*, July 25, 1925, p. 8.

Anderson, George W. "Roads — Motor and Rail." *Atlantic Monthly* 135 (1925): 393-404.

"Auto Shooting in South Carolina." *Horseless Age* 15 (1905): 323.

"Automobile Legislation in the United States." *Horseless Age* 10 (1922): 505-11.

"Automobile Notes." *Scientific American*, January 15, 1910, p. 64.

"Automobile Rides as A Consumption Cure." *Horseless Age* 13 (1904): 522.

"Automobiles Conspicuous at State Fair." *Horseless Age* 30 (1912): 354.

"Automobiles for Physicians' Use." *Journal of the American Medical Association* 46 (1906): 1172-1207.

"Automobiles on Farms Almost Equal Telephones in Number." *Automotive Industries* 47 (1922): 276-77.

Baer, Joseph A. "Transportation of Pupils in Cuyahoga County, Ohio." *Journal of Rural Education* 5 (September-October 1925): 16-21.

Bedford, Scott E. W., ed. *The Sociology of Rural Life. Publications of the American Sociological Society* 11 (March 1917).

Borth, Christy. "He 'Liberated the Women.'" *Think*, National Automobile Jubilee Edition, (December 1946): p. 30.

Brimmer, Frank E. "The Nickel-and-Dime Stores of Nomadic America." *Magazine of Business*, August 1927, p. 151.

Bruce, Robert. "Place of the Automobile." *Outing* 37 (October 1900): 65-69.

Butler, Ellis P. "The Adventures of A Suburbanite. V: My Domesticated Automobile." *Country Life in America* 17 (1910): 417-19.

Canfield, Dorothy. "Tourists Accommodated." *Country Gentleman*, June 1927, p. 23.

Chase, Edwin P. "Forty Years of Main Street." *Iowa Journal of History and Politics* 34 (July 1936): 227-61.

Chesley, A. J. "The Automobile as A Public Health Hazard." *American Journal of Public Health* 14 (November 1924): 917-20.

Clancy, Eugene A. "The Car and the Country House." *Harper's Weekly*, May 6, 1911, p. 30.

Claudy, C. H. "Building Character with A Motor Car." *Country Life in America* 24 (August 1913): 80-84.

———. "Some Practical Points on Motor Touring." *Country Life in America* 19 (January Mid-Month 1911): 248-50.

———. "The Woman and Her Car." *Country Life in America* 23 (January 1913): 41-42.

Clough, Albert L. "The Educative Value of the Automobile." *Horseless Age* 13 (1904): 423-24.

Cole, Phoebe. "The Auto Solves Some Household Problems." *American Home* 2 (1929): 345.

Colwell, M. Worth. "The Worst Roads in America." *Outing* 51 (1907): 246-49.

Crossman, Edward C. "The Gasoline Horse in the West." *Scientific American*, January 5, 1918, p. 17.

M. B. D. "From New York to West Virginia." *Rural New Yorker* 81 (December 30, 1922): 1526; 82 (January 6, 1923): 82; 82 (January 13, 1923): 44.

———. "Tourists' Cabins on the Farm." *Rural New Yorker* 89 (1930): 908.

Dodge, Henry I. "Transportation and the Cost of Living." *Country Gentleman*, February 22, 1919, p. 24.

Dorner, Otto. "Good Roads and State Aid." *Forum*, 26 (1899): 668-72.

Draper, George O. "Advice from A Horse Driver." *Horseless Age* 14 (1904): 608-9.

Duckwall, W. E. "Why the Car Driver 'Moves On.'" *Rural New Yorker* 76 (1917): 188.

"Dunkards Wrestle with the Motor Car Problem." *Motor Age*, June 18, 1914, p. 13.

"Educating the Farmer-Motorist." *Motor Age*, March 18, 1915, p. 12.
"Efficiency Chart." *Journal of Rural Education* 4 (November 1924): 137.
"Everyday Questions on Transportation of Pupils." *Journal of Rural Education* 5 (September-October 1925): 21-23.
J. C. F. "The Passing of the Horse." *Horseless Age* 10 (1902): 218.
"Farmer Buying Power Much Higher than It Was in 1914." *Automotive Industries* 48 (1923): 21.
"Farmer Spends $65 Year in Owning Car." *Automotive Industries* 49 (1923): 1071.
"Farmers and Roads." *Motor Age*, February 9, 1911, p. 10.
Ferguson, Ernest L. "The Rural Motor Vehicle: What Gasoline Means in Agriculture." *Scientific American*, February 10, 1912, p. 133.
Ferguson, Milton J. "Getting Books to Farmers in California." *Bulletin of the American Library Association* 13 (July 1919): 137-40.
Flint, W. P. "The Automobile and Wild Life." *Science* 63, n. s. (1926): 426-27.
Foote, John M. "A Comparative Study of Instruction in Consolidated and One-Teacher Schools." *Journal of Rural Education* 2 (April 1923): 337-51.
"Ford Parts for All Garages." *Motor Age*, January 2, 1919, p. 15.
French, L. E. "A White Mountain Tour." *Horseless Age* 14 (1904): 336-39; 363-66.
"From Physicians East and West." *Horseless Age* 7 (1901): 26-38.
"From the Four Winds." *Motor Age*, September 10, 1908, pp. 28-29.
"From the Four Winds." *Motor Age*, October 28, 1908, pp. 36-37.
"From the Four Winds." *Motor Age*, December 4, 1913, p. 46.
"From the Four Winds." *Motor Age*, March 26, 1914, pp. 36-37.
"From the Four Winds." *Motor Age*, August 3, 1916, p. 50.
"Gas Chariots and Dead Churches." *Literary Digest*, February 28, 1925, pp. 31-32.
Geyer, O. R. "Motorizing the Rural Church." *Scientific American*, May 14, 1921, p. 385.
"Good Roads and Good Health Are Allied Benefits." *Motor Age*, April 6, 1914, p. 15.
Harger, Charles M. "The Automobile in Western Country Towns." *World Today* 13 (1907): 1277-80.
_____. "Automobiles for Country Use." *Independent* 70 (1911): 1207-11.
_____. "The Country Store." *Atlantic Monthly* 95 (1905): 91-98.
Harrison, Herbert H. "Automobile as A Social Factor." *American Homes and Gardens*, July 1915, p. 239.
Hart, Joseph K. "The Automobile in the Middle Ages." *Survey* 54 (1925): 493-97.
"Hawkeye Speeds Up; Buys A Buggy." *Motor Age*, February 23, 1922, p. 30.
Head, T. L., Jr. "Transportation of School Children in Montgomery County, Alabama." *Journal of Rural Education* 2 (December-January 1922-23): 159-66.
"The Healthfulness of Automobiling." *Horseless Age* 12 (1903): 420.

"High School Adds 2-Year Automotive Course." *Motor Age*, February 15, 1923, p. 28.

Hitchcock, A. P. "The Joys of Being A Farmer." *Country Life in America* 20 (1911): 46-52.

Holmes, Roy H. "The Passing of the Farmer." *Atlantic Monthly* 110 (1912): 517-23.

Horseless Age 5 (1900): 5, advertisement.

"Horseless Carriages and Sanitation." *Scientific American*, January 1, 1896, p. 36.

"How Many American People Can Afford Automobiles." *Current Opinion* 72 (February 1922): 264-65.

"How Many More Motor Cars Have We Room For?" *Literary Digest*, October 7, 1922, pp. 60-63.

Howard, James R. "'Automobiles Increase Agricultural Production.'" *Automotive Industries* 47 (1922): 112-13.

"Iowa Repeals Ruling for Nervous Horses." *Automotive Industries* 52 (1925): 885.

Ireland, E. W. "Supervising the One Teacher School." *Journal of Rural Education* 3 (May-June 1924): 414-22.

"Is this Eggsactly Right?" *Motor Age*, December 28, 1916, p. 15.

Kèler, Theodore M. R. Von. "The Farmer and the Motor Car." *Collier's*, supplement, January 9, 1915, p. 34.

———. "Suburban Changes and the Automobile." *Collier's*, January 8, 1916, pp. 60-62.

King, Clyde L., ed. *The Automobile: Its Province and Its Problems. Annals of the American Academy of Political and Social Science* 116 (November 1924).

King, Clyde L., and Tichenor, Frank A., eds. *The Motion Picture in Its Economic and Social Aspects. Annals of the American Academy of Political and Social Science*, 128 (November 1926).

Langford, Walter. "What the Motor Car Is Doing for the Farmer." *Scientific American*, January 15, 1910, pp. 50-51.

Lichtenberger, J. P., ed. *Country Life. Annals of the American Academy of Political and Social Science* 40 (March 1912).

Long, J. C. "Passing of the Hick." *Outlook* 126 (1920): 425-29.

McMahon, John R. "Our Jazz-Spotted Middle West: Small Towns and Rural Districts Need Clean-Up as well as Chicago and Kansas City." *Ladies' Home Journal*, February 1922, p. 38.

May, Earl C. "My Town and the Motor Car." *Collier's*, January 3, 1925, pp. 17-18.

Milburn, George. "Catalogues and Culture." *Good Housekeeping*, April 1946, pp. 181-84.

"The Modern Car and Its Work." *Rural New Yorker* 83 (1924): 906.

Moore, Hollister. "Marketing Data." *Automotive Industries* 42 (1930): 263-68.

Morgan, David. "As A Veteran Rural Pastor Sees It." *Christian Century* 42 (1925): 58.

Morris, C. O. "The Farmer and the Automobile." *Country Life in America* 15 (1909): 636.

———. "The Truth about the Automobile." *Country Life in America* 15 (1909): 259-60.

Motor Age, September 14, 1911, p. 87, advertisement.

Motor Age, May 20, 1920, back cover, advertisement.

"Motor Age's Picture Pages of Automotive Interest." *Motor Age*, August 24, 1922, pp. 26-27.

"The Motor Car and Country Life." *Craftsman*, May 1911, p. 227.

"Motor Cars and Sunday Observance." *Watchman-Examiner* 10 (1922): 519.

"Motor Mail Is Planned." *Motor Age*, January 10, 1918, p. 20.

"Motor Posse Runs Down A Murderer in Nebraska." *Motor Age*, October 8, 1914, p. 15.

"Mount Desert Now Open to Automobiles." *Horseless Age* 35 (1915): 558.

"Much Higher Rates for Increase in Rural Motor Fatalities than in Cities." *Motor Age*, August 26, 1926, p. 40.

Mueller, A. D. "The Health of Rural School Children." *Journal of Rural Education* 4 (November 1924): 106-13.

Mulherson, Anne M. "Rural Library Service to Multnomah County, Oregon." *Journal of Rural Education* 4 (April 1925): 374-75.

"Nantucket's Losing Fight against the Motor-Car." *Literary Digest*, April 30, 1921, pp. 48-51.

Noggle, Burl. "The Twenties: A New Historiographical Frontier." *Journal of American History* 53 (September 1966): 299-314.

"One More Revolution." *Independent* 55 (1903): 1162-64.

"Outlawed Signs Being Torn Down." *Horseless Age* 28 (1911): 360.

H. T. P. "The Return of the Horse." *Bookman* 13 (1901): 425-27.

Page, Logan W. "How Small Communities May Have Good Roads: The Value of Whole-Hearted Co-Operation." *Scientific American*, January 2, 1915, p. 14.

———. "The Motor Car and the Road: The Destructive Effect of High Speed." *Scientific American*, January 15, 1910, p. 46.

Parrott, Hattie S. "Rural School Supervision in North Carolina." *Journal of Rural Education* 5 (January-February 1926): 219-30.

Peck, H[arvey] W. "The Influence of Agriculture Machinery and the Automobile on Farming Operations." *Quarterly Journal of Economics* 41 (May 1927): 534-44.

Peck, Harvey W. "Civilization on Wheels." *Social Forces* 7 (December 1928): 300-9.

———. "The Economic Status of Agriculture." *Journal of Political Economy*, 34 (October 1926): 624-41.

Phillips, Madison R. "The Motor Car on the Farm." *Country Life in America* 19 (1911): 258-59.

Pierce, L. B. "The Ohio Farm Woman's Car." *Rural New Yorker* 78 (1919): 1804.

"Post No Bills Here." *Motor Age*, March 15, 1917, pp. 32-33.

Powers, Marsh K. "The Forgotten Fireside." *Outlook* 130 (1922): 608-11.

Presbrey, Frank. "Opening Up the 'Back Country.'" *Collier's*, January 15, 1910, pp. 16-17.

Pusey, William A. "The Disappearance of Doctors from Small Towns: Irregulars in Small Towns." *Journal of the American Medical Association* 88 (1927): 505-6.

Mrs. T. H. R. "A Day's Auto Outing in New England." *Horseless Age* 13 (1904): 553-54.

Rankin, W. S. "Rural Medical and Hospital Services." *American Journal of Public Health* 17 (January 1927): 15-19.

"Reduction of Noise in Automobiles." *Scientific American*, April 11, 1903, p. 262.

"The Return of the Glidden Tourists." *Horseless Age* 16 (1905): 151-53.

"Rights of Motor Vehicles." *Scientific American*, supplement, January 26, 1901, p. 20967.

"Roads — Good and Bad: How They Came to Be and What They Mean to the User." *Scientific American*, January 5, 1918, pp. 12-13.

Rural New Yorker 71 (1912): 577, advertisement.

Dr. H. L. S. "The Automobile in My Business." *Horseless Age* 7 (1901): 21-26.

Saviers, L. "A Michigan Outing." *Horseless Age* 13 (1904): 502-5.

Scott-Montagu, John. "Automobile Legislation: A Criticism and Review." *North American Review* 179 (August 1904): 168-77.

Shafer, Chet. "The Old Livery Stable." *Saturday Evening Post*, February 5, 1927, p. 20.

Shidle, Norman G. "*The Small Town* — That's Where Biggest Automotive Market Lies." *Automotive Industries* 54 (1926): 397-99.

Slauson, Harold W. "The Automobile and the Smoke Nuisance." *Country Life in America*, 21 (April 15, 1912): 48.

"Some Leading Automobile Suits." *Horseless Age* 10 (1902): 512-13.

"Some Snares and Delusions of Country Roads." *Literary Digest*, September 11, 1920, pp. 101-5.

Speed, John G. "Modern Chariot." *Cosmopolitan*, June 1900, pp. 139-52.

"State Assumes Sanitary Control of Tourists Camps." *Motor Age*, July 20, 1922, p. 39.

Stock, Harry T. "Over the Gasoline Trail." *Christian Century* 45 (1928): 1073-74.

Stone, C. W. "Do We Want the County as the School District?" *Journal of Rural Education* 2 (March 1923): 311-14.

Stoner, Dayton. "Automobiles and Animal Mortality." *Science* 69, n.s. (January 28, 1929): 670-71.

———. "Toll of the Automobile." *Science* 61, n.s. (January 16, 1925): 56-57.

Studebaker, John W. "The Automobile and Rural Education." *Think*, National Automobile Jubilee Edition, December 1946, pp. 28-29.

Sturtevant, Ethel. "Living Off the Land." *Harper's Monthly Magazine* 154 (March 1927): 526-27.

Suhrie, Ambrose L., ed. *New Possibilities in Education. Annals of the American Academy of Political and Social Science* 67 (September 1916).

Sullivan, Lambert G. "Getting Your Story Across." *Motor Age*, June 10, 1920, pp. 7-10.

Taylor, Alva W. "Moving the Country up to Town." *Christian Century* 40 (1923): 177-78.

Tilton, Evelyn E. "The Library in the Rural School." *Journal of Rural Education* 4 (December 1924): 164-70.

"Transportation Problems in Massachusetts." *Journal of Rural Education* 5 (September-October, 1925): 23-27.

Vance, Truman, S. "Why Young Men Leave the Farms." *Independent* 70 (1911): 553-60.

Vickers, Denver M. "One Method of Bringing Metropolitan Service to Country Communities." *Transactions of the American Hospital Association* 26 (1924): 48-55.

Walker, Irma M. "The Book Peddler Glorified." *Public Libraries* 25 (February 1920): 55-61.

Welliver, Judson C. "The Automobile in Our Country." *Collier's*, January 8, 1916, pp. 70-74.

White, Lee Strout [E. B. White]. "Farewell, My Lovely!" *The New Yorker*, May 16, 1936, pp. 20-22.

Wilson, Charles M. "The Country Store Survives." *Outlook and Independent* 157 (1931): 142.

Wood, Quintan, and Cushing, Charles P. "The Return of the Bad Men: The Rural West Arms to Repel City Bank Raiders." *Country Gentleman*, June 1926, p. 8.

Wright, H. D. "The Whipper Whipped." *Horseless Age* 16 (1905): 298.

Wylie, Dalton. "Taking the Library to the People." *Country Life in America* 23 (March 1913): 66.

GOVERNMENT PUBLICATIONS

New York State, Crime Commission, Sub-Commission on Causes and Effects of Crime. *A Study of Delinquency in Two Rural Counties*. 1927 Legislative Document No. 94. Albany, N.Y.: J. B. Lyon Company, Printers, 1927.

U.S., Congress, Senate, *Report of the Country Life Commission: Special Message from the President of the United States Transmitting the Report of the Country Life Commission*. S. Doc. 705, 60th Cong., 2d sess., 1909.

U.S., Department of Agriculture. *County Agricultural Work under the Smith-Lever Act, 1914-1924,* by William A. Lloyd. Miscellaneous Circular No. 59. Washington, D.C.: Government Printing Office, 1926.

_____. *The Farm Woman's Problems*, by Florence E. Ward. Department Circular No. 148. Washington, D.C.: Government Printing Office, 1920.

_____. *Home Demonstration Work, 1922,* by Grace E. Frysinger. Department Circular No. 314. Washington, D.C.: Government Printing Office, 1924.

_____. *Rural Hospitals*, by Wayne C. Nason. Farmers' Bulletin No. 1485. Washington, D.C.: Government Printing Office, 1926.

_____. *Rural Libraries*, by Wayne C. Nason. Farmers' Bulletin No. 1559. Washington, D.C.: Government Printing Office, 1928.

———. *Yearbook, 1914.* Washington, D.C.: Government Printing Office, 1915.

U.S., Department of Agriculture. Office of the Secretary. *Educational Needs of Farm Women.* Report No. 105. Washington, D.C.: Government Printing Office, 1915.

———. *Social and Labor Needs of Farm Women.* Report No. 103. Washington, D.C.: Government Printing Office, 1915.

U.S., Department of Interior, Bureau of Education. *Consolidation of Rural Schools and Transportation of Pupils at Public Expense*, by A[rthur] C. Monahan. Bulletin No. 30. Washington, D.C.: Government Printing Office, 1914.

———. *Consolidation of Schools and Transportation of Pupils*, by J[ames] F. Abel. Bulletin No. 41. Washington, D.C.: Government Printing Office, 1923.

———. *Rural School Supervision*, by Katherine M. Cook and A[rthur] C. Monahan. Bulletin No. 48 [1916]. Washington, D.C.: Government Printing Office, 1917.

U.S., Department of Interior, Office of Education. *Availability of Public School Education in Rural Communities*, by W[alter] H. Gaummitz. Bulletin No. 34. Washington, D.C.: Government Printing Office, 1930.

U.S., Department of Labor, Children's Bureau, Dependent, Defective and Delinquent Classes. *Juvenile Delinquency in Rural New York*, by Kate H. Claghorn. Series No. 4, Bureau Publication No. 32. Washington, D.C.: Government Printing Office, 1918.

UNPUBLISHED MATERIAL

Bradley, James J. Letter to Michael L. Berger, April 7, 1971.

Hatch, David L. "Changes in the Structure and Function of A Rural New England Community since 1900." Ph.D. dissertation, Harvard University, 1948.

Miller, Thomas R. "Some Social Implications of the Central Rural Schools of New York State." Ph.D. dissertation, Syracuse University, 1938.

Mueller, John H. "The Automobile: A Sociological Study." Ph.D. dissertation, University of Chicago, 1928.

BOOKS

Allen, Frederick L. *The Big Change: America Transforms Itself, 1900-1950.* New York: Harper & Brothers Publishers, 1952.

———. *Only Yesterday: An Informal History of the Nineteen-Twenties.* New York: Harper & Brothers Publishers, 1931.

American Country Life Association. *Religion in Country Life: Proceedings of the Seventh National Country Life Conference, Columbus, Ohio, 1924.* Chicago: American Country Life Association, 1925.

American Library Association. *Book Wagons: The County Library with Rural Book Delivery.* Chicago: American Library Association, 1922.

Anderson, Rudolph E. *The Story of the American Automobile: Highlights and Sidelights.* Washington, D.C.: Public Affairs Press, 1950.

Anderson, Wilbert L. *The Country Town: A Study of Rural Evolution*. With an introduction by Josiah Strong. New York: Baker & Taylor Co., 1906.

Armstrong, Louise van Voorhis. *Good Roads: A Play in One Act*. New York: Samuel French, 1929.

Atherton, Lewis. *Main Street on the Middle Border*. Bloomington, Ind.: Indiana University Press, 1954.

Atkeson, Mary Meek. *The Woman on the Farm*. New York: Century Co., 1924.

Automobile Manufacturers Association, *Automobiles of America*. A Savoyard Book. 2nd rev. ed. Detroit: Wayne State University Press, 1968.

Barber, H. L. *Story of the Automobile: Its History and Development from 1760 to 1917, With An Analysis of the Standing and Prospects of the Automobile Industry*. Chicago: A. J. Munson & Co., 1917.

Blumenthal, Albert. *Small-Town Stuff*. University of Chicago Sociological Series. Chicago: University of Chicago Press, 1932.

Bowers, Q. David, ed. *Early American Car Advertisements*. New York: Bonanza Books, 1966.

Brainard, Annie M. *The Evolution of Public Health Nursing*. Philadelphia: W. B. Saunders Company, 1922.

Bromfield, Louis. *The Farm*. Harper's Modern Classics, edited by Winfield H. Rogers. New York: Harper & Brothers Publishers, 1933.

Brunner, Edmund deS. *The Growth of A Science: A Half-Century of Rural Sociological Research in the United States*. New York: Harper & Brothers Publishers, 1957.

_____. *Village Communities*. American Village Studies of the Institute of Social and Religious Research. New York: George H. Doran Company, 1927.

_____, and Kolb, J[ohn] H. *Rural Social Trends*. Recent Social Trends Monographs. New York: McGraw-Hill Book Company, 1933.

_____; Hughes, Gwendolyn S.; and Patten, Marjorie. *American Agricultural Villages*. American Village Studies of the Institute of Social and Religious Research. New York: George H. Doran Company, 1927.

Burnham, Ernest. *Two Types of Rural Schools: With Some Facts Showing Economic and Social Conditions*. New York: Columbia University Teachers College, 1912.

Burr, Walter. *Rural Organization*. New York: Macmillan Company, 1921.

_____. *Small Towns: An Estimate of Their Trade and Culture*. New York: Macmillan Company, 1929.

Burritt, M[aurice] C. *The County Agent and the Farm Bureau*. The Farmer's Bookshelf, edited by Kenyon L. Butterfield. New York: Harcourt, Brace and Company, 1922.

Campbell, Macy. *Rural Life at the Crossroads*. Boston: Ginn and Company, 1927.

Carson, Gerald. *The Old Country Store*. New York: Oxford University Press, 1954.

Chase, Harold B. *Auto-biography: Recollections of A Pioneer Motorist, 1896-1911*. New York: Pageant Press, 1955.

Clark, Thomas D. *Pills, Petticoats, and Plows: The Southern Country Store*. Norman, Okla.: University of Oklahoma Press, 1964.

Cleveland, Reginald M., and Williamson, S. T. *The Road Is Yours: The Story of the Automobile and the Men Behind It*. New York: Greystone Press, 1951.

Clymer, Floyd. *Henry's Wonderful Model T, 1908-1927*. New York: Bonanza Books, 1955.

_____. *Treasury of Early American Automobiles, 1877-1925*. New York: Bonanza Books, 1950.

Cohn, David L. *Combustion on Wheels: An Informal History of the Automobile Age*. Boston: Houghton Mifflin Company, 1944.

Croy, Homer. *R. F. D. No. 3*. New York: Harper & Brothers Publishers, 1924.

_____. *West of the Water Tower*. New York: Harper & Brothers Publishers, 1923.

Cubberly, Ellwood P., and Elliott, Edward C., eds. *State and County School Administration*. New York: Macmillan Company, 1915. Vol. 2, *Sourcebook*.

Davis, Clyde B. *The Age of Indiscretion*. Philadelphia: J. B. Lippincott Company, 1950.

Denison, Merrill. *The Power to Go*. American Industries Series. Garden City, N.Y.: Doubleday & Company, 1956.

Donovan, Frank. *Wheels for A Nation*. New York: Thomas Y. Crowell Company, 1965.

Douglass, H[arlan] Paul, and Brunner, Edmund deS. *The Protestant Church as A Social Institution*. New York: Harper and Brothers, for the Institute of Social and Religious Research, 1935.

Douglass, Harlan P. *The Little Town: Especially in Its Rural Relationships*. Rev. ed. New York: Macmillan Company, 1927.

_____. *The Suburban Trend*. New York: Century Co., 1925.

Eastman, E[dward] R. *These Changing Times: A Story of Farm Progress during the First Quarter of the Twentieth Century*. With a foreword by L. H. Bailey. New York: Macmillan Company, 1927.

Emmet, Boris, and Jeuck, John E. *Catalogues and Counters: A History of Sears, Roebuck and Company*. Chicago: University of Chicago Press, 1950.

Farrington, Frank. *More Talks by the Old Storekeeper*. Chicago: Byxbee Publishing Company, 1912.

Felton, Ralph A., and Beal, Marjorie. *The Library of the Open Road*. Cornell Extension Bulletin No. 188. Ithaca, N.Y.: New York State College of Agriculture at Cornell University in cooperation with the Library Extension Division of the New York State Department of Education, 1929.

Finger, Charles J. *Adventure under Sapphire Skies*. New York: William Morrow & Company, 1931.

Flink, James J. *America Adopts the Automobile, 1895-1910*. Cambridge, Mass.: MIT Press, 1970.

_____. *The Car Culture*. Cambridge, Mass.: MIT Press, 1975.

Fry, C. Luther. *American Villagers*. New York: George H. Doran Company, 1926.

Fuller, Wayne E. *RFD: The Changing Face of Rural America*. Bloomington, Ind.: Indiana University Press, 1964.

Galpin, Charles J. *Rural Life.* New York: Century Co., 1918.

———. *The Social Anatomy of A Rural Community.* Research Bulletin No. 34. Madison, Wisc.: University of Wisconsin Agricultural Experiment Station, 1914.

Gee, Wilson, ed. *The Country Life of the Nation.* Chapel Hill, N.C.: University of North Carolina Press, 1930.

Gillette, John M. *Rural Sociology.* New York: Macmillan Company, 1923.

Glasscock, C. B. *The Gasoline Age: The Story of the Men Who Made It.* Indianapolis: Bobbs-Merrill Company Publishers, 1937.

Griffin, C[lare] E. *The Life History of Automobiles.* Michigan Business Studies, vol. 1, no. 1. Ann Arbor, Mich.: Bureau of Business Research, Graduate School of Business Administration, University of Michigan, 1926.

Grimes, William A. *Financing Automobile Sales: By the Time-Payment Plan.* Chicago: A. W. Shaw Company, 1926.

Groves, Ernest R. *The Rural Mind and Social Welfare.* With a foreword by Kenyon L. Butterfield. Chicago: University of Chicago Press, 1922.

Hale, Louise Closser. *We Discover the Old Dominion.* New York: Dodd, Mead, & Company, Publishers, 1916.

Hanifan, L. J. *The Community Center.* Teacher Training Series, edited by W. W. Charters. Boston: Silver; Burdett & Company, 1920.

Hawthorn, Horace B. *The Sociology of Rural Life.* New York: Century Co., 1926.

Hertzler, Arthur E. *The Horse and Buggy Doctor.* New York: Harper & Brothers, 1938.

Hill, Ralph N. *The Mad Doctor's Drive: Being An Account of the 1st Auto Trip Across the United States of America, San Francisco to New York, 1903, or, Sixty-Three Days on a Winton Motor Carriage.* Brattleboro, Vt.: Stephen Greene Press, 1964.

Hoffer, Charles R. *Introduction to Rural Sociology.* New York: Richard R. Smith, Inc., 1930.

———. *Services of Rural Trade Centers in Distribution of Farm Supplies.* Bulletin No. 249. St. Paul: University of Minnesota Agricultural Experiment Station, 1928.

Holbrook, Stewart H. *Murder Out Yonder: An Informal Study of Certain Classic Crimes in Back-Country America.* New York: Macmillan Company, 1941.

Hulbert, Archer B., ed. *Historic Highways of America.* 16 vols. Cleveland: Arthur H. Clark Company, 1902-1905. Vol. 15, *The Future of Road-making in America: A Symposium,* edited by Archer B. Hulbert.

Janeway, Elizabeth. *The Early Days of Automobiles.* A Landmark Book. New York: Random House, 1956.

Keats, John. *The Insolent Chariots.* Philadelphia: J. B. Lippincott Company, 1958.

Kirschner, Don S. *City and Country: Rural Responses to Urbanization in the 1920s.* Westport, Conn.: Greenwood Publishing Company, Inc., 1970.

Kolb, J[ohn] H. *Service Institutions for Town and Country.* Research Bulletin No. 66. Madison, Wisc.: University of Wisconsin Agricultural Experiment Station, 1925.

———, and Brunner, Edmund deS. *A Study of Rural Society: Its Organization and Changes*. Boston: Houghton Mifflin Company, 1935.

Landis, Benson Y. *Social Aspects of Farmers' Cooperative Marketing*. Federal Council of Churches of Christ in America, Department of Research and Education Bulletin No. 4. Chicago: University of Chicago Press, for the Department of Research and Education, Federal Council of Churches of Christ in America, 1925.

———, and Frame, Nat T., eds. *A Decade of Rural Progress*. Chicago: University of Chicago Press, for the American Country Life Association, 1928.

Lewis, Sinclair. *Free Air*. New York: Harcourt, Brace and Howe, Inc., 1919.

Lincoln Highway Association. *The Lincoln Highway: The Story of A Crusade that Made Transportation History*. New York: Dodd, Mead & Company, 1935.

Long, Harriet C. *County Library Service*. Chicago: American Library Association, 1925.

Longstreet, Stephen. *The Boy in the Model T: A Journey in the Just Gone Past*. New York: Simon and Schuster, 1956.

Lynd, Robert S., and Lynd, Helen Merrill. *Middletown: A Study in Modern American Culture*. A Harvest Book. New York: Harcourt, Brace & World, 1929.

MacGarr, Llewellyn. *The Rural Community*. New York: Macmillan Company, 1924.

McKenzie, R[oderick] D. *The Metropolitan Community*. Recent Social Trends Monographs. New York: McGraw-Hill Book Company, 1933.

Macklin, Theodore; Grimes, W. E.; and Kolb, J[ohn] H. *Making the Most of Agriculture*. Boston: Ginn and Company, 1927.

Maxim, Hiram T. *Horseless Carriage Days*. New York: Harper & Brothers Publishers, 1937.

Mayers, Lewis, and Harrison, Leonard V. *The Distribution of Physicians in the United States*. New York: General Education Board, 1924.

Merz, Charles. *And Then Came Ford*. Garden City, N.Y.: Doubleday, Doran & Company, 1929.

Milburn, George. *Catalogue*. New York: Harcourt, Brace and Company, 1936.

Moline, Norman T. *Mobility and the Small Town, 1900-1930: Transportation Change in Oregon, Illinois*. Research Paper No. 132. Chicago: The University of Chicago Department of Geography, 1971.

Moore, Harry H. *American Medicine and the People's Health: An Outline with Statistical Data on the Organization of Medicine in the United States, With Special Reference to the Adjustment of Medical Service to Social and Economic Change*. New York: D. Appleton and Company, 1927.

———. *Public Health in the United States: An Outline with Statistical Data*. New York: Harper & Brothers Publishers, 1923.

Morison, Samuel E. *The Oxford History of the American People*. New York: Oxford University Press, 1965.

Morris, Lloyd R. *Not So Long Ago*. New York: Random House, 1949.

Morse, H. N., and Brunner, Edmund deS. *The Town and Country Church in the United States: As Illustrated by Data from One Hundred Seventy-Nine Counties and by Intensive Studies of Twenty-Five.* New York: George H. Doran Company, 1923.

Mowry, George E. *The Urban Nation, 1920-1960.* Vol. 6 of *The Making of America,* edited by David Donald. 6 vols. New York: Hill and Wang, 1965-1968.

National Automobile Chamber of Commerce. *Facts and Figures of the Automobile Industry.* New York: National Automobile Chamber of Commerce, 1922.

———. *Facts and Figures of the Automobile Industry: 1925 Edition.* New York: National Automobile Chamber of Commerce, 1925.

———. *Facts and Figures of the Automobile Industry: 1926 Edition.* New York: National Automobile Chamber of Commerce, 1926.

———. *Facts and Figures of the Automobile Industry: 1927 Edition.* New York: National Automobile Chamber of Commerce, 1927.

———. *Facts and Figures of the Automobile Industry: 1929 Edition.* New York: National Automobile Chamber of Commerce, 1929.

———. *Facts and Figures of the Automobile Industry: 1930 Edition.* New York: National Automobile Chamber of Commerce, 1930.

National Country Life Association. *Proceedings of the First National Country Life Conference, Baltimore, 1919.* Ithaca, N.Y.: National Country Life Association, 1919.

Neely, Wayne C. *The Agricultural Fair.* Columbia University Studies in the History of American Agriculture, vol. 2. New York: Columbia University Press, 1935.

Nevins, Allan. *Ford: The Times, the Man, the Company.* New York: Charles Scribner's Sons, 1954.

North, Sterling. *Plowing on Sunday.* New York: Macmillan Company, 1934.

Ostrander, Gilman M. *American Civilization in the First Machine Age, 1890-1940.* New York: Harper & Row, Publishers, 1970.

Partridge, Bellamy. *Excuse My Dust.* New York: McGraw-Hill Book Company, Whittlesey House, 1943.

———. *Fill 'er Up!: The Story of Fifty Years of Motoring,* New York: McGraw-Hill Book Company, 1952.

Phelan, John, ed. *Readings in Rural Sociology.* New York: Macmillan Company, 1920.

Presbrey, Frank. *The History and Development of Advertising.* Garden City, N.Y.: Doubleday & Company, 1929.

President's Research Committee on Social Trends. *Recent Social Trends in the United States.* With a foreword by Herbert Hoover. 1-vol. ed. New York: McGraw-Hill Book Company, 1933.

Rae, John B. *The American Automobile: A Brief History.* Chicago History of American Civilization. Chicago: University of Chicago Press, 1965.

Rankin, J. O. *Reading Matter in Nebraska Farm Homes.* Bulletin No. 180. Lincoln, Nebr.: University of Nebraska Agricultural Experiment Station, 1922.

Reavis, George H. *Factors Controlling Attendance in Rural Schools*. New York: Columbia University Teachers College, 1920.

Reck, Franklin M. *A Car Traveling People: How the Automobile Has Changed the Life of Americans — A Study of Social Effects*. Detroit: Automobile Manufacturer's Association, 1945.

Ringel, Fred J., ed. *America as Americans See It*. New York: Harcourt, Brace and Company, 1932.

Rodgers, Richard, and Hammerstein, Oscar, II. *Oklahoma!* New York: Random House, 1942.

Rowsome, Frank, Jr. *The Verse by the Side of the Road: The Story of the Burma-Shave Signs and Jingles*. Brattleboro, Vt.; Stephen Greene Press, 1965.

Saloutous, Theodore, and Hicks, John D. *Twentieth Century Populism: Agricultural Discontent in the Middle West, 1900-1939*. A Bison Book. Lincoln, Nebr.: University of Nebraska Press, 1951.

Sanderson, Dwight, ed. *Farm Income and Farm Life: A Symposium on the Relation of the Social and Economic Factors in Rural Progress*. Chicago: University of Chicago Press, for the American Country Life Association, 1927.

_____. *The Farmer and His Community*. The Farmer's Bookshelf. New York: Harcourt, Brace and Company, 1922.

Sims, Newell L. *Elements of Rural Sociology*. Crowell's Social Science Series. New York: Thomas Y. Crowell Company, Publishers, 1928.

Smallzreid, Kathleen A., and Roberts, Dorothy J. *More than You Promise: A Business at Work in Society*. New York: Harper & Brothers Publishers, 1942.

Smith, Bruce. *Rural Crime Control*. New York: Columbia University Institute of Public Administration, 1933.

Sorensen, Charles E. *My Forty Years with Ford*. New York: W. W. Norton & Company, 1956.

Sorokin, Pitirim A.; Zimmerman, Carle C.; and Galpin, Charles J., eds. *A Systematic Source Book in Rural Sociology*. 3 vols. Minneapolis: University of Minnesota Press, 1930-1932.

Soule, George. *Prosperity Decade: From War to Depression, 1917-1929*. Vol. 8 of *The Economic History of the United States*, edited by Henry David *et al.* 9 vols. New York: Rinehart & Company, 1946-1947.

Suckow, Ruth. *Country People*. New York: Alfred A. Knopf, 1924.

Sydenstricker, Edgar. *Health and Environment*. Recent Social Trends Monographs. New York: McGraw-Hill Book Company, 1933.

Tarbell, Mary Anna. *A Village Library in Massachusetts: The Story of Its Upbuilding*. Library Tract No. 8. Boston: American Library Association Publishing Board, 1905.

Taylor, Carl C. *Rural Sociology: In Its Economic, Historical, and Psychological Aspects*. Rev. ed. New York: Harper & Brothers Publishers, 1933.

Turner, E[rnest] S. *The Shocking History of Advertising*! London: Michael Joseph Ltd., 1952.

University of Illinois, College of Commerce and Business Administration, Bureau of Business Research. *The Automobile and the Village Merchant:*

The Influence of Automobiles and Paved Roads on the Business of Illinois Village Merchants. Bulletin No. 19. Urbana, Ill.: University of Illinois, 1928.

University of Nebraska, Committee on Business Research of the College of Business Administration. *The Influence of Automobiles and Good Roads on Retail Trade Centers*. Nebraska Studies in Business No. 18. Lincoln, Nebr.: Extension Division of the University of Nebraska, 1927.

Vaile, Roland S., ed. *Small City and Town: A Conference on Community Relations*. Minneapolis: University of Minnesota Press, 1930.

Vidich, Arthur J., and Bensman, Joseph. *Small Town in Mass Society: Class, Power and Religion in A Rural Community*. Princeton, N.J.: Princeton University Press, 1958.

Vogt, Paul L. *A Rural Survey in Southwestern Ohio*. Miami University Bulletin, Series 11, No. 8. Oxford, Ohio: Miami University, 1913.

West, James [Carl Withers]. *Plainville, U.S.A.* New York: Columbia University Press, 1945.

Wheeler, Joseph L. *The Library and the Community: Increased Book Service through Library Publicity Based on Community Studies*. Chicago: American Library Association, 1924.

Wik, Reynold M. *Henry Ford and Grass-roots America*. Ann Arbor, Mich.: University of Michigan Press, 1972.

Willey, Malcolm M., and Rice, Stuart A. *Communication Agencies and Social Life*. Recent Social Trends Monographs. New York: McGraw-Hill Book Company, 1933.

Williams, James M. *The Expansion of Rural Life: The Social Psychology of Rural Development*. New York: F. S. Crofts & Co., 1931.

Wilson, Warren H. *The Evolution of the Country Community*. 2nd rev. ed. Boston: Pilgrim Press, 1923.

Wyman, Arthur C., ed. *Automobile Laws of the New England States, New York, New Jersey, and Pennsylvania*. Legislative Reference Bulletin No. 2. Providence: E. L. Freeman Company, State Printers for the Legislative Reference Bureau of the Rhode Island State Library, 1908.

Young, James H. *The Toadstool Millionaires: A Social History of Patent Medicines in America before Federal Regulation*. Princeton, N.J.: Princeton University Press, 1961.

Index